Daytime Stars

Daytime Stars

*A Poet's Memoir of the Revolution,
the Siege of Leningrad, and the Thaw*

Olga Berggolts

Translated and edited by

Lisa A. Kirschenbaum

Foreword by

Katharine Hodgson

The University of Wisconsin Press

The University of Wisconsin Press
1930 Monroe Street, 3rd Floor
Madison, Wisconsin 53711-2059
uwpress.wisc.edu

3 Henrietta Street, Covent Garden
London WC2E 8LU, United Kingdom
eurospanbookstore.com

Printed in the United States of America

This book may be available in a digital edition.

Library of Congress Cataloging-in-Publication Data

Names: Berggol'ts, Ol'ga, 1910-1975, author. | Kirschenbaum, Lisa A., editor, translator. | Hodgson, Katharine, writer of foreword.
Title: Daytime stars: a poet's memoir of the revolution, the siege of Leningrad, and the thaw / Olga Berggolts; translated and edited by Lisa A. Kirschenbaum; foreword by Katharine Hodgson.
Other titles: Dnevnye zvezdy. English
Description: Madison, Wisconsin: The University of Wisconsin Press, [2018] | Includes bibliographical references and index.
Identifiers: LCCN 2017049163 | ISBN 9780299316006 (cloth: alk. paper)
Subjects: LCSH: Berggol'ts, Ol'ga, 1910-1975. | Poets, Russian—Soviet Union—Biography.
Classification: LCC PG3476.B45 D613 2018 | DDC 891.71/44 [B]—dc23
LC record available at https://lccn.loc.gov/2017049163

For my students

The voice of memory sounds like a pledge and a promise.

Andrei Sinyavsky
"The Poetry and Prose of Olga Berggolts," 1960

Contents

Part II

Illustrations

Foreword: Finding Memory in the Margins

Katharine Hodgson

For any Soviet writer in the early post-Stalin years, writing autobiographical prose was a challenging undertaking, particularly for a writer like Olga Berggolts, who had personal experience of arrest and imprisonment in the late 1930s. It was almost inevitable that an account of her life would need to leave out a good deal so as to avoid running into trouble with the censors. There were other concerns to bear in mind: autobiography brought with it a focus on the individual at a time when an emphasis on personal experience could lead to charges of bourgeois individualism, of setting oneself apart from the collective. Authors would also have been aware of the model life stories that had been told in classic Socialist Realist novels such as Nikolai Ostrovsky's *How the Steel Was Tempered*; such narratives presented the hero's progression toward higher political consciousness—a process ending with the hero's renunciation of any individualistic concerns as he embraced his proper place in a socialist society.[1] Berggolts does gesture in the direction of Socialist Realist convention in the final episode of part I of *Daytime Stars*, set almost entirely on a single day in February 1942, when, grieving at her husband's death from starvation, and severely weakened by hunger herself, she walks through the frozen and surreal landscape of her besieged city back to the factory clinic where her father still worked as a doctor. This episode is reminiscent of the "death and resurrection" motif that is a common feature in the Socialist Realist "master plot" outlined by Katerina Clark.[2] The book ends with the poet's acceptance of her duty to stay alive and do what she can as a writer to help others to endure.

In general, however, Berggolts's life did not lend itself easily to the ideal Socialist Realist pattern of a Communist biography. In the late 1930s she had been subjected to political persecution. Following the arrest of her former husband, the poet Boris Kornilov, as an "enemy of the people" in March 1937, she was excluded from the Writers' Union and the Communist Party, and, although reinstated in both the following year, she was arrested in December 1938, accused of involvement in an alleged anti-Soviet conspiracy, and remained in prison until July 1939. She also suffered appalling losses in her personal life, including the deaths of her two daughters in childhood and the death of her second husband, Nikolai Molchanov, in the siege of Leningrad. A publishable linear, chronological narrative would have had too many awkward gaps in it, so Berggolts found a creative solution for *Daytime Stars*. She put together a nonchronological narrative in which connections between different stages of her life were established through the author's own memory. This approach enabled her to select moments that marked key points in a process of inner growth and linked together childhood, youth, and maturity, emphasizing the wholeness and coherence of her development.

This emphasis that autobiography placed on the author as an individual was entirely in line with Berggolts's polemical defense of lyric poetry in an article published shortly after Stalin's death.[3] The principles of "self-expression" (*samovyrazhenie*) that, she argued, were essential to a lyric poet were deeply rooted in her own practice as a writer, both of poetry and prose, where she did what she could, within the constraints of censorship, to convey her own lived experience to readers who shared those same experiences. Her reputation as a lyric poet who "told the truth" about the siege of Leningrad won her many admirers among her contemporaries, while her poems about her imprisonment, circulating in manuscript form in the early post-Stalin period, impressed emerging young poets who found in them "the truth about the desperate restlessness of our hungry and makeshift world."[4] In an article of 1936 she had already put forward ideas about lyric poetry that she would return to after the war, when she had become a well-known and authoritative figure.

Berggolts was among the first writers and critics whose challenges to the literary and cultural norms of the Stalin years precipitated the Thaw that lasted, intermittently, into the 1960s. In her article of April 1953, and in her polemical speech at the Congress of the Soviet Writers' Union the following year, she argued vehemently that much Soviet lyric poetry was unfit for its purpose. Lyric poetry, in her view, should be an expression of the poet's individuality, which readers could accept as an expression of their own thoughts and feelings. By suppressing their individuality, poets had failed to express emotions with which readers could identify, so that readers could not see their own experiences and feelings in literary works that purported to represent faithfully the world in which they lived. At the beginning of the third chapter of *Daytime Stars* Berggolts reflects on her task as author of an account of one person's life that was at the same time the story of her entire generation, citing readers' responses to the first installment of her book as evidence that they had found themselves in it, and saw themselves as its cocreators. Strangers had written to her with stories of their own lives, she felt, because they were concerned that their individual experiences were not being reflected in the literary works they read. Here was justification of Berggolts's emphasis on "the lyric": by sharing her personal experience she was expressing experiences shared by a generation. Because she believed that she spoke for many, she felt justified, too, in trying to create an honest and open statement of the spiritual legacy of her generation, including things that went wrong as well as the positive aspects of this shared past.

In spite of her explicit determination to speak openly of past mistakes, Berggolts did in fact have to rely heavily on the ability of her contemporaries to read between the lines, drawing on the memory of their own experiences. She signaled this to her readers, telling them that even though many important aspects of the lives of Soviet people had been treated superficially or even distorted, "we remember all." It is this insistence on memory that is the key both to the way *Daytime Stars* is written and the way Berggolts hoped it would be read by her contemporaries. Like a lyric poem, the book emphasizes the present moment, in which experiences from the present and the past coexist. This living memory provides the structure of the narrative. The readers' own memories enable them to weave their personal experience into the story, to understand, as Berggolts did when discovering poetry as a child, that "everything was about me!" Their own memories were to fill in the gaps, following the author's hints and allusions, just as readers in Leningrad during the siege had understood, from isolated details about daily life in the starving and frozen city, that the poet knew far more of their reality than she could acknowledge openly.

Memory is a recurring and dominant theme in Berggolts's work. In a poem of October 1939, written a few months after her release from prison, the poet's memory is described as "insatiable," like a "molten asphalt path" that bears indelible impressions of everything that has passed along it.[5] In her prewar poetry most of the things that were painfully imprinted on her memory were largely those that could not be spoken about openly; Berggolts represents herself as someone who remembers but cannot share her experiences except through oblique allusions or silence. In her diary, however, she makes no attempt to conceal the way that traumatic events continue to haunt her. In October 1939 she writes: "When I'm on my own at home I speak out loud to the investigator, the commission, to people, about the shameful case they cooked up against me. Everything—poems, events, conversations with people—reminds me of prison. It stands between me and life."[6] On the anniversary of her arrest, 14 December 1939, she reports in her diary that since her release in July she has been experiencing vivid flashbacks of her time in prison: "After five months of freedom the sensation of prison is something I feel even more keenly than when I was released. It is precisely that same sensation, i.e., I don't just actually feel, smell the oppressive smell of the corridor in the 'B[ig] house,' a smell of fish, damp, onions, the sound of footsteps on the stairs, but also the state of mind, a mixture of detached curiosity, fear, unnatural calm and the sense of foreboding, inevitability, that I felt when I went for interrogation." Later the same month she writes: "I've been free for almost six months, but not a day or night goes past when I don't think about prison or dream about it," and she wonders repeatedly whether she should seek psychiatric help.[7]

Her siege diaries report similar experiences. In July 1942 she notes that she is haunted by images of victims of the siege, including those of her dying husband and a little girl she saw begging in the street. Berggolts associates these recurring images with feelings of guilt about her own selfishness and unworthiness, and with fears that her wartime success is nothing more than a mirage.[8] The image of her husband, starving and delirious, persists in her diary, as, for instance, when she remembers him in the hospital several months after his death: "But he stands before me just as I saw him that last time, with his arms folded across his chest, naked, wet (he folded his arms because of the cold), with a painful grimace, trampled down and crushed by the merciless machine of war."[9] By contrast, in the poems she wrote for publication about the siege of Leningrad, Berggolts recast herself as a conscious and purposeful guardian of memory, rather than as a victim who was powerless to escape repeated confrontations with images of a disturbing past. These poems understand memory as a duty to bear witness to the suffering of the city's people rather than an oppressive burden; in them, Berggolts portrayed herself as someone committed to preserving the memory of the siege against the efforts of those who would have preferred to erase it.[10]

A reading of Berggolts's diary from the years of the siege of Leningrad shows just how carefully constructed the memory of the siege offered to readers of *Daytime Stars* is, compared with the immediate record of her feelings and experiences. Some aspects of her life under siege feature prominently in her diary, but only obliquely in her memoir. For example, although *Daytime Stars* includes the death of her husband, which prompts her to set out on foot across the city to tell her father, it does not mention the affair Berggolts began in autumn 1941 with her Leningrad Radio colleague Georgy Makogonenko, or the guilt that she increasingly felt about it as her starving husband grew weaker, was admitted to the hospital, and died in January 1942. Her diary shows repeated attempts to persuade herself that her affair with Makogonenko was not a betrayal of her husband, that she loved them both, and loved her husband above all. On 26 December 1941, for example, she wrote: "O, if only Kolka [Molchanov] can keep going, if I can get him to Arkhangelsk and get him into hospital. He's the one who is most important, the one I love the most, and I am faithful to him with my whole heart, in spite of Iurka [Makogonenko]. I am faithful to them both and am not betraying either of them."[11] On 20 May 1942, already living with Makogonenko, Berggolts writes: "Not that long ago Iurka hurt me dreadfully: he said that in November Nikolai had said to him, about me: 'If you want her, you'll have to get her away from Leningrad, if she stays here she'll die and then neither you nor I can have her.' O, surely he didn't know that I was living with Iurka then? My God, just the awareness that he was happy with me, happy to be together, is the only thing that justifies, in my own eyes, my behavior toward Kolya,—can it really be that this awareness was mistaken?"[12] In *Daytime Stars* the relationship with Makogonenko is simply excised; the journey to see her father becomes the focus of dramatic tension, while in her diary it is an episode that is not described at all.[13]

A comparison of the way in which Berggolts writes about the siege in her diary and in her memoir reveals further significant differences. The horizons framing her diary account of the siege are narrow, in terms of both space and time. Very rarely does she describe moments of escape from these constraints. Her diary entry for 26 December 1941 records feelings of joyous intensity in terms that echo the impression, described in *Daytime Stars*, that she is living "all of life at once":

How I recognize and understand this state of strange, piercing, unthinkable happiness when you sense that you are on the verge of destruction and are living all of life—good, generous, and open—at once.

No, it's not something you can explain to anyone, this sense of supreme freedom and happiness that is outside everyday, ordinary life, a freedom from everything that is not life, nor life itself, that cannot be captured by words.

I know this sense of supreme freedom from when I was in prison, in isolation cell number nine, when, suddenly living all of life at once—past, present (the scrap of sky above the metal sheet blocking off the window) and future, and I laughed from astonished joy, from a sense of full and absolute freedom.[14]

Most of her diary account of the siege as she lived through it day after day is understandably focused on immediate events and feelings, concerned most of all with the present. She frequently expresses doubts and uncertainties about the near future, as plans for evacuation are made and then come to nothing, and she can find no way to resolve her emotional dilemmas. In the cold and starving city her diary is increasingly preoccupied with plans to obtain more food, with her own growing weakness and her difficulty in working when she struggles to think about anything except her hunger.

The narrative of the siege in Berggolts's diary during the winter of 1941–42 is predominantly a story of the author's awareness of her own powerlessness, even as she desperately formulates plans to save her husband from death by starvation. In *Daytime Stars* the Leningrad siege is assigned a key role as a turning point in the author's life, a moment of insight that draws on her past experiences in order to set her on her future path. Her diary account is fraught with doubt, questions, and conflicting emotions, and shows no sense of how her ordeal might end or, if she should survive, how she might live in the future.

In *Daytime Stars*, Berggolts uses memory selectively as a way of constructing a sense of purpose and direction in her narrative, connecting childhood, youth, and adult experience through associations that allow the author to move freely from her earliest childhood memories to Leningrad in February 1942, or from the cold and hungry years of the civil war in Uglich to the present day of the Soviet Union beginning to emerge from the Stalin era. Woven into the story are episodes from Berggolts's idealistic youth of the late 1920s and early 1930s. The author looks back to the day of Lenin's death in January 1924, when she was thirteen years old. This event is written into the story of her development not just as an idealist but also as a writer, and so becomes part of the author's reflections on what it means to be a Soviet writer, which again connect her earliest memories with the present day. It is Lenin's death that inspired her to write her first published poem, but her poetic genealogy reaches back further, to childhood encounters with the poetry of Alexander Pushkin and Mikhail Lermontov, which showed her that everything in poetry was alive, and it was "about me."

Both the opening chapter of part I of *Daytime Stars*, "Journey to the Town of My Childhood," and the final chapter, "The Nevsky Gate Campaign," range across many different stages in the author's life. In between them is the only chapter of the book that is set entirely in a single period of time: two days in autumn 1937. Unlike the other two chapters, which were written either in a single year or over two years, the middle chapter was written between 1939 and 1957. It recounts an episode in which the author is reluctantly taken out by her father to visit the zoo, which fills what would otherwise be a large gap in the narrative between the early 1930s and the start of the siege of Leningrad.

The circumstances in which this outing takes place are somewhat opaque: we are given to know that some of the author's colleagues had denounced her (but we do not know the nature of the accusations made against her), and that she is preoccupied with attending meetings and writing documents that might resolve her problems. As she follows her father around the zoo, the animals that she views are at first perceived only as a reflection of her own unhappy situation: she sees a resemblance between one of her accusers and a prowling hyena; she identifies a group of ill-assorted birds sitting glumly around a filthy pond as "a meeting of our editorial committee." Gradually she begins to extricate herself from her misery, realizing that her father is attempting to distract her from her troubles by taking her back to her childhood and his own youth. They share memories: her own of a visit to the zoo in very early childhood when he returned briefly from his service in World War I as an army surgeon; his of Olga and her sister crying, fifteen years ago, when their parents forbade them to go out in the rain and pick mushrooms in a woodland clearing. The narrator's mood moves conclusively from disillusion to hope when Betty the elephant finds the coin she throws into the cage, an event that she interprets as a sign that everything will be resolved, that her current difficulties are transient.

In *Daytime Stars* there is no further explanation of her alleged misdeeds, or any mention of their consequences, beyond saying in passing that an unjust accusation was made against her in the years 1937–39. Yet Berggolts's contemporaries, even without any knowledge of the author's personal circumstances, would have been able to make an educated guess about the kind of troubles that she was likely to have faced in 1937, drawing on their own experience, or that of family, friends, or colleagues. The situation she alludes to in *Daytime Stars* is just part of a series of accusations, meetings, and confrontations that led to the poet's exclusion from the Communist Party and the Writers' Union. Berggolts's ordeal began in May 1937, when accusations were made against her in the Leningrad Writers' Union, from which she was then excluded. Its officials passed her case on to the Communist Party organization in the Elektrosila factory, where she was a candidate member of the party and worked on the factory newspaper. Her expulsion from the party duly followed.[15] This was far from the end of her ordeal. In late June 1937 Berggolts was summoned by the Leningrad secret police, the NKVD, to be questioned about Leopold Averbakh, the literary functionary who had been arrested in April. It was her connection with Averbakh that had first prompted her persecution; they had an affair in the early 1930s. Her accusers in the Writers' Union and in the Communist Party would not accept her claims that she knew nothing of the alleged counter-revolutionary plot that Averbakh was leading. After her interrogation by the NKVD Berggolts suffered a miscarriage; a later document found in her file said that the statement she had made in 1937 that she was a member of a Trotskyite counterrevolutionary organization had been forced from her when she was "in a very difficult moral and physical condition, as can be witnessed by the fact that immediately after questioning Berggolts was taken to the hospital in premature labor."[16]

Through the months that followed Berggolts petitioned for her re-instatement in the Communist Party. Her diary for the early months of 1938 shows intermittent despair about her exclusion, and moments when she felt she was coming to terms with it. Her reinstatement in the party and the Writers' Union came in summer 1938, but in December she was arrested and imprisoned; she suffered a further miscarriage in prison, most probably after being beaten during interrogation. Berggolts was released in July 1939 when a review of her case found it to be without any basis. She returned home with the knowledge that the prisons were filled not with the "enemies of the people" but with loyal Communists, and that the system that had put them there was far from fulfilling the noble ideals that she believed in.

The details of her persecution have emerged only gradually. In the completed text of *Daytime Stars*, Berggolts approached the problem of talking about her persecution and arrest the only way that was then avail-able to her: obliquely. While she skirts cautiously around the subject in her account of the 1937 visit to the zoo, she suggests more, indirectly, by setting up a chain of associations that connect her with the image of the bell in Ler-montov's poetry, and then by recalling the fate of a bell that was sent into exile from the town of Uglich in the early sixteenth century. She recalls the particular personal significance that Lermontov's poem about a poet whose work would ring out like a bell had for her in her rebellious youth.[17] A few pages later the narrative switches back to Uglich and the story of the bell that was rung to summon the townspeople to the scene of the tsarevich Dmitry's murder, where they killed the murderers. Without comment, Berggolts notes what followed: the execution of two hundred townspeople, the mutilation of many others whose tongues were cut out for "bold speech," and the arrest and exile of sixty families. The Uglich exiles were made to drag their bell, which she calls their "herald," their "singer," and "poet," with them to Siberia, after it had been taken down, whipped, mutilated, and silenced. The bell's "voice" was only restored when it returned to Uglich in 1892, to be rung each year by the people of the town in a ceremony commemorating the murdered tsarevich, a ceremony that Berggolts remembers taking part in as a child. On her return to Uglich after Stalin's death she rings it once more, hearing its voice as that of a poet warning those who threaten children with war, hunger, and orphanhood that retribution awaits them. The identity of these perpetrators is left deliberately vague; however, the identification of Berggolts the poet with the bell that bore witness to savage injustice is perfectly clear.

The poems Berggolts was able to publish in her 1965 collection *Uzel* (The knot) revealed something of her persecution and imprisonment but could not supply any context from her biography or do much to reveal the wider implications of the terror for her contemporaries. The scenario for the 1968 film version of *Daytime Stars*, which Berggolts coauthored with the director Igor Talankin, originally contained explicit reference to her prison experience, including a conversation with a doctor in the prison hospital. Not all of this material was filmed, and the prison episodes that were filmed were excluded from the final version.[18] Berggolts's role as both witness to and victim of persecution is underlined by the way the *Daytime Stars* film scenario places the Uglich exiles dragging the bell along a street in the middle of modern-day Leningrad. None of the passersby, except Berggolts, appear to notice them, but she takes up the place of one of the men hauling the bell when he falls to the ground exhausted, presumably about to die. The parallels between the Uglich exiles and the people of Leningrad's recent past are striking: during the first winter of the siege of Leningrad, the sight of people falling dead in the street was not uncommon; in the years that preceded the war, large numbers of people were sent from the city's prisons, unseen, or unacknowledged, to execution, or to the labor camps.

Having published *Daytime Stars*, Berggolts made occasional notes for a second volume of autobiographical prose that would address the subject matter she had only hinted at in the first volume. During her lifetime the publication of a book that confronted the Stalinist terror and its effects on a generation was unthinkable, and writing it was too painful a task for Berggolts, whose health was failing. Her experience of imprisonment could not easily be woven into a narrative about her growing insight that Communism was the only proper goal to be pursued by humanity. In her notebooks, however, Berggolts considered the way in which terror created invisible links between friends and acquaintances. In *Daytime Stars* she recalls her childhood friend, Valya Balkina, with whom she stood listening to the factory sirens sounding on the day of Lenin's death; in notes for the second volume she recalls hearing from a literary scholar, Yulian Oksman, a former prisoner in the Gulag, of the death of Valya's second husband, Nikolai Barshev, a prison camp inmate who refused to labor and so starved to death. Berggolts reflected on her feeling that she was destined to find out about Barshev's fate, then still unknown to his widow.[19]

Another note relating to *Daytime Stars* states that far from being marginal, the terror of the 1930s was a key part of her generation's experience: "but if I don't talk about the life and experience of my generation in 1937–38 that means I won't talk about what is most important and everything that went before—the description of childhood, the call of the revolution, Lenin, joining the Komsomol and the party, and everything that followed—the war, the siege, my life today—will be almost devalued."[20] She agonized in her diary only months after her release from prison about how she might show in her writing the centrality of the terror for the development of those who lived through it: "How can I write about the subject of consciousness, and leave out the main thing—the last two or three years, i.e., prison? The situation is that you can't leave 'prison' out, but you can't put 'prison' in. [. . .] But the last few years have been the strongest, most tragic experience of our generation, and this is something I know not just because of what happened to me."[21] What emerged clearly from her thinking about a possible second volume of *Daytime Stars* was that it must "connect prison and the blockade inseparably."[22] It seems as though she came to understand, even before the war, that endurance of and resistance to the terror would be a preparation for the war that was coming: "Prison was the source of the victory over fascism. Because we knew that prison was fascism, and we were fighting it, and we knew that there would be war tomorrow and we were ready for it."[23]

Daytime Stars devotes many pages to the siege of Leningrad, and allows only a few words to hint at the author's experience of persecution. Berggolts's allusive style of writing relied on the ability of her readers, her contemporaries, to fill in the gaps by drawing on their own experience and memories to decode the meaning of the images and associations she used. Reading her autobiographical prose without having the knowledge and experience of her contemporaries, we need help not just to fill in the gaps, but to know where they are. The image of the daytime stars that gives the book its name is an eloquent reminder of its author's attempt to make visible that which is unseen.

Preface

This translation of Olga Berggolts's *Dnevnye zvezdy* (Daytime stars) was inspired by a desire to provide a compelling introduction to a unique work of Soviet autobiography and to an author well known in the Soviet Union whose work has rarely been translated into English. Immediately, the project ran up against the problem that *Daytime Stars* is not a single, delimited work. Berggolts began writing *Daytime Stars* immediately after Joseph Stalin's death in 1953. She published the first three chapters (part I) in 1959. This translation (based on the Russkaia kniga edition, 2000) includes the finished part I along with the two chapters Berggolts completed for a projected part II. But Berggolts never considered the book truly finished, and she left much additional material. My interest in producing a readable translation of manageable length—not a definitive scholarly edition—argued against including this material. The problem is that leaving out these unfinished pieces of *Daytime Stars* means leaving out much of Berggolts's reflection on a key moment in her autobiography—her arrest and imprisonment during the terror of the late 1930s.

Ultimately, I opted to solve the problem not by appending disconnected, unfinished fragments and diary entries at the end of the more polished and carefully structured text but by making silence about the terror a central component of the presentation of the memoir. The foreword by Katharine Hodgson focuses on Berggolts's attenuated discussion of the purges. It provides narrative details regarding Berggolts's experience of the terror and highlights the complexities of her response. It also includes and analyzes excerpts from Berggolts's recently published diaries.

My introduction explores the use of *Daytime Stars* as a historical source, and from this perspective again highlights the importance of Berggolts's oblique discussion of the purges. It addresses the broad question of how historians approach memoirs as historical sources as well as more specific questions raised by Berggolts's text: the tensions between memory and forgetting; the narrative construction of identity; and the historical context of the Thaw.

Berggolts herself characterized *Daytime Stars* as a collection of notes, a "draft of a draft" of her "Essential Book." In translating these notes, I have tried to capture their diverse tones, from the philosophical to the colloquial, from the deeply personal to the stereotypical. I have retained Berggolts's uneven chapter divisions as well as her chapter and section titles; I have added chapter numbers. Except where they might confuse the English-language reader, I have also retained the suspensions (. . .) that Berggolts employed so liberally as an important element of the style and structure of the text. In a few cases I have taken the liberty of breaking up paragraphs that seemed excessively long.

The editorial notes function primarily to clarify references—to books, movies, songs, people, and events—that would have been familiar to Berggolts's Soviet audience in the mid-1950s and early 1960s but that may be lost on readers unfamiliar with Soviet history and literature. The cultural context provided in the notes allows readers to understand Berggolts's efforts to construct a respectable literary lineage for her modernist experiment that—however tame by Western standards—marked an important departure from Socialist Realist norms. The scholarly references are not exhaustive but are intended to direct readers to recent and relevant resources in English. So far as possible, I tracked down the sources of Berggolts's quotations and provide information on English translations for the reader who wishes to follow her intertextual references. In cases where Berggolts elides parts of her own story, as she notably does in the case of her experiences of the purges, I have used the notes to fill in some of the details that she omits. The fullest discussion of Berggolts's life and particularly her experience of the purges can be found in the foreword.

In the pages that follow, I have deliberately mixed two systems of transliteration. In order to make bibliographic and linguistic references as useful as possible to readers undertaking further research, I have used a modified Library of Congress system (with hard and soft signs, but no other diacritics) for references in the notes. In the text itself and in the annotations, I further simplified the transliteration in order to render Russian names and places in a manner more familiar to non-specialists. I have omitted soft signs (so Ol'ga Berggol'ts becomes Olga Berggolts); substituted "y" for "ii" at the end of names and adjectives; and replaced the combinations "ia" and "iu" with "ya" and "yu" (so Maiakovskii becomes Mayakovsky). Where there exists a well-known English version of a name or place, I have used it. In references to non-Russians, I have restored the original spellings of names. Following Joseph Brodsky's lead, I have transliterated the city of St. Petersburg/Leningrad's nickname as "Peter."

Acknowledgments

This project is the fruit of a long-ago conversation with Barbara Walker. It turned out that we both harbored a desire to include Olga Berggolts's memoir *Dnevnye zvezdy* in our courses on Soviet history. And so we decided to undertake a translation. Barbara's help was essential in putting together the proposal and the initial sample translation. Unfortunately, she got too busy with other projects to finish this one. But had she not been there at the start, I never would have dared.

I could not have finished the translation without the thorough and thoughtful assistance of Yuliya Kalnaus, who helped unravel many translation puzzles and caught numerous errors and inconsistencies. Any that remain are, of course, my own.

I owe an immense debt to Katharine Hodgson for her good advice and good cheer, her crucial help with the technical details, and her beautiful foreword.

Gwen Walker has been an ideal editor, offering excellent suggestions and just the right amount of prodding. I am grateful for her enthusiasm for this project.

I thank Victor Lebedinsky, the late Mikhail Iur'evich Lebedinskii, and Fyodor Vladimirovich Ianchin for permission to publish an English translation of *Dnevnye zvezdy*.

As always, none of this would have been possible without the support and love of my family. My parents, Diane and Barry Kirschenbaum, continue to amaze and encourage me. I am thrilled that my mom still enjoys reading everything I write. I thank John Conway for listening, loving, and looking for the diurnal stars.

My students inspired me to undertake this translation. I dedicate this book to all of them—past, present, and future.

Daytime Stars

Introduction

Daytime Stars *as Historical Source*

Lisa A. Kirschenbaum

Olga Berggolts was a complex figure: a citizen of passionate Soviet loyalty who was purged, a former prisoner who became a significant public figure during the siege of Leningrad, a sensitive and eloquent woman who survived the brutalities of the war in Leningrad to challenge the orthodoxies of Socialist Realism by writing and publishing *Daytime Stars* in the wake of Joseph Stalin's death. The memoir is at once a tantalizingly vivid historical source promising insight into the everyday life and feelings of this remarkable woman and a constrained and evasive document. This introduction explores the variety of interpretive strategies that historians interested in understanding Berggolts and her times can apply to such a source.

Describing the memoir as documenting a spontaneous surge of living memory, Berggolts herself invites readers to interpret the book as a detailed and authentic account of Soviet life. At the same time, she suggests that the memoir illuminates the narrative construction of Soviet subjectivity, exposing her efforts to "collect myself as something unified" (75).[1] Complicating both of these interpretations is the fact, highlighted in Katharine Hodgson's foreword to this volume, that the memoir tells only part of Berggolts's story, eliding in particular her experience of the Stalinist terror. Implied references to the purges coupled with nostalgia for the revolution's "childhood," which was also the author's childhood, mark the memoir as an artifact of the post-Stalin Thaw. Told out of chronological order, it offers an idiosyncratic and incomplete narrative of Berggolts's life that historians can read as a reflection of real events, an imaginative act of self-construction, and a commentary on the historical period from which the text emerged.

Daytime Stars as True Story of the Blockade

Especially in the vivid and powerful chapters that describe what she saw, felt, heard, and smelled during the siege of Leningrad, Berggolts encourages us to read for "facts." The "900 days and 900 nights" of the blockade of Leningrad during World War II constitutes one of the most tragic and mythologized episodes of the war. It began on 8 September 1941, when German and Finnish troops cut the city off from the rest of the Soviet Union. Relatively few Leningraders left the city before the blockade closed, when it became nearly impossible to evacuate civilians or resupply the city. During the late fall and throughout the winter of 1941–42, the city's population—predominately women, children, and the elderly—faced conditions that defy imagination. In January 1942, temperatures reached forty degrees below zero (the point at which centigrade and Fahrenheit converge). Leningraders suffered the bitter cold in a city without heat, electricity, running water, or public transportation. Between 20 November and 25 December, the daily bread ration for office workers, dependents, and children fell to a low of 125 grams. Thousands died of starvation every day, and corpses piled up in the streets and courtyards. The next two winters of the war were not as deadly, although the city and the route out of it along the so-called Road of Life across frozen Lake Ladoga remained vulnerable to German artillery and bombs. In January 1943 the Soviet offensive pierced the blockade; it was fully lifted on 27 January 1944—after 872 days.[2]

Berggolts and her husband declined an offer to evacuate the city in September 1941, and they remained in the city as the starvation winter set in. As she relates in her memoir, he died at the end of January 1942. Evacuated to Moscow in March 1942, she returned in April and remained in the city until the end of the war. Her radio broadcasts during the first winter of the war indelibly linked her to the blockaded city. Survivors remembered her voice and her poetry as powerful spiritual resources in the most extreme circumstances.[3]

For historians of the blockade, Berggolts's account of the effects of hunger are particularly compelling and convincing. In recounting the journey to her father's house in February 1942, the most painful moment of her blockade experience, Berggolts makes palpable the "extreme bodily weakness," the "constant icy chill," the "gnawing hunger" (125), and the psychological numbness born of starvation: "I had almost no feeling then, no human reactions" (130). Her description of the blockade bathhouse provides a searing picture of the physical and spiritual effects of starvation: "desecrated," inhuman bodies beside whom a well-fed woman appeared "nauseating, repugnant, and disgusting" (165).

Here Berggolts appears to provide privileged access to the truth of the blockade as she survived it. Grounded in the authority of experience, such claims are easily taken at face value.[4] However, few historians would be inclined to do so. Instead, most would cross-check the author's account against other memoirs, diaries, testimonies, and official documents, asking whether and how Berggolts's descriptions of the blockaded city and starving Leningraders chime with those produced by differently situated individuals. Thus, for example, historian Alexis Peri compares "diary-like" published accounts of the blockade, including *Daytime Stars* and also literary critic Lydia Ginzburg's *Notes of a Blockade Person*, to a large and varied sample of "unpublished accounts penned by amateur writers." Peri finds that for diarists, who reported similar confrontations with healthy bodies in the bathhouse, "the 1941–42 bathhouses emblematized the horrors of starvation and stratification."[5]

When undertaking such comparisons, historians handle the memoir less as a straightforward repository of facts about the author's life than as a life made into a story. Like any story a memoir is necessarily partial: things are left out, magnified, and misremembered (intentionally or not). Authors narrate and structure events in a particular way—intentionally, especially in a literary memoir such as *Daytime Stars*, but also perhaps unconsciously or unreflectively. Thus historians often use autobiographical texts cautiously, even skeptically, on the lookout for language and narrative choices that signal the assumptions, agendas, or constraints shaping the author's account of what "really happened."[6]

Berggolts's stated commitment to telling the "whole truth" (74) notwithstanding, the attentive historian can find important hesitations and gaps in her story of the blockade. Asserting that most of the starving "become boundlessly polite and quiet," she also grants that a few "became brutal"; however, she never follows up on her promise to "somehow [. . .] return to them later" (128). Quoting the starving women in the bathhouse who were certain that a well-fed stranger was either a thief or the mistress of some privileged, criminal man, Berggolts seems to acknowledge that many Leningraders pilfered and stole. Still, her account provides no direct confirmation of criminal activity and ignores entirely the crime of cannibalism. All told, about two thousand people in Leningrad were arrested for cannibalism, but the topic remained taboo in Soviet publications about the blockade.[7] Even where she seems most unsparing, the historian may detect a refusal or inability to say all she saw and felt. Berggolts's account of the bathhouse is intimate and revealing but also distanced, as she describes the "profaned, emaciated, blemished, and spotted" (165) bodies of the women around her—but not her own pain, her own desecration.

Most striking, perhaps, is Berggolts's omission of the torments caused not by hunger or cold or artillery but by the political police (NKVD). In lovingly describing her father as continuing his selfless work as a factory doctor, she neglects to mention that after surviving the first winter of the blockade he was deported to Siberia for refusing to become a police informer. He returned in 1947, and died a year later.[8] Yet Berggolts's list of the traumas that finally "finished him off"—"civil war typhus, the famine and the misery of the blockade [. . .] and hypertension" (141)—omits exile.

These gaps do not necessarily indicate an intention to deceive, distort, or cover up. Instead they can be understood as marking the point beyond which, for reasons personal or political, Berggolts could not take her story. Berggolts herself warns readers that although "we remember all," she might nonetheless "leave something unsaid." She counted on her readers, equipped with their own memories of the war and the purges, to fill in what remained unspoken, confidently predicting that "the reader, who together with me writes our Essential Book, will understand me to the end" (74). Historians, lacking the memories of Berggolts's contemporaries, can accomplish something similar by reading the memoir against additional sources to identify and perhaps fill in abridgements and erasures. Doing so, we learn more about her world and also about her self.

Daytime Stars as Act of Self-Construction

Approaching the memoir as a life made into a story allows us to understand it as a "complex rhetorical and artistic performance" that offers insight into the author's consciousness or subjectivity.[9] As historian Barbara Walker argues, the value of Soviet memoirs for historians "lies at certain key moments less in their accurate reflection of what actually happened in the past, and more in how they reflect the ways their authors, as participants in Russian culture, view the world."[10]

Applying this insight to Soviet memoirs raises the question of how to understand an author who often articulates her worldview in stilted, stereotypical ideological language. Can such language be taken as an authentic and essential reflection of the author's consciousness? Addressing this question in the context of diaries from the 1930s, historian Jochen Hellbeck argues against dismissing overtly ideological or propagandistic language as an external imposition on the author that obscures his or her "true" self. Instead, he maintains, historians should read such language as evidence of a really existing and "widespread urge" among diarists (and perhaps memoirists) "to ideologize one's life." From this perspective, a narrative's ideological language is not a sign of perhaps coerced "outward compliance" but rather a central element in the process of self-definition.[11]

In *Daytime Stars*, Berggolts seems to encourage this sort of reading, often underscoring the affective power of propaganda and the formative importance of thoroughly ideologized Soviet "models of self."[12] For example, she recounts emotional responses to even the most seemingly banal slogans. Witnessing the revolution as a seven-year-old in Petrograd, she was fascinated by the name "Lenin" and the other "awesome, beautiful" words on everyone's lips: "decree," "Sovnarkom," "revolution" (98). At thirteen, participating with her schoolmates in a demonstration, she experienced every revolutionary song as the "absolute truth" (101). As an adult during the blockade, discovering the faded remains of a slogan remembered from 1917— "Defend the Revolution!"—moved her to tears, to "happy sobs" (114).

Berggolts suggests that such reactions require no special explanation, that they are the natural consequence of the fact that she and her generation grew up with the revolution. Although she presents her story out of chronological order, her narration is guided by a "need to begin from the beginning, with the origins of consciousness, with the distant, but unfading past—mine and my country's" (41). And at the beginning, "from earliest childhood" (96, 107) she finds two keys to her identity: Lenin and poetry. The two come together in her recollection of Lenin's death, the moment that she, her generation, and indeed the revolution itself crossed "from childhood directly into young adulthood" (102). Standing in the snow with the whistles of the Nevsky Gate's factories blaring in deafening, mournful homage to Lenin, thirteen-year-old Lyalya decided to join the Komsomol and, "almost suffocating with a strange new happiness," pledged to become "a professional revolutionary. Like Lenin" (103). Almost immediately, the political commitment became linked to her aspirations as a poet. She wrote a poem in Lenin's honor that succeeded in bringing her to tears and that became her first published piece. Signed Olga, not Lyalya, it marked the end of her childhood. Seeing her published work, torn between pride and embarrassment, she amended her vow. She would become a "professional revolutionary poet" (106).

Thus Berggolts narrates the love of Lenin that might be taken as "outward compliance" as a moment of transformation and fundamental self-definition. Indeed in an oblique reference to her arrest she claims that her "belief that I didn't break my sworn adolescent oath, the consciousness that I belong to the party, fused with Lenin's name" gave her "the strength, despite all the misfortunes, to live fully, to live with all my being" (103). In this narrative Berggolts seems to realize her stated aim of subverting the "alien and harmful" (38) differentiation of propaganda ("sermon") and the most intimate and unsparing truth ("confession"). In her terms, the story of lifelong devotion to the party of Lenin is persuasive propaganda because it is deeply personal, linked to the origins of her identity as a Soviet writer.

The memory of her inviolable adolescent oath may well have offered, as Berggolts suggests, a resource and refuge in the 1930s. And yet it is difficult to reconcile the power ascribed to her oath in *Daytime Stars* with the diary entry made in 1939 just months after her release from prison (and discussed in the foreword) in which she asked, "How can I write about the subject of consciousness, and leave out the main thing—the last two or three years, i.e., prison?" This juxtaposition is not meant to suggest that the diary expressed "the truth" while the memoir distorted truth into something fraudulent but publishable. Instead, if we recognize both as legitimate expressions of the poet's "consciousness," the comparison offers a way to consider the complexity of the self as constituted in different narratives at different times. Perhaps, as historians Choi Chatterjee and Karen Petrone suggest in their analysis of Soviet models of selfhood and subjectivity, "faith in the revolutionary utopia" could coexist with "disbelief, irony, and even resistance to certain aspects of the system."[13] Is the "me" Berggolts narrated in *Daytime Stars* like the "me" her younger self saw in Lermontov's poetry, more wish than reality, "the me that I had to become" (111), the "me" that she needed or wanted to conjure after Stalin's death?

Daytime Stars as an Artifact of the Thaw

Whether understood as a potentially true story or as an act of self-construction, the memoir is always a product of the time in which it was written. Writing about the past, the author works in a particular present. Thus memoirs can serve as indicators of broader changes and continuities, as historians look for connections between the text and contemporary social, political, and cultural discourses, practices, and conditions.[14]

In the case of *Daytime Stars*, the "present" is the years of what has come to be known as the Thaw, the period of on-again, off-again cultural openness and "coming to terms with the Stalinist past" that followed Stalin's death.[15] These were years in which some of Stalin's crimes were revealed by his successor, Nikita Khrushchev, and in which the memory of the Great Fatherland War began to be systematized and sacralized in a war "cult" that ultimately took on vast dimensions.[16] Among the works that charted new territory were Evgeny Evtushenko's 1961 poem "Babi Yar," which condemned the Soviet regime's failure to commemorate the Jewish victims of the Nazi massacre, and Alexander Solzhenitsyn's stunning 1962 Gulag novel *One Day in the Life of Ivan Denisovich*. Among the works that marked the shifting, erratic borders of disclosure stood Vasily Grossman's epic novel of World War II, *Life and Fate*. In 1961 Mikhail Suslov, one of the old Stalinists in the party leadership, told Grossman that the novel, which centered on the battle of Stalingrad and drew extended parallels between Stalinism and Nazism, covered ground so forbidden that it could not be published for two hundred years.[17] Berggolts's memoir was a product of these exciting and uncertain times. She was among the first to intervene in post-Stalin cultural debates, making an impassioned defense of lyric poetry (discussed in the foreword) in 1953, just a month after Stalin's death. The first section of *Daytime Stars* was published in 1954, the same year as Ilya Ehrenburg's *The Thaw*, the novella that gave the era its name.

Berggolts also contributed to the burgeoning cult of the war. Her verses, inscribed at the center of the memorial dedicated in 1960 at Piskarevskoe Cemetery, where hundreds of thousands of Leningraders had been buried in unmarked graves during the siege, became the watchwords of the cult: "Nothing is forgotten, and no one is forgotten." The phrase clearly echoes the memoir's "we remember all." Both can be understood as at once a mythic whitewash and a call to remember. Given that the war cult effaced, ignored, and distorted so much of the Soviet war experience, "nothing is forgotten" can be read, as historian Nina Tumarkin notes, as a galling bit of hypocrisy.[18] Yet in the context of the cemetery, the verse called attention to the fact that the official monument did not tell the full story. Providing what any survivor would recognize as an attenuated description of the city's suffering, the poem pledged that the horrors would not be forgotten—"neither the hungry, cruel, dark / winter of forty-one-forty-two, / not the savagery of the shelling, / nor the terror of the bombs in forty-three." At Piskarevskoe as in *Daytime Stars* Berggolts suggested that she (and by extension, her audience) remembered more than she could say.[19]

The Thaw gave writers, albeit unevenly, flexibility to criticize the Stalinist past and to experiment with new literary forms, shifts that have been linked to a new, post-Stalin Soviet subjectivity. Writing in 1960 as a near contemporary of the literature he analyzed, George Gibian dubbed the Thaw an "interval of freedom," a time when Soviet writers were able to express, however fleetingly, opinions that in Stalin's time "would certainly have been repressed by the writers themselves—or by the men in charge of controlling Soviet cultural life." He saw in Thaw literature an "encouraging similarity" to "our," that is American or Western, "values" as the "nonpolitical contemporary Soviet man" sought what Gibian called an "island of private of life."[20] More recently, historian Anatoly Pinsky has critiqued this vision of a "liberal" post-Stalinist self. Emphasizing writers' and critics' growing attraction to the "diaristic form" in this period, he argues that they valued diary writing not as a means of constructing "islands" of private life but rather because they "longed to reform Soviet socialism." The seemingly private form of the diary offered writers a forum for "meticulous and critical empirical investigations of Soviet life" and a means of transforming themselves and their readers "into courageous and independent citizens" capable of realizing the revolutionary dream of building communism. In their diaries, writers constructed a post-Stalin Soviet person whose self-expression and independent criticism served the party.[21]

Berggolts's memoir participated in this turn to the diary as a form that constructed the individual's life as "inseparable from universal life" (40). Strictly speaking, of course, the memoir is not a diary. But Berggolts characterized the work as an "open diary" (74), and linked it to the temper of the times in which the "need to keep a diary" was felt by writers and non-writers alike (40). When *Novyi mir* (New world) published the first piece of *Daytime Stars* in 1954, the editor Alexander Tvardovsky placed it in the section "The Diary of a Writer." For Tvardovsky, who oversaw *Novyi mir*'s publication of some of the most important products of the literary Thaw, the key attribute of the "writer's diary"—a rubric under which he published essays, sketches, and poems—was "free expression."[22] In his 1960 review of Berggolts's work in *Novyi mir*, writer (and future dissident) Andrei Sinyavsky argued that *Daytime Stars*, despite its deliberate abandonment of "chronological principles," retained essential elements of a diary: "intimacy with the reader" and an "intense immediacy" in its recounting of experience.[23] Berggolts's "empirical investigations" turned inward. But as she took great pains to emphasize, intimacy and free expression did not mean "contemplating [one's] own navel" (39). To the contrary, she asserted that the writer telling about her own heart "necessarily tells about the heart of the people" (39). She bared her soul in the "open diary" so that it might reflect universal life, just as a deep well might reveal daytime stars.

Written between 1953 and 1962, the memoir represented de-Stalinization as a project of recovery—in both the sense of retrieving submerged or lost fragments of memory and of returning to an earlier state of health and idealism. Berggolts structured it around a number of metaphoric and literal "return" journeys. In literary terms, the memoir "returned" to the early Soviet modernism exemplified by the poet Vladimir Mayakovsky. Although she nodded to the influence of the Socialist Realist novel, Berggolts's work constituted a departure from its pedantic "master plot." Among the literal journeys recounted in the memoir, the one most closely tied to the memoir's present is the return to Uglich, the town of Berggolts's childhood. Explicitly motivated by Stalin's death, Berggolts sought by this return to recapture her childhood faith in the revolution. Optimistic hope in a bright, neo-Leninist future suffuses this section of the memoir. She describes not a thaw in the Stalinist winter but the morning after the deluge, when "a high, clear rainbow might stand over a plain washed by a storm" (55). She writes ecstatically of feeling connected to the whole of the Soviet people and its history, of long dormant memoires beginning to live once again. Written before the 1956 Secret Speech that revealed some of Stalin's crimes, this section does not broach the question of the terror. Instead, Berggolts emphasized that the "great work" of the revolution was "now unfolding anew, was making a new historical ascent" (55).

And yet it is also in Berggolts's account of Uglich that the memoir comes closest to striking a note of despair. The poet mourns the "fairy-tale beauty" (45) sunk to the bottom of the reservoir created by the hydroelectric dam on the Volga. In a later section of the memoir, she laments another submerged city, the petty-bourgeois but beloved "Atlantis," her early childhood home, whose "geological destruction" she herself had facilitated as a young communist committed to the destruction of the bourgeois past. (76). These losses could be traced not only to Stalin, as the official Thaw narrative dictated, but also to her earliest, purest, and most cherished understandings of the revolution. Realizing the "Fairy Tale of Light" in which hydroelectric dams brought light and power to the whole country turned out to have unexpected and devastating costs. The wonders of the new world did not prevent a deep sense of longing for the land of childhood, always tied in the memoir to the "childhood" of the revolution, "a wondrous landscape" "to which the path has been lost" (76).

Approaching Berggolts's memoir as a narrative thus allows us to rethink the larger historical context. She tempers optimistic hopes for the revival of revolutionary idealism with pictures of the revolution's destruction of treasured landscapes and (implicitly) lives.[24] Berggolts's story encourages us to understand the Thaw as facilitating not only a working through of the Stalinist past but also an accounting, however attenuated, of the costs of trying to make fairy tales come true.

Part I

Journey to the Town
of My Childhood
1954

The Dream

Perhaps everyone has one dream more joyful and beloved than any other, a dream that returns again and again all one's life. You can't call it up, or demand its appearance: it turns up on its own, whenever it pleases. It may vanish for whole years at a time, but then it returns again without fail, generously imparting the same bliss that it always has.

I have a dream like that. I dream of the town of my childhood—Uglich, to which our mother took me and my sister from Petrograd in 1918, and where we lived for almost two and a half years while my father fought against the Whites far away in the South. We lived first in one street, then in another, in various houses, but by order of the city commune we lived longest of all in a cell of the Epiphany of the Virgin Monastery, our final dwelling in Uglich. Our building was in a remote corner at the end of the monastery wall, near the dense garden, by a deep pond concealed by enormous lindens. Sometimes we walked to school not along the street, but instead through a dark corridor inside the thick stone monastery walls. Walking that corridor was terrifying, even though doing so during the spring thaw kept one's felt boots dry. And the school was also inside the monastery, at the other end of it from our building, in a red brick structure that had earlier been known as "the chambers" and that stood directly opposite the high white cathedral with five deep blue domes covered with great golden stars.

The blue domes with gold stars of the Epiphany of the Virgin Cathedral in Uglich, 2015. The cathedral was restored in the post-Soviet period. (Ekaterina Bykova, Dreamstime.com)

We lived in the cell during the summer, fall, and winter—above all in the winter of 1920 . . . oh, but those were slow, icy evenings, with the blind, stinking oil lamp, with the threatening boom of the nearby monastery bells, with the burning anguish for Petrograd! Mama would tell us that she had taken us away from Petrograd so that we wouldn't die of hunger there, but we remembered that two years before in Petrograd we had eaten better than we were eating now, that there had even been sausage there, and that in our dining room glowed a hanging lamp with a lampshade. We remembered that lamp as if it were a living, much loved human being, and it seemed to us that it continued to burn in Petrograd, even though mama had told us that grandfather, grandmother, and our nanny Avdotya had long since been using an oil lamp, and that they were eating even worse than we were: At least we have *duranda* to eat; there's *vobla*, and lots of oatmeal bran that can be made into *kissel*, but *there* . . . and she fell silent.[1] But it was impossible to believe that in each and every town, and especially in our dear Petrograd, it was just as hungry, cold, and dark as in our cell. No, surely the lamp in Petrograd was still burning . . . And every evening, our mother went to work at our school, to the "liquidate illiteracy" program, where the old women were learning to read, like children, and we stayed alone, locked into the freezing vaulted cell.

The bells tolled menacingly; the semicircular windows darkened; the cemetery was all too near, with the graves of some monk elders; the nuns on duty in our school told us that the elders sometimes "rose out of their graves" for some reason, and had it not been for Tuzik—a hungry ginger-colored dog who had attached himself to us that winter—it would have been truly terrifying. What a good thing that we had talked mama into bringing the dog into our cell, quietly dividing our meager food with him; he rewarded us with a deep love and watched over us jealously. Wrapping ourselves in the blanket and pulling the stinking oil lamp right up to our books, terrified that the lamp might go out and therefore hardly breathing (to be on the safe side, mama left us only one match from her store) we studied our lessons, and Tuzik sat directly opposite the door, his triangular ginger-colored ears pricked up aggressively, prepared to hurl himself at the elders at any moment should they suddenly rise from their graves and force their way in.

Even so, one time Muska put out the oil lamp by sighing heavily. The single match broke between my fingers, and of course we couldn't find its head. We were rooted to the spot by fear, by the sudden blackness.

"Now we're going to die," Muska said in a deep voice.

"Don't worry," I whispered, "mama will be back soon. There go the bells for vespers, which means that the liquidate illiteracy class is already over. Because the old women have to go to vespers . . ."

But I was even more frightened than my little sister.

Tuzik approached us, and, laying his paw on my knee, licked our faces efficiently. His tongue was rough, hot, it smelled of warmth. He behaved like the oldest member of the household.

"Soon it will be spring," I said. "We'll go to the forest again . . . with the Saturday work brigade . . . to collect lilies of the valley for the pharmacy and pinecones for the electric plant.[2] Would you like to go to the forest, Muska?"

"I want to go to Petrograd," she answered in the same deep, sad voice.

"It's all Kolchak's fault," I explained, "they told us in class! And the hunger and everything, everything . . ."[3]

And a sweet convulsion of hatred squeezed my throat.

We fell silent. But the cell was already a little bit less dark than it had been when the oil lamp first went out and the match broke: the outlines of the bench along the stove, the pillows on the bed, and the tub with water were growing dimly visible; those semicircular little windows, brightening miraculously, poured the sad, snowy moonlight of deepest winter into the cell.

Thus we whiled away the winter with Tuzik, greeted the sweet Volga spring, waited for papa, waited for the end of the war and for our return to Petrograd, to our loved ones, to bread, to the bright hanging lamp.

. . . And then, during my youth in the thirties, it was precisely that dark, calamitous time of childhood and civil war—the cell, the corner of the monastery yard with the mighty lindens, and, most important, the high white five-domed cathedral opposite the school—that for some reason became for me a dream-place of the purest, most triumphant, definitive happiness.

I would dream: I arrive in Uglich and walk along the long, wide street overgrown with low sparse green grass. And it's neither early dawn, when gloom turns into light, nor glowing evening passing into night, because not only the sky, but all of the air and even the houses and the trees around them radiate some kind of flickering silvery-milky light, almost a blueness—way up there, up above. There I go along the green glimmering street, and in the distance the white mass of the cathedral also glimmers and glows. I absolutely have to get to it, because beyond it is our school and garden, and in the garden the giant lindens agitate and roar with all their round, ringing, tin-like leaves, and I know that when I reach the cathedral, the lindens, an astonishing, instantaneous, complete happiness will commence. I wander along the strangely dusky streets, and the cathedral gets ever closer, ever brighter, and a premonition of happiness grows ever more deeply in me, something wonderful, glittering, almost piercing trembles and shakes inside, closer and closer to the cathedral, and suddenly—that's it: I wake up! Thus over many years I've never succeeded—in my dream— in reaching "my cathedral." And it's been thirty-two years since we left Uglich . . .

Last year I decided to travel to Uglich in waking life, and reach the cathedral, reach the school, reach that quivering happiness, of which I had dreamed for so many years. I had to do it.

But before I tell about that, I should tell the story of how we returned to Petrograd. I remember our journey back to Petrograd not as a dead memory, knowing that thus and such happened, thus and such took place in the past, but rather with the living memory of feeling the events and feeling my own emotions. With the kind of memory that binds separate memories into a whole, complete life, allowing nothing to die out, but keeping everything eternally alive, eternally contemporary. That kind of memory, they say, is either a punishment or a blessing, but maybe it's both at the same time. But even if it were punishment alone, I still wouldn't resist it.

Papa's Back

I was ten years old, and my sister eight, when one morning I woke up and saw all at once that some soldier stood in the middle of the cell with his back to our bed. His Red Army overcoat was unbuttoned; in his right hand he carried a kit bag, and with the left he embraced mama and, quickly patting her on the shoulder, spoke quietly:

"There, there . . ."

An unbelievable realization dawned on me.

"Muska," I shouted, "Get up! The war is over! Papa's back!"[4]

At that papa turned around, stepped over to our bed, and we froze with shock: his head was shaven, his face thin, dark and without a mustache, though we knew that he should have a beautiful mustache and wavy hair: for almost seven years—since he had gone to war against the German emperor Wilhelm—we had known him by the student portrait and had long forgotten what he was really like, living.

"Are you our papa?" asked Muska politely.

"That's right," he replied, and in his overcoat sat down on the edge of the bed; he smelled of the unknown: of heavy, coarse cloth, of cheap tobacco, of smoke—he smelled of war and papa. Probably he didn't recognize us either and didn't know what to do with us. He cautiously touched the crown of my head and then Muskina's with his left hand, and with his right hand he kept on holding onto and holding onto his kit bag: After all, he had come from far away, from the war, and probably he had held onto his kit bag like that the whole way, so that marauders or speculators wouldn't steal it from him. Finally mother took the bag out of his hand and said:

"So, why don't you kiss the kids . . ."

But papa didn't kiss us.

"Give them some sugar," he said, staring fixedly at Muska.

We ate sugar for the first time in three years, crunching fiercely and choking, staring at our papa and getting used to him.

"Papa," I asked, "the hungry time is over, too? Right, papa?"

I wanted to keep saying "papa" over and over.

"It's over," he said.

"And we're going to Petrograd, papa?"

"Well, of course. That's why I came, to get you."

"Soon, papa?"

"In three days."

We squealed and clapped our hands. They were sticky from the sugar and stuck together. For the first time papa smiled—he had begun to get a little bit more used to us—and suddenly began to look more like his student portrait.

"But the steamboats aren't going on the Volga," exclaimed Muska. She was stubborn, a skeptic, and didn't believe in all this good luck. "How can we do it?"

"So we'll go straight to the boat. One of those big ones, you know? To the Volga Station. And from there—lickety-split—straight to Peter by train."[5]

He started to laugh, and we started to laugh and gasped with delight, staring adoringly at papa.

And preparations for the journey to Petrograd began the very next day. Unfamiliar men carried plywood boxes and bundles of bast matting right into the cell, and to the smell of papa was joined the smell of travel, departure—the melancholy smell of fresh wood, fresh air, and bast. We quickly came to appreciate these new things that did not belong indoors: we climbed into the boxes and sat in them, wrapped ourselves in bast matting and marched around the room, and papa shouted at us sternly to stop making a nuisance of ourselves. We enjoyed even that because it meant that papa wasn't just with us, but was already our real true actual papa, because he added:

"You'd do better to start figuring out what you want to take to Peter."

We threw ourselves into sorting out our meager children's household, books and toys, and right away almost everything that only yesterday had delighted us and was beloved turned out to be unworthy of Petrograd: the stick soldiers, the broken bits of colorful crockery, and the big wooden spoon, swaddled in a rag, that we called "Little Vanya."

Of course we chose Teddy Bear with one button eye and a squashed stomach—because Teddy was from Petrograd, he had come to Uglich with us—but we decided to leave the bits of crockery, the soldiers, and "Little Vanya" behind.

"And what about the little old man?" my sister asked me in a whisper.

I started whispering too:

"The little old man—yes!"

And tossing our assemblage aside, we ran to find our little old man.

We had discovered him in early spring in the monastery garden, among the still bare branches of the dogrose; squatting, hunchbacked, dark, his gnarled arms hanging right down to the earth, his angry, pensive little face with a pointed beard twisted at an unnatural angle. Stealing closer, we saw that this old man was not real, not alive, but a very strange wooden root. That is to say, he was in fact alive; only, in our presence, around human beings, he was motionless and pretended to be a tree root. But we saw through his clever ruse.

Underneath a small but surprisingly dense and gloomy fir tree, resembling a lean-to, we built the little old man a house (for it was impossible to drag him home, as he wasn't a plaything but an inhabitant of another world that was unattainable by human beings), and he lived under the fir tree, as in a pagan temple, in silence and secrecy. He ate the tiny bits of bread that we brought him, and drank water from the lids of jars, although not, of course, when we were around. And no one besides us knew of the little old man and his secret life, well, actually even we never caught a glimpse of it, however much we tried. But we guessed it all! We even told each other about how our little old man ran around the garden at night and touched everything with his gnarled hands, every now and then for some reason digging little holes. But he had to run like a pestle, waddling from side to side—because he didn't have any sort of legs! And it was so interesting and terrifying to believe in all this that we were actually a little afraid of our little old man, and quite loved him.

We took along an old checkered rag, and reverently, a little fearfully, we pulled the little old man out from under the fir tree. Glancing into his now empty temple, I had to convince myself yet again that we were really going to Petrograd. But the little old man was indifferent, hunchbacked, and dark, thinking his own thoughts, and his unnaturally twisted face was as always angry and pensive. I wrapped him in the rag very quickly, so that no one would see him. The whole time we were in his presence we spoke in a whisper.

"We aren't going to unwrap him in the house, are we, Lyalka?"

"No, no, we won't unwrap him. Or else mama might see him."

"And papa."

"Right, papa too. Papa's back!"

"Ah. Papa's back. And where is the little old man going to live in Petrograd, Lyalka?"

"What do you mean, where is he going to live? In our garden! Muska, you remember our garden—how huge it is? Right?"

"Ah. I remember, it's colossal. And our Petrograd house is even bigger. You know, in three days we'll be living in it!"

We stared at each other in amazement and laughed out of happiness.

"Let's get going and pack faster!"

I clasped the wrapped-up little old man to my chest, and we rushed off to our building. The lindens in the monastery garden, rejoicing, rattled their round leaves above us; the honeyed, radiant, hot wind blew in our faces. Purely for the fun of it we ran all out, headlong, gasping for breath because of the wind and happiness, when all of a sudden Tuzik leaped out of the bushes.

He hurled himself first at my chest, then at Muska's, barking loudly and offendedly, and we came to a standstill as if rooted to the ground, for we understood: Tuzik *knows everything*. Both that we were leaving for Petrograd, and that yesterday mama and papa had told us firmly that it was impossible to take Tuzik along with us. He had figured it all out from the new, strange smell of papa, from the smell of the boxes and bast—from the melancholy odor of departure. He had also figured out, of course, that we would not be taking him along with us . . . but even so he hoped!

And on the day of our departure, while we cunningly and unnoticed by the grown-ups tucked our little old man into a big box right underneath the bast, while strange men nailed the boxes closed and carried them off in a wheelbarrow to the landing, while we walked behind the wheelbarrow— Tuzik ran busily along beside us, not allowing himself to be distracted for even a minute. He had absolutely decided to go along with us to Petrograd. Muska and I were silent, dispirited by our treachery, and I didn't even look back at the monastery, at the cathedral, which later and for so many years I would dream about as something so wonderful and unattainable.

The big boat was already weighed down by our baggage, and papa, very thin and sweaty, embraced his Uglich friends and acquaintances and pressed us to sit down. But we, exchanging hugs and kisses with our friends, just couldn't say goodbye to the dog who had spent those hungry, dark, frightening evenings with us in the cell, and we started hugging him, crying and crying . . .

One of the peasants pushing our wheelbarrow to the landing sang out: "Whose doggie is this?"

"Ours," I answered, and glancing at the man, I saw that he had a round, kind face. "Do take him with you, uncle.[6] But please feed him, or he'll starve to death."

The man nodded his head:

"Ok, I'll take him for the kids. He's a nice little dog, just right for children."

He pulled a rope from out of the depths of his striped trousers and tied it around Tuzik's neck, taking the other end of the rope in his hand.

"Now sit down, sit down," papa urged us. "Don't howl, girls, you're off to grandma and grandpa, to Peter!"

We sat down and the boat cast off. Desperately straining to get to us, Tuzik began to bay, to yelp, to wheeze, even downright sobbing. We both started howling.

The view of Uglich and the Church of Dmitry-on-the-Blood from the Volga, c. 1910, as Berggolts would have seen it as a child, before the dam raised the level of the river. (Library of Congress, Prokudin-Gorskii collection, lot 10340)

"Well, God bless you, children," said mama, "you should really look back at Uglich for the last time. You went through so much there."

I raised my face, swollen with tears. Shimmering through the tears, looking as if it was about to slide down toward the water, Uglich sat way up high on the slope, ornamental, ancient, green; and "our cathedral" towered over it all, white, with the five dark blue star-covered domes, and the Tsare-vitch Dmitry Palace reddening gloomily on the bank,[7] and, a little in the distance, the Resurrection Monastery; and it was all covered by a sultry summer haze, shimmering through the shroud of my tears, and some kind of soft white fluff from the trees drifted endlessly through the air. And all at once an unprecedented tenderness blazed up in me toward the town that was vanishing before my eyes: because here we had experienced not only the "hungry time"; here we experienced the first proud bursting joy of going out with the Saturday work brigades together with real Communists and members of the Komsomol,[8] singing the "Internationale," feeling ab-solutely just like "grown-ups," honest-to-goodness participants in the war against the Whites, against the hated Kolchak . . . And what about our school? What about Tuzik? And what about the holidays, especially the spring holidays? . . .

I remember—I remember with my heart—how I felt then, without recognizing it as clearly as I do now, that something very good, very bright, remained behind in Uglich, something that would never ever come again, not even in Petrograd. And a shining, sharp, delicate string jerked to life and began to moan, to quiver inside my chest.

. . . We traveled along the Volga for a whole day and a whole night, and at first it was very interesting at night: it looked as if it was even possible, if one could just figure out how, to hook a silvery little star out of the dark warm water, like a little fish; and warm, homey lights clustered along the banks . . . but then we got very sleepy. It took us a long time to find a comfortable spot, boxes stuck out everywhere; then, snuggling up to each other like puppies, we dozed off somehow or other. However, we had to wake up again almost immediately—we were approaching the Volga Station. All around there was a dark pink fog: we landed right at the shore. We desperately wanted to sleep, and everything was as in a dream: clambering endlessly along a slope, wet, cold, blue-gray with dew; and then sitting in some sort of smelly hut, then traveling in an unbearably squeaky cart, and when the sun had already risen, we arrived at the Volga Station and— evidently—entered the train hall.

And there I was so shocked that the dream seemed to blow away, and that delicate string moaning inside me suddenly fell silent, as if it had snapped. So many people, so many people were all around—and right in the train station with its dull, half-smashed windows, and on the platform, and right on the ground against the wall of the train station—so many people and the main thing, all of them, all of them had the very same face! It wasn't masculine or feminine, old or young, but simply a face, yellow like a church candle, with dark blue shadows around the eyes, with sticky strands of gray hair . . . Later I recognized that face in the Aid the Hungry posters. And—whether they lay in exhaustion, right on the floor or on the ground, or sat, or stood, they all somehow swirled, swarmed, shrieked; and a wild calamity, a wild power emanated from those yellow-blue swirling people with a single face, from the endless, pitiful incessant clamor, from the piercing crying of nursing infants, from the penetrating odor of urine and cinders.

"It's because the war's over . . . This is everyone going home . . . to Petrograd, like us. Everyone, everyone to Petrograd . . . and we are just the same as they are, we're all going to Petrograd together," went swiftly through my mind, and all at once I felt myself utterly caught up by the power of that wildness, sensed clearly that I myself—as an individual—did not exist.

And we sat down on the floor with mama, in the thick of the people, closely pressed against an aunty with a yellow face, horrifyingly like our own mama. I could not take my eyes off our neighbor. We sat in the railway station for a long time, all the way till evening, and with an insatiable curiosity new to me, I looked around at the people gnawed away by hunger. With all my being I devoured the rumble and groan, and with greed, with horror, with a strange delight I listened to the new, bewildering, incomprehensible, and vast—sensation of being.

Getting ourselves seated in the train was terrifying. Everyone pushed so hard that it seemed as if any minute it would end in death. Papa handed me and Muska to some uncle straight through the window, and the uncle threw both of us on the top berth, like bags. Then those who had gotten into the train car began to push away those who were still trying to creep in through the window, and in the quivering yellow light of candles, the people moaned and groaned, cried out, and made a racket even more terrible, more pitiful, than in the train station. But I fell asleep instantly, hardly had my head touched the berth . . .

Fairy Tale of Light

It seemed to me that someone was quickly stroking my face with a cool, furry little paw.

"Squirrel," I thought, not surprised, and at the same time I was dreaming about an orange pine grove, where the pines stood very straight and bright orange, the mirrored patches of sunlight and shadow hanging motionless between them. It was very hot; hands and cheeks stuck to the resin; it was stifling from the hot, glowing resin, from the sun, from the clear color of the pines, but the squirrel tickled my face, quickly, quickly, coolly, gently, with all its tiny hairs, lightly pawing the hair on my forehead.

"Squirrel, dear," I murmured inarticulately, laughing and loving the squirrel very much. "I'm going to catch you and bring you to Petrograd."

I raised my hand to my face and opened my eyes. And instantly, with the same insatiable greed that had erupted in me yesterday at the station, I began to look and listen, look and listen . . .

The train pounded. The dim dawn, puzzled and uncertain, lit the train car. I glanced down: people who were incomprehensibly arranged, who had shouted hysterically through the night, rudely pushing each other, now slept. Everyone slept; they slept sitting, tightly, trustingly pressed against each other; they slept with their heads on their knees or burying their face in their hands or with their hands behind their head. I couldn't distinguish papa and mama from those all around, the identical bent backs, sleeping, like everyone. All sat as though they were frozen in a deep, difficult meditation, motionless, gray, bent over, and from above they resembled big round stones, timidly lit by the gray dawn.

"And King Arthur is asleep, and the knights of the round table are fast asleep,"—suddenly this phrase, which I'd picked up somewhere, solemnly and sadly sounded in my mind, and how apt it seemed!

They slept, tired, silent, as if forever frozen in an important thought, and sleeping this way, sped to Petrograd. Only occasionally I heard a groan or fragmentary, half-delusional mutterings—probably many had already come down with typhus . . .[9]

"And the knights of the round table were fast asleep . . . And what about the squirrel?" Its paw was still running across my face. But it was the slightly open window; light early morning air rushed into the hot train car. Holding my breath, I put my open, burning mouth under this living stream . . . No, not everyone was sleeping: below, under my berth, invisible from above, two men were talking quietly. Outside the window, an empty, gray, foggy field unfolded. A burned-out hut slipped past. The fog became thicker, the iron rumbled: we slowly crept across an iron bridge. Black, wet beams floated past the window; a morose sentry, standing on some kind of strange ledge on the bridge, raised his eyes and looked straight into my pupils, and our gazes met, merged . . . And far below, behind the beams, water glowed dimly—it was the river. Cold, colorless, all in steam, it passed through the empty fields, where shrubs were faintly visible in the fog and the first morning light. And in a sharp, almost painful instant it seemed to me that all this had already happened in my life: the land and water in fog, and the unwavering gaze of a stranger straight into my pupils—from the emptiness and fog . . .

". . . And here, my good fellow, masses of people are working on this river," a male voice spoke under my berth in a singsong; storytellers probably talked through the night with such a voice—hoarse, mysterious, a bit raw. "Folk from all over Raseya,[10] masses of all sort of working people—stonemasons, stonebreakers, tilebreakers, ore haulers . . . like under Peter the Great."

"We heard," answered a younger voice, tired and brittle.

"And an amazing machine was brought there . . . It's . . . it's the cleverest machine in the world, my good fellow! It'll pick up and lift earth with a sort of claw, like a scoop . . . So, how much do you suppose it'll lift?"

"And how much?"

"Up to one hundred cartloads at a time! Do you hear? And it takes any earth—summer or winter. And what kind of winters do we have? Hungry and cold, and the ground is like iron in these winters. But it's not afraid of that ground. It digs and digs, gnaws down to the wildest stone and it scatters the tallest mountain . . ."

"So, and what's it for?"

The storyteller sighed deeply, joyfully, and his voice became soft and tender, exactly as if it glowed in the dawn light; so, I suppose, storytellers' voices brightened when they embarked on a story about the breaking of an enchantment.

"Eh, you're a silly kid. 'For what?' There will be a waterfall there! Understand, a colossal waterfall. And of such violent force, that light itself will appear from this waterfall. Like from God. It's called Volkhovstroy, my good fellow, remember that—Volkhovstroy.[11]

"And will there be a lot of this light?"

"Uh, kiddo! Such a question! It will flood all of Raseya with light, to the last crack. White light, clear, like daylight. In a word—scientifically, well, simply speaking, electrical . . . only you probably can't pronounce it yet."

"Why's that?"—the young voice was suddenly offended. "I'm very able to pronounce it: e . . . e-lectrical . . . Oh, you, grandpa, think . . ."

"I don't think!"—the storyteller exclaimed, almost gleefully. "I'm just saying: study, my good fellow, understand . . . Because the power of this light from electricity will be a frightening power. Everything is subject to this power: it can grind the hardest iron and drive machines and plow, it can plow, kiddo, and what's most important, not as we now putter around with a wooden plow, but turning up thousands of versts at a time.[12] Power and light, like from the Lord God—power and light."

The storyteller seemed to sigh and paused. The train pounded. As if frozen in deep thought, everyone slept, exhausted, on the lookout for typhus, round and motionless, and sleeping, sped to Petrograd.

"Starving and cold, at least let there be light," the young voice said mdly, wearily. "It's easier in the light than in the dark, right, grandpa?"

"Could be," he indifferently agreed, then once again boomed enthusiastically: "How it will gush from Volkhovstroy, how it will begin to shine over all of Raseya, how it will begin to splash. Lenin so ordered it."

Petrograd

At noon we arrived in Petrograd, at our own Nevsky Gate.[13] And suddenly it turned out that our Petrograd house wasn't at all enormous, as we'd remembered it for almost three years, but small . . . It was so very small, and it was absolutely incomprehensible why it had shrunk so much while we were living in Uglich and dreaming of it.

And the garden wasn't there at all—only four birches around a half-destroyed arbor, even the greenish fence with hearts carved on its planks wasn't there.

"During the hunger it was chopped down for firewood," said grandma, and for the first time she cried over the garden. Instead of the flower garden there was a kitchen garden, fenced by rusty beds and rusty tin signboards, very small—so even the garden was small back then; new tenants, strangers hilled the potato plants.

So our little old man had nowhere to live.

For three days, wrapped in a checkered rag, he lived behind the stove in the dining room. Then, when we were alone, we pulled him out with great reverence, unwrapped him, and put him on a chair. We set him down, looked at him and—were stupefied: the old man *wasn't there*. It was just an ugly, dark root, true, the same one as in Uglich, with the same shoots protruding from its sides, which in Uglich were the little old man's arms, and the same gnarl on top, which before was his angry, pensive little face—everything, everything was there, but the little old man himself was gone. It was as if he'd disappeared on the way to Petrograd, leaving in his place something homely and absolutely dead. We turned him this way and that, looked at him from the sides and from behind, we laid down on the floor and looked up from there, squinting deliberately: no—a root, not the little old man! Muska could still make out his small beard and the little old man's general vague outline, but I couldn't see anything anymore except an ugly root, and this, as I later understood, was a great loss.

I myself shoved the former little old man into the stove, on the sly . . .

And perhaps this happened to the little old man or also to us because in our Petrograd house we encountered an unexpected and great joy: shortly before our arrival electricity came to our house, and the old hanging lamp now burned even brighter than before we left for Uglich! How good it was that we didn't believe mama that in those years it was everywhere as dark and cold as our cell. True, light was supplied only in the evening, but when grandpa quietly clicked the switch and the friendly light flared up under the old greenish shade, it seemed to me that something within me had also clicked and lit up—how nice it was!

"Grandpa," I asked quietly, timidly, as if giving away a big secret, "grandpa, this . . . this is from Volkhovstroy?"

"What's with you, Olyushka! Volkhovstroy is still being built . . . And when it's built, will we really have these kinds of bulbs? This is a dark little sixteen candlepower thing . . . But then there'll be big, round, bright ones, and all day long it'll be, and everywhere, not just our house . . ."

And I became even happier. Our grandfather said almost the same thing as the old man under my berth, that meant that the old man didn't lie, that Volkhovstroy—is true, and will be . . . and bright light will be everywhere, and if there will be light then there won't be cold, darkness, hungry times; there won't be a train hall like at the Volga Station; there won't be the frightful people that were there; they won't be anywhere, not in Petrograd, not in Uglich! A momentary vision of the past, the night-time conversation in the train car—the trip to Petrograd, everything in its entirety, sharply and clearly flashed before me, and I understood, not intellectually but in some other way, that now all of this will forever remain in me, as a part of myself, as something eternally alive . . .

In My Memory

And so it was. The trip from Uglich to Petrograd remained in me not just as a recollection—over the course of my life, this recollection, alive and sharp, became increasingly full, enriched, increasingly lived, and everything new that flowed into it or came into contact with it, everything that I learned, became my own personal past.

Many years later, I learned that in roughly the same years when we returned to Peter, almost in the same days, the famous English science fiction writer H. G. Wells visited my homeland, and I read his book about this trip.[14]

He traveled on the very same railway as us; he saw the same women, men, and children as we did; he saw us. But we lived, while he looked. He looked as if at a scene, from a window in a private compartment in a good train car, where he traveled with his son, with his English coffee set, a blanket, and canned goods brought from England. They were accompanied by a sailor "assigned in Petrograd," wrapped in an ammunition belt, who kept a sharp eye out so that no one insulted the famous guest, and at station stops ran to get him boiling water, carrying the boiling water in a "silver teapot with the tsar's monogram," a teapot so "charming" that Wells remembered it . . . The sailor went for boiling water at stations like the Volga Station. And the English writer was horribly displeased that he traveled not by the express but by the fast train, crossly and continuously harassing the Baltic sailor carrying the silver teapot with his political complaints . . ."my lips were unsealed," he later wrote. "I spoke to my guide, as one mariner might speak to another, and told him what I thought of Russian methods."[15] The writer also mentions that he felt acutely irritated by the sailor's answer: upon hearing "my rich incisive phrases" he answered very respectfully with a single, stereotypical phrase, very "significant of certain weaknesses of the present Russian state of mind. 'You see,' he said politely—'the blockade!'" The fourteen-power blockade . . .[16] And the author of *War of the Worlds*, which describes a war between people and Martians, couldn't understand what the sailor put into this "stereotypical" polite phrase, "You see, the blockade . . ." I still think how much self-possession it took the sailor not to answer the grumbling writer "Baltic style" . . . In those days back in Uglich, even we, the children, sang that Kolchak wore an "English uniform."[17] Oh, how my childhood loves this unknown sailor, recognized many years later, how it doesn't forgive the famous writer anything—it's stronger than maturity!

Herbert Wells did not, of course, hear a conversation such as the one I heard on the way to Petrograd, but at the very same time Lenin talked to him about Volkhovstroy! And the famous science fiction writer condescendingly took pity on the "dreamer in the Kremlin," who succumbed to "the Utopia of the electricians."[18] And he titled his book about my homeland in those years *Russia in the Shadows*; he saw it only in the shadows, and he saw its future as a shadow, though he wasn't the worst of the foreigners; he in some measure sympathized with us. How proud is my childhood of the nameless people traveling with me in that train car—Russian peasants, who saw the future of their homeland as radiant. How proud is my childhood and my whole life of Vladimir Ilich Lenin, not only dreaming, but, even then, in those years, beginning to carry out the people's dream of light and power. My life is eternally proud of them, with a deep, virtuous, silent, open pride—be proud always, remember them always, no matter what happens to you, to the country, to the people!

In December 1920, the GOELRO plan was ready, and reporting on it at the Eighth Congress of Soviets, Gleb Maximilianovich Krzhizhanovsky switched on a map of the Russian Soviet Federated Socialist Republic "with centers and circles" and it lit up before the delegates' eyes, almost blinding them.[19] Perhaps this was the same evening when in our cell the oil lamp went out because of my sister's careless breath, and the only match was broken, and we, in darkness and fear, snuggling together, didn't know that at the same time, far away in Moscow the map of the Future lit up and shined—our future. It was already determined by the party, it was already seen by it.

All of this is almost legendary now: Wells's trip, the conversation with Lenin, the shining map at the Eighth Congress of Soviets—it was familiar to me—and associated with childhood, organically and proudly included in it as something belonging to it, as its property—in the days of my Komsomol youth, during the First Five-Year Plan in the period of ardent work at the Elektrosila factory on the orders for the Great Dnieper.[20] And my childhood and my life grew richer and richer—moreover, twenty years later I heard all about this from Gleb Maximilianovich Krzhizhanovsky himself, when in January 1952 I spent a whole evening with him before my first trip to the Volga-Don.

The Knight of Light

Rather short, wizened, animated, in a black academician's hat, with a dark-swarthy face on which the white triangular bushes of his eyebrows shined brightly, the same bushes as his small mustache, and the same bush as his small beard, with very big, dark eyes full of life and intelligence—so appeared before me the man who started working with Vladimir Ilich Ulyanov in the Union of Struggle for the Emancipation of the Working Class.[21] He was exiled together with Lenin to Siberia; wrote the immortal "Warsawian";[22] was one of the leaders overseeing the establishment of GOELRO—one of the zealots of electrification, whom Lenin called "the knights of light."

At Gleb Maximilianovich's request, I told about how Alexandrovskaya Street in the Nevsky Gate, down which he and Lenin walked at the end of the nineteenth century to a meeting of the first workers' circles, looks today: the little wooden house where they met has been preserved, and the middle part of the street paved with large cobblestones has settled a bit, so that the walls of huge poplars that stand on both sides of it are strongly and evenly bent toward one another, the crowns almost closed, as if a living green tent covered the road along which the young Lenin once walked.

"Oh, how I remember him—then!" Gleb Maximilianovich quietly exclaimed, and so much tremulous, deep love sounded in his voice and was expressed on his living face that it seemed to light up everything all around. "I am proud that even back then I followed him. And you know, followed him, followed him, closely, as they say, like a rooster—all my life . . . And how much heart he put into this GOELRO plan of ours, how much we discussed it in this very room . . ."

"Vladimir Ilich was here? In this room?"

"Yes, of course," Krzhizhanovsky merrily confirmed. "He was here quite often, alone and with Nadezhda Konstantinovna[23] . . . And he always sat in the very place and on the very chair on which you're sitting now . . ."

I involuntarily jumped and saw the modest, smart room in a new light, and a slight chill ran through my body.

"Sit, sit," my host waved his hand at me, "don't worry . . . For me, everything here is connected to him . . . He was a bold dreamer, a brilliant dreamer, sometimes . . . somewhat mischievous—in a Russian way! You know he understood what electrification meant not only as a statesman, but also somehow as a young man in love with it, with his Volkhovstroy . . . Yes, it was his child. His favorite." And looking at me sternly, he asked: "You've been to Volkhovstroy, I hope?"

And here I couldn't but tell Krzhizhanovsky, at least briefly, that I was at Volkhovstroy—just three weeks before, when electrification's first born celebrated its twenty-fifth anniversary. And it happily turned out that there I caught the living and beautiful conclusion of the legendary tale, overheard in childhood, in the hungry year's calamitous train car: I met the son and grandson of the person who in 1919 brought from red Peter that very same "cleverest machine in the world" that gnawed the earth down to the wild stone, about which the old man in the train car spoke with such inspiration and hope. He was from the Putilov works,[24] an old Petersburg worker named Alexei Vasilevich Vasilev, and the "cleverest machine" was Excavator No. 25, lifting half a cubic meter of earth. How far from today's giant self-propelled excavators! . . . But in those years it seemed enormous for my country—as our Petrograd house seemed to me . . . When Volkhovstroy was built, Alexei Vasilevich returned to Peter—already Leningrad—to his native "Red Putilov works," but his son, Vasily Alexeevich, arriving there in 1920, stayed to work on the new-born power station. He got married to a "Volkhovstroy mermaid," a girl from the village of Duboviki—a village that sank to the bottom, flooded by the Volkhov River after the construction of the dam. In the year of Volkhovstroy's launch they had a son named in honor of his grandfather—the first builder of Volkhovstroy—Alexei. During the Great Fatherland War, the Vasilev family did not leave the station, they protected it, ready to fight for it to the last breath against the enemy.[25] And although the Germans were literally right beside them, shelling and bombing Volkhovstroy, the small band of Volkhovites—workers at the station—nonetheless solemnly celebrated the fifteenth anniversary of Volkhovstroy in December 1941, and in January were already beginning to restore the station in order to supply current to Leningrad. The old Putilov worker Alexei Vasilevich worked at this time at the Kirov plant—in blockaded Leningrad. In January 1942 he died of hunger at the factory, at his workplace.[26]

I told Gleb Maximilianovich this story, worthy of a poem, even more briefly than I have here—I couldn't wait to question and listen to him. Becoming more animated, and seemingly younger, he told about Lenin and about his meeting with Wells: "Lenin laughed at him and said, 'He understands nothing at all!'" He told about the Eighth Congress of Soviets, where he turned on the map of the Russian electrification plan. I asked him nevertheless if it was really true that they'd had to shut off the current to all of Moscow in order to light the map.

"No," he answered seriously, "not all of it: in one room in the Kremlin one sixteen-candlepower bulb stayed on . . . God, how I worried that evening! I was asked to keep to forty minutes . . . And the plan—after all it's volumes and volumes, you see? . . . But forty minutes! I say to Vladimir Ilich: 'Vladimir Ilich, I'll fail.' He chuckles: 'Nothing to worry about. Drink a strong cup of coffee right before the presentation—I myself sometimes do the same when I'm worried before a presentation.' Well I followed his advice, but my worry didn't abate . . . And here I make the presentation and I feel that so much was unsaid, so much . . . Finishing—I felt as though I'd said nothing! I turn on the map of the Russian Federation, already the whole map, pronounce the last phrases, and I understand absolutely clearly: so, I've failed!" (Gleb Maximilianovich grabbed his head with his hands; real terror flashed in his eyes.) "I failed! And I'm looking sidelong, from the corner of my eye—at Lenin, Lenin! And I see . . . Vladimir Ilich nods his head at me and smiles, and Nadezhda Konstantinovna smiles . . . And from the hall, from the semidarkness—some kind of strange rumble . . . I look—it's the delegates standing one after the other, looking, riveted, at the lighted map, applauding it . . . you understand, they applaud! And Lenin is so pleased, he smiles and also applauds . . . Well, I think, seems to have gone over well . . ."

He laughed youthfully and happily, shaking his head in the academician's hat, clearly reproaching himself for his past doubts—all this difficult and beautiful past lived in him as an eternally living memory, a memory of feelings and blood . . . He paced around the room, paused and added with strong emotion:

"Y-yes . . . we had to go through a lot drawing up the plan . . . It was all tapped out on that typewriter—can you see?" And he indicated a big old-fashioned Remington under a crumpled and rather shabby cover. "Things happened. Sometimes with those old specialists I had to behave like a tiger tamer . . . One night I'll never forget! That night I was finishing the preface to the 'Electrification Plan' . . . I was ending it with words addressed to our distant, happy descendants. I wrote that the wonderful, highly developed, bold, and intelligent people of the future will probably find plenty of errors, mistakes, deficiencies in our work . . . And I asked them to excuse us all this, because, constructing this first, imperfect plan, we worked in difficult circumstances, during a fourteen-power blockade, fighting off foreign intervention, suffocating from destruction, cold, and hunger. And, you know, imagining this amazing, happy person of the future, mentally conversing with him, I cried . . . Yes, I stood alone in the middle of this same room and here, clenching my hands like this, I cried out of love for this future person, out of admiration for him, out of an incredible desire to get at least a glimpse of him, of that future whose foundations we are laying—the distant future . . ."

He stood in the middle of the room, a rather short, very old man—older than the electric light bulb, the automobile, the airplane, an assistant of the immortal Lenin, a valiant knight of light—stood, with clenched hands, with moist, shining eyes, reliving his night of rapture in the face of the future. And looking at him with some sort of austere agitation, I wanted to say:

"And after all you were crying then for yourself, yourself today . . . For our present days—for the way it is now . . . for everything in it . . ."

But I didn't say anything—the virtuous agitation of the moment was bigger than words.

The Essential Book

And so from that year, from that night when Gleb Maximilianovich Krzhizhanovsky, rooted to the spot, dreamed of "getting a glimpse" of the future, and soon thereafter switched on his visible, matter-of-fact, shining map; from the year we left Uglich; from that first dim feeling at the hungry Volga Station of *being*; from that night in the typhus train car, where I overheard the fantastical tale of Volkhovstroy; from the arrival in our Petrograd, where our dear house had shrunk, and the little old man (magical childhood vision) disappeared, and an anxious, trembling adolescence came into its own, like the dawn, along with the first electric light bulb gleaming in our old house—since that day thirty-two years have passed. And if there is something that I want to write about more than anything, it is about those thirty-two years of life—my own life, meaning also everyone's, because I can't separate one from the other, just as it's impossible to separate breath from air.

I'm certain that most if not all writers have an Essential Book that is always ahead. It is his favorite, most cherished, beckoning irresistibly. Perhaps, occasionally, in solitude, the writer trembles with delight before the vision of it, accessible to no one but himself . . . The writer can't know in advance in what *form* it will materialize—whether as a poem, verses, a novel, a memoir, but he knows for certain *what* it will be in its main essence: knows that the core of it will be *himself*, his life, and first of all the life of his soul, the journey of his conscience, the formation of his awareness—and all of this is inseparable from the life of the people. In other words, the writer's Essential Book—in any event *my* essential book—is made visible by me as a book saturated with the truth of *our universal everyday life*, transmitted through *my* heart.

The Essential Book, it seems to me, must begin with childhood itself, with the origins, with the first pure and fundamental impressions that for my generation in particular so happily coincide with the first years—also childhood!—of our new society. The Essential Book must reach the peak of maturity at which the writer works with full and gratifying inner freedom and fearlessness, unconditionally trusting himself, in view of everyone and alone with himself; when his only concern is taking care that the whole of life, his and in general, be expressed fully and as one, appearing not as random episodes, but as a whole, that is—in its essence, not as the partial truth of separate events, but as the guiding truth of history.

At its foundation, the Essential Book rests on a single, all-encompassing, and clear feeling, that is, on the foundation of our great idea, which became all five human senses, and it integrates them by means of the writer's special artistic sense. The Essential Book openly and truthfully displays the formation, maturation, and ripening of this idea-feeling—or put another way, of the communist worldview and the person's view of life; it reveals his struggle—with circumstances, with himself, with remnants of the past within him and around him, with enemies, with opponents, and sometimes even with friends.

Does the dream of creating such a book run counter to the writer's fundamental task—reflecting objective reality in artistic form and nurturing the reader's communist worldview? No, it isn't a contradiction, because the most important thing that literature must reflect (more precisely—express) is the internal, spiritual world of our person, the complex and multifaceted movement of this world that is defined by the actions of the public-spirited person and that defines his actions. No higher or nobler task exists for the writer. There's no need to discuss what universal human victories (and not simply successes!) great Soviet literature has achieved on this field; its victories are widely known, and we, moving forward into the future, can boldly draw on it. Were I asked if I could point to a particular example of this sort of book, I would first of all point to works of poetry like Mayakovsky's "About This" and "At the Top of My Voice" and of prose like Nikolai Ostrovsky's *How the Steel Was Tempered.*[27]

With insurmountable and calm force these works destroy the absurd contrast between confession and sermon.

The passionate, thoroughly propagandistic final chapter of the poem "About This"—"Application on Behalf of . . ."—with its fiery and unshakeable faith in the future, in the "thirtieth century" that will "overtake the pack of trivial things that rend the heart," and in the wonderful people of this future, a plea addressed to them—"resurrect me," thirsting to be with them, at least as "a keeper for your beasts" ("At least get a glimpse of them," dreamed Krzhizhanovsky)—this whole chapter supported by the whole previous course of the poem in which the poet, with the utmost ruthlessness toward himself, bares his heart, his inner world with all its turmoil, sorrows, its struggles "with that which is beaten into us by the departed slave," that inner world that not only reflected the most complex social processes of those times, but through which they passed, with pain and joy. The poet experiences the petty-bourgeois attempt to attack "our red-flagged order" during NEP as something deeply intimate, as jealously toward a lover (with real, human jealousy).[28] The poem is written, as Mayakovsky himself said of it, "for personal reasons about universal everyday life." The propagandistic, the sermon-like *persuasiveness* of its final, particularly life-affirming chapter relies on the poet's own deepest *belief* in his ideals, enduring belief, proven by ordeal, expressed by him with ruthless—indeed confessional truth.

All of this applies to an even greater degree to the poem "At the Top of My Voice," a poem that not only propagandizes but directly agitates for militant, socialist, party art—precisely preaches it. But Mayakovsky preaches this art not as something beautiful but external, existing outside of himself, but instead as an affair of his *own personal life*; he agitates by strong personal example. His heart is wide open, open to its depths before the reader; he is so convinced of the rightness of his cause, of the truth of the art he is preaching, that he is not at all afraid to say, "And agitprop is stuck in my teeth." And after that, an open, severe confession:

> But I
> > subdued
> > > myself,
> > > > standing
> > on the throat
> > > of my own song . . .

or the equally open address to distant and happy descendants:

> For you,
> > who
> > > are healthy and agile,
> The poet
> > licked up
> > > tubercular spittle
> with the rough tongue of a poster. —

It does not contradict the poem's proud concluding lines:

> I will raise,
> > like a Bolshevik party card,
> all one-hundred volumes
> > of my
> > > party books—

And unshakeable authority is imparted with these lines, evoking in the reader unconditional, unlimited trust.

The enormous, enduring educational value of Nikolai Ostrovsky's book *How the Steel Was Tempered*, a party book through and through that is still forming the souls of whole generations (already more than Ostrovsky's own generation!), rests on the fact that as Ostrovsky was creating the image of Pavel Korchagin, propagandizing it, he poured into it his whole life, his whole soul. And this soul was the great soul of a communist, the best child of the century. And it's not important that the "confession of the child of the century" comes in this case not from the author himself, and not even in the first person—I've already said that the forms embodying the Essential Book can be quite varied . . . I don't know what percentage of the beautiful trilogy by Fedor Gladkov (*Childhood, Outlaws, Evil Days*[29]) is speculation and fiction, but I'm convinced that here the author succeeded in writing his Essential Book, that in it he really writes about himself and his life—"for personal reasons about universal everyday life"—such a big, human, joyful truth, such personally lived existence emanates from the pages of this trilogy; it is written with such high artistic freedom.

And the Essential Book shuns neither collective heroes, nor speculation, nor fiction; it does not refuse any of the wonders of art, and above all—not for a moment does it refuse the great task of communist propaganda. But communist propaganda-preaching in these books is above all the effective transmission of the personal spiritual and life experience acquired in the whole people's struggle for the creation of the new, just society, and therefore it is necessary to fellow citizens; this is the insistent suggestion to the reader of the great truth of life that the writer grasped personally. We, propagandists, "mobilized and called by the party," are proud of this, and the dream of the Essential Book is the dream of the maximum output of strength for the party's, for the people's cause. Demanding not the maximum but the minimum—that is what clips the wings of the artist, who feels in himself true strength and dreams of a heroic act in the name of art. But the people demand the maximum from us, and all our writers' thoughts, arguments, discussions are subordinate to exactly this demand.

Attempts to separate confession from sermon, to juxtapose them, finally to prefer the confession to the sermon—or vice versa—provokes an active inner protest not only because such attempts are clearly alien and harmful to the work of Soviet literature but also, I would say, because of their somehow belligerent illiteracy. These attempts are made by people who clearly don't love, don't value, and don't even know the background of great classical Russian and Soviet literature that never separated confession from sermon but, on the contrary, always sought to use a form of confession as the most powerful instrument of propaganda, that is sermon. I have already spoken about the majestic personal example, or more precisely— about Mayakovsky's heroic feat. And isn't the autobiographical trilogy by Gorky, the founder of Soviet literature—*Childhood, My Apprenticeship,* and *My Universities*[30]—at the same time splendid, devastating propaganda of hatred for the world of philistines and hucksters, who distort the human face, a fiery sermon of humanity striving for the future?!

Gorky remained here the same publicist, tribune, propagandist as in "Song of the Falcon," as in *Mother*, and in all his other works.[31] For the genuine writer, connected by blood to the life and struggle of the people, there can be no danger in writing about himself and his own life. No, and here he won't sink into contemplating his own navel, won't engage in vain revelations, but, telling of his own heart, even about its secret movements, he necessarily tells about the heart of the people.

. . . *Past and Thoughts*—here is a book with which I, and probably most literary people, can converse almost every day, each time with new excitement and new surprise.[32] What a fearless and natural fusion of the most intimate narrative of the "swirling heart" with pictures of European social turns; what intelligent and exacting love permeated the creation of the image of the progressive people of that time, the fighters against tsarist tyranny, and alongside them—what devastating, pamphleteering characterizations and "portraits" of tsarist satraps, and incinerating hatred of Nicholas I, and pain on behalf of the Russian people, and belief in its unlimited strength! Everything in this book is described with that ideological directness, with that personal, passionate attitude, with that "subjectivity" that is also one of the essential aspects of the artist's party spirit. And everything is saturated with the blood of the heart, and with the shattering force of propaganda! Here one cannot oppose the confession and the sermon, and this is, I affirm, the tradition that Soviet literature, with a new ideological basis and new means, has continued and deepened, and that it must continue and deepen!

I repeat and stress: I absolutely do not want to say that the Essential Book can *only* be a diary or memoir, only directly autobiographical, and certainly not every writer can and must come out with such a book, in such a form. But if we speak about the form of the Essential Book, the appearance of which I together with many writers and readers ardently await, the creation of which I myself dream about as about the work of my whole life, then I imagine it as closest of all to *Past and Thoughts*, a brilliant *novel* of the human spirit, a novel unlike any in world literature. But Soviet literature must create it. It seems to me sometimes that everything has already been prepared for its appearance. It seems to me sometimes that I feel an elbow next to me, the touch of "our Herzen," who is no less essential to us than Gogol or Shchedrin.[33] I am ready to give him everything, everything that he demands, let my life and my name dissolve without a trace into his name, I will be happy if only one line written by me will be useful to him, only one diary entry, only one thought or feeling! . . .

The writer writes his Essential Book unceasingly, sometimes from childhood. Most often it is a diary, certainly written without the expectation that it will be solemnly published in his lifetime. For some a diary is a necessity. Not a demand of "self-admiration" or "self-absorption," as literary philistines, Hiders and Eunuchs, think.[34] And at first it's instinctive, but with maturity comes an ever greater awareness of the significance of the universal life passing through one's own life, or perhaps, it would be truer to say—an awareness of the significance of one's own life as inseparable from universal life.

Of course not only writers keep diaries. This need to keep a diary arises in certain periods with particular sharpness among both writers and non-writers. Thus, in the days of the blockade a huge number of Leningraders, of the most varied ages, professions, and circumstances kept diaries.[35] I've read lots of blockade diaries, written by the dark of oil lamps, in gloves, with hands almost too weak to hold a pen (more often—a pencil: the ink froze); the entries in some diaries were cut short at the moment of the author's death. Now scorching, now freezing, the triumphant Leningrad tragedy breathes from the many, many pages of these diaries, where a person writes with total candor about his or her own every day cares, efforts, sorrows, joys. And, as a rule, one's "own," the "deeply personal," is at the same time universal and general, the national becomes deeply personal, indeed humane. History suddenly speaks with a living, simple human voice.

I said that the writer writes his Essential Book unceasingly, always going toward it, tirelessly dreaming of it. Very often it seems: "This, what I'm writing is, finally, the most essential, exactly where I will express all that is most secret and precious, necessary to my fellow citizens. Here it is—the Essential Book, I am writing it . . ." But the book is written, and you see that, once again, it's not it, or only an approach to it, or a retreat from it. That is why the Essential Book is as if always in draft, an eternal draft. Because it is in perpetual motion, coinciding with the motion of life, with the growth and motion of the writer's consciousness. Whatever it may be about, through the motion of life and consciousness, it absorbs more and more; it demands additions all the time, even retroactively, even additions from the past rising up in a new way. Life itself and the truth found in it always rigorously proofread the Essential Book. It branches out, produces separate independent works that are no more than a detail of it; it becomes overgrown with footnotes, a mass of notes in the margin— besides what is written, besides what is published, and sometimes only planned or outlined. And perhaps precisely these footnotes, marginal notes, diary reflections will become the foundation, "will breathe the living soul"[36] into the future book and make it Essential. Maybe it will remain just a draft, or maybe it should just be published as is?

. . . And I, like other writers, have an Essential Book that is always ahead, excerpts from which are scattered in what is published as verses and prose, in what still remains in draft, in the desk, or only in my heart, in my memory. But increasingly I want to gather all of this, try to consolidate it, materialize it. Probably this will once again not be it, but the time has already come in my own life and the general life, when, beginning any work, even for the newspaper, one can't help but think about the Essential Book, can't help but hope that this is the way to it, an approach, let it be at least a step, but already a real approach.

I have already said that the Essential Book must begin from childhood itself, from the first pages of life . . . And that's why last year I traveled to the town of my childhood, to the town of my happiest dream—in the footsteps of the Essential Book that is always ahead, only in draft . . . More than ever, there is a need to begin from the beginning, with the origins of consciousness, with the distant, but unfading past—mine and my country's. But that which you've already read and will read in these pages, is not yet the Essential Book, it is still not from it, but only for it, only a step toward it, only a draft of a draft—an eternal draft. But so many now go toward it, toward their Essential Book, perhaps this will in some way aid the general search?[37] For now I only want to describe the trip to the town of my childhood—no more . . .

"It's Mine!"

And so on a blue July day last year, the small ship *Georgy Sedov* cast off from Khimok and headed down the Moscow Canal, along the Volga to Uglich.[38]

I waited with patient submissiveness for the end of the numerous locks that I'd experienced once before on this canal and, just like the first time, when the ship sank into the dark cave of the lock, it seemed to me that we'd never get out of there. When we entered the Big Volga, a huge, heavy, dark gold moon was rising in the transparent and calm sky and the pink light had not quite faded in the west. An inexpressible peace reigned all around, and Russian nature—dear, kind, not oppressing, not astounding with its wild beauty, but caressing with its vastness—eagerly, openly, generously unfolded before my eyes and heart . . . "Shelter yourself in the vast expanses! How can I live and cry without you!"[39] I repeated these lines of Blok's as my own plea. Oh, it's true, it's impossible even to cry, even to grieve without you. Nothing is possible without you. And if you are, then everything will be, everything will return, even that which now seems un-recoverable. And even love will return . . . Lines of verses—others' and my own—boiled up and escaped, and they were about different things, about many things . . .

> About the motherland and about love—
> They are inseparable in me . . .

About "the golden wedding anniversary"—

> It is clear to everyone that I won't stay with you,
> Neither to the silver, nor to the gold.
> But we had an iron one—
> on the edge of death during the war.
> I will not give it up for all the gold:
> I love you all the same, as the iron one . . .

About the Kalyazin Bell Tower[40]—

> About how all of it, white,
> rises from the quiet-quiet waters,
> and clouds pass overhead
> and at its feet.
> It stands, reflected in the mirror-like,
> fathomless-pure heights,
> as if marveling at its sad
> ancient Russian beauty;
> as if saying: "Look,
> I am with you—in all my glory . . ."
> O, city of Kitezh,[41] city of Kitezh,
> fearlessly rising above the water!

Our little ship carefully, quietly, as if with deep respect, rounded the bell tower of the half-submerged town, and in the clear and kind moonlight, the whole tower to the onion dome was reflected in the water; it was so beautiful that, as in childhood, I wanted to reach out my hand and exclaim: "It's mine!"

The Kalyazin Bell Tower, c. 2002. (Luciano, CC BY 2.0, Wikimedia Commons)

We had in childhood, in Uglich, a sort of game . . . and no, not really a game, but something more serious: so if you see something that strikes your imagination—a beautiful person, an unusual little house, some wonderful corner of the forest—and if you're the first to reach out your hand and cry: "Dibs, it's mine!"—then it'll be yours, and you can do whatever you want with it. For example, if it's a building, a house, you can populate it with whomever you want, describe them and how they live, what kinds of rooms there are or how you're going to live there yourself. If it's a person, you can imagine anything you want about him, give him any sort of life— in short, you could do everything in your imagination with what became yours. But most importantly, this—picture, city, person—is yours and none of the other kids could encroach on it, because everyone knows that it's yours, and you yourself know. And there wasn't any doubt that this really belonged to you. I still remember the amazingly absolute confidence we had then in the right of inviolable ownership. The painting *Moonlit Night on the Dnieper* by Kuindzhi was "mine";[42] also "mine" was Tanya Kozlova, a senior girl from school with a round Russian face and quiet, big, gray-blue eyes, not a beauty, even a little snub-nosed, but so sweet that you couldn't take your eyes off her; even she didn't know that she was "mine." When we read the books by Lukashevich and Stanyukovich about the defense of Sevastopol, Sevastopol became "mine," also the sailor Koshka and Admiral Nakhimov;[43] Muska was terribly jealous, and even though I magnanimously conceded the French and even Napoleon to her, she said: "What am I gonna do with them? . . ." Later, also "mine" was a certain little brook in the forest, clear, fiercely luminous, terribly grouchy, that ran out from under a green, mossy, seemingly plush rock. It grumbled and muttered almost like a human being; in any case, one phrase, which it obstinately repeated in a weak bass voice—"will be-will be-will-be-will be . . ."—could be heard quite clearly. What it would turn out to be—it didn't say . . . Probably, some kind of wondrous waterfall, but somewhere so far away that we couldn't get to it. And much of what I had in childhood, so many riches, so much "mine," I don't even remember . . . And the Valdai *duga* in the Tsarevich Dmitry Palace in Uglich was also "mine," but I will tell about it separately . . .[44]

Two Meetings

And the town of childhood appeared in the early dawn, in the fog, behind a gauze of the lightest warm rain, with the same strange twinkling that I'd dreamed about for so many years. And not agitation, but a wary silence arose in me when I saw it, even from afar and even before the entrance under the grand gateway arch with the lush, tidy flowerbed next to the huge, rectangular building, almost bare architecturally, of the famous hydroelectric station.

My little town no longer soared on a precipitously steep green slope: the water raised by the dam reached almost all the way to the boulevard, to the Tsarevich Dmitry Palace, to the ancient little church on the shore; it seemed very small to me, achingly small, as if it had descended into the water, as if it had settled heavily into the earth. I had long understood that it should seem that way, but I later learned that Uglich really is sinking into the earth, and part of it sank into the water. This exact terminology is used at hydroelectric sites—to sink into the earth, to sink into the water, to sink to the bottom. The old-old Paisevsky Monastery that repelled Polish raids during the Time of Troubles sank into the water;[45] the village of Spasskaya sank into the water, the ancient pine forest thinned out on that side. And many of Uglich's buildings, especially the ancient ones, sank into the earth: with the advent of the reservoir the groundwater rose in the town, and the soil softened, became different than it had been a few hundred years ago when these churches were built, all this fairy-tale beauty, these bell towers and monasteries, meekly and irreconcilably raising their darkened little heads above the water.

. . . It was about five o'clock in the morning when the sleepy woman on duty at the town's hotel—a single-story wood building with carved window casings and lintels—took me to my room; in the small elongated room there was a bed, where the pillow was standing with one of its corners pointing up, a table covered with an old tablecloth, a couch, above that an antique mirror in a walnut frame, and on the windowsill of a big window—tall, lush, bright pink geraniums. And from the window, behind the clump of trees and roofs could be seen the three tented roofs of the "Wondrous"—the church of the Alexeevsky Monastery, thus named by the people three and a half centuries ago for its truly wondrous architecture—rising austerely, sadly, and harmoniously into the just-turning-blue sky. It was very quiet, only the barely audible whisper of the gentle, luminous rain in the leaves, and the smell of wet grass pouring through the open window, and occasionally a pink geranium petal falling noiselessly to the windowsill . . .

"That's good," I thought, "as if I've always lived here. Now I'll wait for nothing, no one's letters, no one's telegrams—even with the call to return, I won't hurry here and there, even to our cell and school . . . I'll have time."

I conscientiously tried to fall asleep, but lying motionless on the bed for nearly an hour, I jumped up: no, I must go "to it." I have to, I have to. Go and get there, although for some reason it was suddenly frightening. And I went toward "my cathedral." It was visible from everywhere—the domes now not deep blue but almost black with barely visible rusty stars, and all the same for a long time, as in the dream, I went toward it, turning in forgotten streets. The light rain stopped, the town woke up little by little, the uncertain pearly dawn turned into morning. From the windows of houses that had settled into the earth, sleepless old women, pushing the lush geraniums aside with their hands, looked at me, and the wide streets, as in childhood, were covered with downy green grass and numerous geese leisurely strutted about the streets with their endearingly ugly juvenile goslings. A great fiery-feathered rooster—undoubtedly the descendant of that very rooster that left a print of its giant talon on the Cockfighting Rock that at one time lay at the end of Rooster Street—the fiery-feathered and fiery-tailed rooster flew up to a closed wicket gate with an iron ring and began to crow deliriously from there. And I was still walking, and the cathedral was still closer . . . And the closer I got to it the more clearly I saw that nothing in this place resembled childhood and the happy dream. No, the building with our cell wasn't there. It simply wasn't on the earth.

There was no dark pond and no lindens that should have been rattling their round leaves; there was no garden where the little old man lived; there was no wall extending between the cathedral and the school. Nothing was the same. I reached the cathedral itself: deeply settled into the ground, shabby, as if covered with lichen, the cathedral now held a state grain procurement warehouse and a petroleum depot, as attested to by the ugly signboards above some kind of jury-rigged plank doors covering the entrance. And only the red brick building opposite the cathedral, our school, my first school, was as it had been then (although, of course, shrunken), and it was still a school. But it was vacation, and the school stood empty and quiet.

I sat on a bench in the small flower garden laid out in front of the school, across from the grain procurement warehouse, and thought that the meeting with childhood and happiness hadn't come off. It was gone, and what was behind it was gone, sunk into the earth, sunk into the water, sunk to the bottom.

> And the land, its deep blue and stones and ashes,
> dear and sweet, repeated to me:
> "You came back, to what you sought.
> Be now at peace. You came."

Probably, I sat here a long time, because the sun flared up, and drops of rain on some light lilac-tinged and pale blue flowers in the school's flowerbeds sparkled in the sun, and their petals began to shine. A young woman, adjusting a small basket with vegetables, sat down on the bench next to me.

"Excuse me, how do I get from here to Annunciation Street?" I asked her.

I still wanted to track down the house of our friends from those years.

"To Annunciation? I don't know anything like that . . ."

"It intersects Holy Cross, this one that goes through here."

"Uh? This was really Holy Cross? That's interesting, how all these names were divine . . . It's October Street. And the one you need is probably Freedom Street. I don't know the way, I live on Zina Zolotova Street."

"And Zina Zolotova—who's she?"

She looked at me, cocking her head like a bird, with dark serious eyes:

"You really don't know? So, you've just arrived. She's our remarkable Uglich native. The first woman tractor driver around here, a member of the Komsomol. The kulaks savagely murdered her, still quite young.[46] So they named the street in her honor. I live there with mama and an old woman."

"So you were born here?"

She shook her head and sighed briefly.

"No, we're not from here . . . We're Leningraders. But we've already been here a long time—eleven years. Our papa worked there, on the construction of a hydroelectric station, as a fitter. He had only just returned from work, and then war, the blockade . . . Well . . . he died in the blockade, from hunger, couldn't bear it. And dying—he ordered us and mama to come here. In February we traveled across Lake Ladoga on the Road of Life.[47] At that time many traveled across the Road of Life, and a few just walked . . . They're pulling sleds behind them, in the sled—little kids, the kids will freeze to death, already dead, and the mother pulls as long as she doesn't fall or as long as they don't give her a lift . . . And we went by truck . . . I'm ten years old, my sister a little younger, mama barely alive, all black, like death . . . How we managed to make it to the Main Land,[48] I don't know. All the same, in our truck a few people froze to death along the way . . . And we still managed to get here, as father ordered. There are a lot of *blokadniki*, Leningraders here.[49] And they greeted us warmly here, fed us well, and at first we couldn't eat enough, couldn't eat enough food; we were even ashamed. I was just a girl, and even I was so ashamed. But—I was eating!"

She was talking as almost all Leningraders, survivors of the blockade, talk about it—with a flat, muffled voice, as if listening to themselves and not believing themselves . . .

"So since then we've lived here. I finished this school, and my sister is still studying, in the ninth grade. Well, many of the blokadniki went back, to Leningrad, but we remained here. You understand, mama was afraid to return to Leningrad—I can't say, I can't, after all, what we lived through there, you can't imagine . . ."

"No," I answered, "I can imagine."

"Oh," she exclaimed, as if delighted. "You were there, in the blockade? To the end?"

"Yes. To the end."

"Oh . . . And now . . . not from there?"

"From there. Just two weeks ago."

"From there!" she exclaimed, and suddenly tears streamed from her eyes. Becoming embarrassed, she tried to laugh. "So tell me then, how is it?"

"Well, how could it be? Wonderful, the most beautiful city! This year the trams were removed from Nevsky . . . and from Bolshaya on Vasilevsky Island, too. And from Kirov Prospect . . . and beyond Moskovsky, the Victory Park is already quite dense. Yes, so you'd already left when we planted it. But it's beautiful! The traces of the blockade have almost completely disappeared . . ."

I spoke in good faith, and still as it were not about the most important thing, but she greedily asked and asked, occasionally interrupting with exclamations: "Really?" "Wow"—her blockade childhood was for her exactly what my Uglich childhood was for me!—and all at once, beginning to bustle, she pulled a photograph from her bag.

"And here after finishing school I got married, and this is my son, Vovochka, already three years old, want to take a look?"

Looking at me from the photograph was a boy with a fat little face, his lips stretched into a little roll, bulging way out, and very astonished dark eyes: the photographer must have showed him some kind of especially astonishing "birdie."

"And he's already a true native of Uglich," said the young mother, admiring her astonished son. "But I will definitely bring him to Leningrad," she added hotly, "definitely bring him, only that way will he begin to understand. And I'll show him everything, and read to him, and tell him about his grandfather . . . Children shouldn't be allowed to forget such a thing . . . That is, of course, those who can't remember . . . I want to say—children must know that before them we survived, right? If you don't mind, give me your address, we will be sure to visit you."

I figured it would be at least seven years before that astonished little boy "will begin to understand," but I gave her my address and said that she must stop by when she comes, she must.

. . . I again walked around the area where childhood once was, where the small, ancient Russian city of Uglich sheltered us as children, in the years of the civil war, the years of the struggle for Soviet power . . . and it once again sheltered Leningrad mothers and children during the years of the Great Fatherland War . . . but our generation was already fighting, defending Leningrad, and the cold, hunger, and darkness of the blockade were one hundred times more frightening than in childhood, in Uglich . . . and I was at war, in Leningrad, together with papa, as an equal . . . and the sparkling Day of Victory came, and in honor of it we began to lay out a park, now already almost dense . . . And between these two wars was the tractor driver Zina Zolotova, murdered by kulaks, and hundreds like her—and I remember them from my work in Kazakhstan, in the first Bolshevik springs. And the Uglich hydroelectric station was constructed— constructed very differently than Volkhovstroy—and a part of ancient Uglich sank irretrievably into the water, and the hydroelectric station's power exceeded the dream of childhood, the first love of the young republic—Volkhovstroy, but even it, this hydroelectric station in Uglich, was only one of the first steps of the great "Volga staircase" . . .

Oh, what epic time abided in the life of each one of us, epic![50] It would have been enough for several generations, but was taken by this one—alone . . . How many events, and almost every one—your life, how many sorrows and joys, inseparable from the sorrows and joys of the whole people. And so it isn't the shining feeling of happiness about which I had dreamed that I am meeting here, but something greater—the almost fearsome, open feeling of my organic *belonging*, by blood, a vital connection with all that surrounds me, with what has sunk into the earth and into the water, and with what was raised and is now rising up above the earth and water; with those who in various times died for the motherland, for communism; with those who built the Uglich hydroelectric station; with those who are being born, growing up, and working here, in Uglich, in Leningrad, in the whole country—this powerful, all-embracing feeling, familiar to many, many Soviet people, enveloped my consciousness and heart. And if my life is so inextricably intertwined with the life of the country, then everything survives in it, including the losses, and together with the native earth, it is directed toward the future, new losses, new beginnings. "It's mine." No, it's ours. And all of ours—is mine! It's mine!

. . . And I nonetheless found the monastery building where we lived during the long winter of 1920 and the lindens and the little pond and, looking ahead, I will tell about it.

Pen and Ink

I found all of this because I first found an old teacher of mine, the drawing teacher. He, of course, didn't remember me, but I remembered and even recognized him, when I arrived at his little brick house right on the banks of the Volga.

Ivan Nikolaevich Potekhin, an artist, an Uglich old-timer, my old drawing teacher, was showing me, one after the other, watercolors, oil sketches, drawings in pencil and in ink depicting old, fairy-tale Uglich, and suddenly, without any ceremony he placed before my eyes this delicate pen-and-ink drawing, and in it was—childhood, winter, happiness, what I had dreamed about for so many years, the cherished place that I was unable to reach in my dream and had not reached in reality . . . And it turned out to be alive. And now it looks at me with all its unsunken charm. It's alive, saved by the old artist—this building with our windows overlooking the lindens and the winter yard. How could he have guessed that this humble drawing would be so necessary to someone's heart? The joy in encountering this, this art received as a gift, was deeper, probably, than any I expected from life . . . No, in rendering this corner of the monastery yard and the fifteenth-century Paisevsky Monastery now standing at the bottom of the Uglich reservoir, in recording Uglich's appearance before the dam, the power station, and the lock were constructed next to it, the old artist didn't hold onto the past. He thought about our descendants, about the future, about our heirs, who will come here to take all their inheritance and will want to see what was here many, many years ago, and seeing it, will truly appreciate our stormy times, the changing face of the Russian land . . . he thought, like most of the people I met, not only about tomorrow, but about the Great Time, stretching far into the future. This doesn't hamper him, but helps him to creatively, luminously work for today. So he goes to villages, making drawings of old carvings, still preserved here and there, from window casings and lintels, cornices, and roof ridges—after all the wood carvers, like the potters, have almost disappeared here. The patterns are disappearing, too. But they must be preserved—these patterns wondrous in their ancestral simplicity and natural grace! Skilled young craftsmen have to reappear; the art of carving must not disappear, because it serves human joy; ornamenting a peaceful dwelling, it can't be replaced by something manufactured by machine—here the wise and free human hand is needed . . .

So he, a rather short and strongly built old man with a dark complexion, a tireless local historian, wandering through the forest, discovers bricks under the roots of an age-old pine toppled by the wind . . . Old, massive bricks . . . He bends down, investigating the bricks, discovers a hole, fearlessly slides into it on his back, strikes a match, and sees that the brick vault above him shines with dozens of dazzling colors, dominated by pale blue, yellow, and green—as if a lush rainbow, sinking into the earth, hid itself here and turned into stone. It's clear to him—this kiln fired the famous, unfading Uglich tiles that decorate the ancient churches near his little brick house, the tiles out of which the stove benches and stoves in Uglich's old log houses are made. Here they were fired—the traces of glaze on the vault, the secret of which is still not unraveled, would be so necessary for us and for the facings of our buildings and in contemporary ceramic production. Because it was indeed in Uglich, and it can also be revived, especially as there are huge deposits of excellent, rich, pliable clay and kaolin clays of rare quality.

And thus Ivan Nikolaevich molds test figures, vases, and utensils from these splendid clays, and, with great difficulty, fires them using artisanal methods, and it still gives beautiful results. Here nature itself, historical traditions themselves suggest: revive ceramic production, and the old artist offers to create a studio, to bring together and nurture a cadre of artists—carvers, ceramicists—of workers, who would now be able to enrich the everyday lives of people in the towns and on the collective farms. No one obliges him to undertake these drawings, discoveries, experiments (just as no one helps him with anything!)—his personal, public consciousness of a duty to the present day, to the future, to our heirs binds him to undertake it.

. . . But I was at Ivan Nikolaevich's a few days after the meeting with "my cathedral," and on that morning, bidding farewell near his place to my fellow Leningrader, I returned to my hotel.

"Silver Night"

I returned to my room with the antique mirror that was growing dim and the lush geraniums, and once again felt with delight that I'm in my place, at home, more "in my place" in the present time than anywhere I've been. I opened my notebook to record the meeting with "my cathedral," with the young Leningrader, and suddenly and irresistibly I wanted to write not about that but about a night at the end of September 1941 . . .

. . . The Badaev warehouses had already burned down—Leningrad's food reserves, and when they burned, a dense, oily cloud rose into the sky and covered the evening sun; an alarming, almost red twilight fell over the city, as during a total solar eclipse—the first herald of the hungry plague already entering our besieged city. Be we still didn't know about that. In those days I was a political organizer (a commissar) in our building, and Nikolai Nikiforovich Fomin was the leader of the self-defense group. We were anxious about a strange leaflet that was scattered during the last German bombing raid, after the fire at Badaev; it consisted of a single phrase: "Wait for the silver night," and, of course, below the despicable vignette also the letters "b. i. g.," which meant "bayonet in the ground." We were afraid that the leaflet nevertheless got to the population because a few women in our courtyard began to say "he promised gases" . . . But there were, of course, no gases, and after a few days, at about midnight, Fomin knocked on my door and said that the self-defense group received an order to go "on standby." We set reinforced posts and stood by the entrance.

There was no shelling, no air-raid alarm, a clear, clear moonlit September night ruled in the city; the traffic had already ceased, and suddenly in that quiet we heard, weakly but distinctly, the roar of field guns.

"The Germans have taken Strelno," the head of self-defense said to me through his teeth. "They're breaking through to the Red Putilov works." And suddenly he groaned, and snorted: "Shame . . . oh, shame, shame . . . how far they've advanced . . ."

"Silver night, Nikolai Nikiforovich?" I asked him, also through my teeth, suppressing a sudden nasty tremor. "Maybe someone will substitute for you?"

"Nonsense," he cried, "I'm not a little boy! Take the post by the entrance, I'm going to the roof . . . Oh my God . . ."

(He died three months later from exhaustion on the way to work, on the Liteiny Bridge.)

I stood by the entrance, and prepared the "on standby" first-aid kit and gas mask; the courtyard's caretaker, Aunt Masha, a wizened, quiet old woman, approached me and reported that the bottles with gasoline were ready (in the event that tanks broke through to our building), and stood next to me, becoming sad in a village way. A murderous silence reigned in the motionless moonlit city; the sounds of the deadly battle going on in the outskirts reached here, the center, as a weak, restless rumble . . .

I looked at our house; it was the most absurd house in Leningrad. Its official title was the Engineers' and Writers' House-Commune.[51] Later a facetious nickname became quite popular in Leningrad—the Teardrop of Socialism. As for us, its initiators and residents, we were widely known as the "tear-droppers." We, a group of young (very young!) engineers and writers, set it up as a cooperative at the very beginning of the thirties as part of a categorical struggle against the "old way of life" (kitchen and diapers!); thus not one apartment had a corner for cooking, much less a kitchen. There wasn't even a place to hang coats in the entryway—there was a communal coatroom downstairs, and also there, on the first floor, a communal children's room and a communal lounge: from the first preliminary meetings we'd decided to organize our free time collectively, without any individualism.

We settled into our house with enthusiasm, ecstatically handing over our food ration cards and "obsolete" individual pots and pans to the communal kitchen—enough, liberate us from cooking!—we immediately created a huge number of collective commissions and "troikas," and even the house's architecturally charmless exterior "in the guise of Le Corbusier," with a multitude of tall, tiny, iron cage-balconies didn't trouble us: the extreme wretchedness of its architecture seemed to us some kind of privileged "austerity" that met the requirements of the new way of life . . .[52]

But after a while, not more than a year or two, when ration cards had been abolished, when we'd grown up, we discovered that our life was so rushed and communal that we had no beachheads even for a tactical retreat . . . except for the windowsills; and it was on the windowsills that the first "apostates" began cooking what they pleased—the communal dining room by now was unable to satisfy the varied tastes of the house's inhabitants. The situation with the diapers, which for some reason kept multiplying in the house, was simply awful: there was nowhere to dry them! We had a wonderful solarium, but the attic was totally useless for drying diapers. Moreover, the building's acoustics were so perfect that if downstairs, on the third floor, at the writer Misha Chumandrin's place, they were playing tiddlywinks or reciting poetry, everything could be heard at my place on the fifth floor, right down to the bad rhymes![53] This overly intimate, forced interaction, together with incredibly small room-kennels, was very irritating and fatiguing. "The phalanstery at 7 Rubinstein hasn't come off," one of us joked, and—what's there to hide?—we often fumed at the "teardrop" and at our own precipitousness.[54]

And so I was walking with the courtyard's caretaker Aunt Masha from the entrance to the little gate, and listening intently to the unnaturally quiet night, I looked at our house, quiet-quiet, without a single lamp, visible in the September moonlight with all its cage-balconies on flat gray walls . . .

"It's a good house," Aunt Masha said all of a sudden, gently as about a child and, sighing, added in the same tone: "It's nothing . . . we'll beat them off."

"True, it's a good house," I thought, and all of a sudden an ardent, frenzied wave of love for this house, exactly as it is, surged in me and completely swept away the remnants of fear and tension.

No, it's not a good house—it's an excellent house, no, most importantly—a beloved house! In the winter it was always light and warm, and what nice collective evening entertainments we had: Boris Chirkov—the living Maxim from *The Youth of Maxim*—came and sang his songs; Babochkin—the living Chapaev—came and showed us his new work—both films had then just come out.[55] Not infrequently at our table, "Aunt Katya"—the most wonderful Korchagina-Alexandrovskaya—would improvise, "playing" things you'd never see at the theater;[56] once even some handsome Indian progressive, whom they said was a "former maharajah," and Misha Chumandrin energetically propagandized him for the revolution—mainly with gestures and slogans uttered in an absolutely invented Esperanto: "Imperialism must be—fini! Comprende, comrade? . . ." In general when Misha Chumandrin drank, he would always toast a wide range of people, in a mysteriously tight voice, joking: "Long live our dear red China! Long live our dear red Bulgaria . . . Long live our dear red Germany . . ."[57] We laughed a lot listening to these toasts—in 1932! . . . But how wonderful was the evening in the communal lounge when the antifascist singer Ernst Busch sang us the song "The Reds from Wedding," and nodding his head gave us the sign to pick up the refrain, and we, with sincere belief and blazing eyes, joined in singing at his march tempo: "Left! Left! Join us, comrade . . . Join our workers' united front, because you are a worker, too!"[58]

"No, we will not surrender our house. We love it. Not for its comforts, which are few—there are so many more discomforts! We love it just as it is, because it's ours, a part of our lives, our dreams, our aspirations, maybe not always well thought-out, but always sincere, and, after all, inconveniences . . . can be corrected! We ourselves heaped them up, and we ourselves will fix them, we'll fix them, all of them, everything is in our hands . . . and if we don't fix this house, then we'll simply build another, a better one! We will, we will!"

And the night was moonlit silver, incredibly quiet, and only at dawn were we given the order to leave our customary posts—the enemy had been stopped on the near approaches to Leningrad.

For some reason I remembered precisely this night after the meeting with the cathedral and the conversation with my fellow Leningrader, and I wanted to make a note about this night and about the history of our house in general, but I didn't note anything down then, just sat terrified, almost in tears, once again enduring that night, looking at the geraniums.

I wrote "for some reason," but that was my feeling then. Now I know why I remembered precisely that night, as I know why for three full weeks I lived in Uglich an extraordinary life—I lived my whole life, past, present, and future, at once.

Last Summer

Of course this was because I was in the town of my childhood during momentous days for the whole country: not five months had passed since Stalin's death; the truce in Korea had only recently been concluded; it had just been reported that Beria was an accursed enemy of the people . . .[59] Together with the people of Uglich, I listened to and discussed the theses issued on the occasion of the fiftieth anniversary of the Communist Party of the Soviet Union; I celebrated this great fiftieth anniversary together with the Uglich Komsomol.[60] Like everyone, I not only understood but felt with my whole consciousness that the great work that Soviet power had begun in the years of my childhood—when the Uglich city commune resettled workers in aristocratic mansions and monastery cells; when notwithstanding the fourteen-power blockade and the darkness and the cold, the Soviets aspired to make the whole country literate, and elderly women in classes at our school began to read, with excitement, surprised at themselves: "We are not sl-aves, sl-aves we are not"; when the worker Alexei Vasilev came to Volkhovstroy from Peter with the first half-cubic-meter excavator in order to start laying the foundation for the first source of light and power—this great work was now unfolding anew, was making a new historical ascent.

In Uglich, Yaroslavl, and Rybinsk I met dozens of diverse people, most of all members of the intelligentsia—newspaper professionals, architects, teachers, librarians, young artists, engineers; I met with workers at the Uglich hydroelectric station, among whom were veterans of Volkhovstroy and people the same age as Dneprostroy—and even if we didn't talk about them, the enormous events of the last year that I've just outlined were woven into our conversation or stood above it as a high, clear rainbow might stand over a plain washed by a storm.

. . . And each time I returned to my room with the geraniums, I recorded not only what I'd experienced and seen that day (much of this was later published in essays in *Literary Gazette*), but I also had to note down on today's margin all that had again begun to live in me. And what began to live again was varied and unexpected. For example, suddenly I once again lived through the evening before the twentieth-fifth anniversary of October in blockaded Leningrad, when after a long, exhausting darkness the first current was supplied—light to the first three thousand residential facilities, that is, houses, and this light was from Volkhovstroy, the first born of electrification, Leningrad's offspring: it was the first to break through to us from outside the ring of the blockade. And on that evening, when light was supplied, the windows of deserted apartments lit up, after all they weren't blacked out, and the Germans bombed, and the lights had to be immediately put out in these dwellings—breaking down doors in order to get in . . . But the most important thing was that through the entire blockade little Volkhovstroy nourished the cradle of revolution with its light and power . . . But this needs to be written in detail, in great detail! Because all of this is also for the Essential Book, like everything else that happened in Uglich. I remembered in the same way as those who assembled our first electric power generator at the Dnieper hydroelectric station—they named it Voroshilov, because almost everyone who assembled it had served during the civil war under Voroshilov's command—but that was in their early youth.[61] And so all my youth went through me, with all its white nights, with its clear, simple love, with its fanatical belief that you can make the bright, perfect future arrive tomorrow, easily, right in this house—and all my youth went through me, breaking off abruptly with the great and terrible—ordeals of the end of the 1930s.

. . . Then after meetings with architects and artists, I would record what the silhouettes of future Volga cities should be, how we will reveal and master all the ancient secrets of the nameless, brilliant Russian architects and artists, and learn their glorious names, and what outstanding, varied painting we'll have, and we'll hand down all of this to our heirs, to our descendants (among whom will be my fellow Leningrader's astonished Vovochka, who will already "understand everything"). And sitting by my-self, imagining their rapture and awe in the face of our epoch, our years, our party, us . . . I couldn't hold back a broad smile.

So, together with the whole country I experienced the tremendous events of 1953, my heart together with it prepared for some new ascent.

And here I'll break off my notes on the journey to the town of my childhood . . .

2

That Forest Clearing
1939–57

Late in the evening, my papa arrived and announced that he was spending the night at my place.

"And tomorrow I will take you to the Zoological Garden," he added sternly. "Yes, yes. In the morning. Definitely."

"He's tipsy," I noted. "I hope he's not going to start singing 'Gaudeamus.'..."[1]

My papa was rarely tipsy, but when he was, his tipsiness was very varied. When just slightly tipsy, so-called "under-drunk," he's grumpy and quarrelsome: criticizes the way things are done in the surgical department (which he himself heads!), harshly scolds the local committee to which they "always intentionally elect him," thunders at the regional health department, and importunately demands that I—yes, I—explain "why are all these outrages happening?"

A little tipsier, he is focused, serious, remembers with tenderness the terrible fronts of the world and civil wars—on which he worked as a military field surgeon from the first days of the world war right down to the Kronstadt ice[2]—discusses issues of world politics—"my prognosis is..."— and becomes very angry if you dispute his prognoses.

Most congenially tipsy, he loudly and merrily gets up to mischief: he applauds for no reason; sings old Nevsky Gate songs,[3] all like this one— sadly merry:

> And Alesha wore golden curls!
> He sang perfectly the city's songs![4]

at the same time shaking his still wavy golden-gray hair; declaims fragments from Derzhavin's "God" and—the old Dorpat student—must try to perform (in a bass voice!) "Gaudeamus."[5] In this state, he is overcome with the most unusual desires: "to have another baby," "to write a tragedy in verse," or, like today, in haste to drag me—a responsible adult member of the editorial staff, who is furthermore overwhelmed by "personal affairs"—to the Zoological Garden.

"Oh, papa," I said, "you know I'm busy. And . . . I'm not in the mood for that!"

"Well, well! None of your games. Am I your father or not? I gave you life. I said I'm taking you, and I'm taking you."

He hesitated and temptingly, significantly added:

"We'll see the lion. The king of the beasts."

I couldn't help smiling. Noticing this, papa went into raptures and clapped his hands.

"Little mother of mine, I'm a tractor driver after all!"[6] he cried, making mischief, and then suddenly became completely serious and asked in a low voice: "So, how are your affairs?"

I became animated. At that time, two people had lodged slanderous allegations against me, and the proceedings had already lasted a long, long time[7] . . . This plagued and tortured me; it was relentless; I could talk about "my affair" at any time of the day for as long as you like. I mentally delivered endless pathetic speeches and carried on bitter internal dialogues with the editor, the secretary of the party committee, with my accusers, and even when I dreamed, I saw only this . . .

"You know, papa," I began to say, "they postponed the final investigation again! And at the last meeting of the editorial board that Klimanchuk carried on so . . . so . . . I just . . . No, I won't give up! I myself will lodge an accusation against her, you understand, myself! And immediately, to the highest authority . . . And now I'm writing a new, very detailed explanatory note about that article. In the note . . ."

Worked up and tormented, I outlined the essence of the note, and papa looked at me intently, completely soberly, continually interjecting only with his doctor's generic rejoinders: "well, well," "yes, yes," "there, there."

"Oh, you've become terrifying to look at!" he suddenly exclaimed, not hearing me out to the end. "Oh, ladies and gentlemen, you're really psychopaths . . . Well, okay. Get some sleep; we'll go early tomorrow. I'll get some sleep, too . . . 'I'm a king—I'm a slave—I'm a god—I'm a worm.'"[8]

"Go to bed. I'm going to sit and draft a statement. Not that one, something else. In relation to a different article of mine . . . I'll bring you a mattress."

"No need. I'm an old soldier; I'll manage without a mattress. 'In a tricorn hat and a gray camp coat.'"[9]

"Papa, only without the singing! I've got such a screeching headache."

"Well, okay, okay. Am I your father or not? Oh, it's a hard case."

He laid down on the hard, very narrow couch, while I covered the lamp with a shade made out of newspaper and settled down with a sheet of paper. I felt very alone because papa didn't listen to "my affair" to the end; in any case, he understood nothing about it or my condition, and he was pleased about something—I didn't know what, but I . . . How obnoxious—not even listening . . . and I . . .

And he suddenly called out to me, affectionately and sadly:

"Lyalka! Little girl . . ."

"What is it, papa?"

"And do you remember how in Zarucheve your mother and I didn't let you and Muska gather mushrooms? In some forest clearing of yours . . . It was a long time ago . . . You howled like anything, lord."

"Ah, papa, just leave me alone. What's there but a clearing! Don't bother me . . ."

He fell silent.

I sat a long time, cleaning up the wording, mentally quarreling with Klimanchuk, smoking to the point of palpitations. I was choked with resentment—I was terribly sorry for myself, repeating in a whisper: "I'm weary, weary, completely worn out . . ."

I fell asleep at dawn and dreamed about some kind of meeting, and suddenly, in the midst of this meeting, I heard papa's voice:

"Lyalka! Wake up! We're going to the zoo!"

I could barely open my eyes: "He didn't forget . . ."

"Papa, it's not even ten. Where are we heading so early?"

"It's good that it's early: they open right at ten. Get up, look—how sunny it is! So, get going, hurry up . . ."

He was cheerful, in good spirits, unusually energetic; his face with its big blue eyes was roguish, like someone who planned to astonish the world, and he irritated me to the point of exhaustion.

In his old military cap, which I remembered from childhood, in his short raglan coat that looked like a woman's skirt, papa ran down the street exactly like someone late for a train. I trotted behind him, swearing quietly. We jumped into the tram on the fly.

Near the Zoological Garden it smelled not like the city but of cool fall earth; the trees, still bronze, were austere and motionless, transfixed, as if they understood that the barely warm, pale golden sunlight was pouring down on them for the last time. The austerity, tranquility, and lovely transparency of the fall day stung me like a piece of ice, with a distinct sadness—and also with austerity, tranquility, and transparency.

"I'm already quite old," I thought.

And papa sweetly narrowed his eyes, turned his face to the sun, drew the sharp air into his round nostrils, shivered, and grunted blissfully:

"Oh, it's good! How good it is! So? Are you happy that you came, little girl? It's a shame that Muska isn't with us. You remember how in the fall, in Zarucheve, we didn't let you and Muska gather mushrooms? In some special forest clearing of yours?"

"Yes, I remember. What about it?"

He annoyed me endlessly.

"Hyenas," he noted with pleasure when we reached the cages. Just look at these bastards. They can laugh. Look how that one there prowls, eh? And that nasty smell from it, holy cow . . ."

"Typical Klimanchuk," I specified to myself and smiled grimly.

"And here are the tigers, Lyalka, look, tigers. Magnificent beasts, aren't they?

"It looks like they're sewn out of a tiger blanket," I answered. "Improbable."

"Well, no, you're mistaken. Beautiful beasts. I like them. So, here are your lions. They'll be fed soon." (Suddenly terribly concerned, papa pulled grandfather's onion-domed watch out of his waistcoat pocket, looked at it, and even listened to it.) "Yes, the feeding will definitely be soon. Well, never mind, I'll show you how they're fed."

"Good lord, I don't need that. Waiting around here . . . for feeding time. You're better off looking at how bald they are. Like worn-out door mats. And they've got foolish snouts. Also—royal! Like Nicholas II had . . ."

Papa chuckled uncertainly.

"So, let's go, papa. We looked. And there's not much to see."

"These lions here are really a bit . . . ," said papa, embarrassed, but still cheerful. "And here are the bears you like. You know they play, make faces. Now we'll look here at the birds, then we'll drop by the different cows and—then to the bears. Okay? And maybe then a little more. So? Good?"

"As you like, papa."

We stood by the cages with the birds. Smelling nauseatingly of bird droppings, the water in the shallow round pool was foul and filthy. And the birds were settled around the pool in a neat circle: a potbellied pelican motionlessly contemplated a crust floating in the water; next to him, rooted to the spot, craning its neck, its eyes closed with a whitish film, was an untidy chicken; behind the chicken, sticking up on one leg, was some kind of sharp-beaked, malicious-looking little bird with a crest, and so on. For some reason all of them were in a complete daze, as if deeply perplexed by something.

I immediately and despondently identified the scene, "A meeting of our editorial board."

Papa heaved a sigh and said nothing. We silently approached the fence with the pony.

"Well, here's the pony," papa said, "of course, it's not much. A little horse . . . You won't like them either . . ."

Something in papa's voice surprised me. I briefly looked at him: papa's face was old, disappointed, and . . . yes!—ashamed.

"What's made him sour?" I thought, and then it suddenly hit me: papa wants me to be astonished and delighted, as in childhood! Because he wasn't contriving to stroll in the Zoological Garden—but in my childhood, in his youth. And I'm so busy grumbling, that I'm not seeing anything— not the golden trees or the funny animals, nothing but the terrible images of my anguish, and I'm—old . . .

"Well then, let's go," said papa despondently.

But I exclaimed with enthusiasm:

"No, papa, dear, wait, wait! I still want to see the horse!"

"So look," said papa mistrustfully but somewhat mollified.

"No, at last I like these," I enthused, trembling with pity and love for my father, and being careful not to overact. "It's so small! Why's it so small, papa?"

"It's just the breed—a pony."

"And this is an 'English pony,' papa. You know it's better than the other one, more beautiful."

"Yes, it seems a bit nicer. It's all muzzle!"

"No, not a bit nicer, most definitely more beautiful. Here's what I'm interested in—is riding it comfortable? I really want to ride it . . . Is it true that they ride them in England?"

I couldn't think of any other way to please him!

"So, why just in England? The kids over there are riding!" papa said happily.

In fact a cabriolet was approaching us; it rattled like a tin can, pulled by an angry, very shaggy pony. And deep in the carriage, way in the back, sat four children in fuzzy berets, a boy-employee smacked his lips and drove; and behind the cabriolet trotted a small shaggy-shaggy dog with tufts of fur covering its eyes. All of them—the pony, the children, the boy-employee, and even the furry eyeless dog—were very serious, inflated, important; they all seemed somehow businesslike, as if hurrying to work or a highly responsible task.

"Well, shall I take you for a spin?" papa repeated and winked. "I can!"

"I really want to! Only . . . but papa dear, this probably isn't entirely convenient?"

"Well then, we'll move on. There's still a lot for us to see."

"Yes, yes, we'll move on. I want to see the monkeys," I exclaimed, rejoicing that I'd managed to fool papa. "You know I really love monkeys. Especially the humanlike ones . . . I've long wanted to see them."

We set off to the monkeys. I took papa by the hand and purposely lagging a little, I walked with him like a model daughter. Papa beamed.

"Do you want me to buy a waffle," he asked. "A big one, with cream?"

"Well, of course. Very much."

"So, is it tasty?"

"You have to ask? Marvelous!"

By smell, and probably by taste, the cream reminded me of strawberry soap, and the waffle itself was undoubtedly made of wood. I ate, choking with disgust, showering myself with plywood crumbs; papa was smoking; the golden trees stood motionless over our small bench, enjoying the last sunshine. Near the bench, a young woman was putting dull, square-toed galoshes on her three-year-old son. The boy's fat little foot was dangling like cotton wool, and the mother couldn't catch it in the galosh, and trying to grab it, she asked gently and melodiously:

"So, Vovochka, what are we going to tell granny—what did we see at the Zoological Garden?"

And the boy answered, diligently wrinkling his round forehead and stretching his lips into a little roll:

"We saw . . . the big ele-phant . . . the big camel . . . and the teeny little horse."

Talking about the elephant and the camel, he spoke in a deep voice, but about the "teeny little horse"—he squeaked in a shrill-shrill voice.

I finally polished off the waffle.

"Wonderful. Now, dear papa, a drink. Only, please, with syrup."

"What kind of syrup do you have?" papa sternly asked the saleswoman.

The saleswoman, with lush, deep red cheeks, answered, ratcheting up her voice in rapture with each new name:

"Cranberry. Cherry! Fresh hay!! Tea nectar!!!"

I chose "fresh hay" mixed with "tea nectar." If you're gonna splurge, splurge!

While I drank, papa looked at me with anxiety:

"Not too cold?"

"No, not at all."

"And do you remember, Lyalka," he asked for third time—"how you howled when your mother and I wouldn't let you gather mushrooms?"

I nodded my head. He laughed happily.

"How you and Muska howled, how you howled, lord! For three hours straight. I'm thinking—how much longer can they howl?"

"Still would! What a day it was! Perfect for mushrooms. Drizzling, so bright-bright, the smell of wet fir trees, that clearing was full of boletus mushrooms, and you . . . What? Now, I suppose, after fifteen years, you feel sorry for us?"

"Sorry . . . I was sorry then, and your mother was afraid—the rain. Well, we wouldn't let you."

Papa looked at me apologetically and happily. How I loved him! I wanted to take him further, still further into his youth, and good memories suddenly opened up the path:

"And do you remember, papa, how we went to the zoo when you visited from the German front?"

He was amazed.

"What? You really remember that? You were just a pup then."

"Really—I remember. Back then there was some kind of kiosk near the gate—shaped like a huge gold bottle, selling lemonade. And more than anything I wanted to see Gray Wolf, who carried the Tsarevich Ivan[10] . . . And I even remember the wolf! And you were in your military uniform . . . And then we all had our picture taken, and I was photographed next to you, kneeling and holding on to your sword. And that made me feel that I was terribly brave. Do you remember, papa?"

"Yes, I certainly remember, I remember, but you . . . Lyalka! And how handsome I was then, eh? Curly hair!" And, shaking his head, he softly sang:

And Alesha wore golden curls!
He sang perfectly the city's songs . . .

Oh! And I had a mustache—you remember, what kind of mustache?"

"Well of course, Muska was always saying: 'pigtails grow under papa's nose . . .' And you always twisted it and sang: 'My mustache, my little mustache no longer curls, my wifey, a fine lady, spruced herself up.'"

"Wait, wait!" Papa waved his hand. "'Wears a cap, asks for tea, one mustn't go near.' Just so?"

"That's not all!" I said triumphantly. "'They gave the broad a full uniform, and the broad became a commander!'" That was a military, frontline song . . .

Laughing, happy, and both young, we went to the monkeys.

As usual, the monkeys had the biggest crowd. Numb, blue-gray boys, leaning across the barrier, like Petrushka marionettes,[11] followed with admiration and envy the fight between two young macaques, encouraging them with advice and shouts:

"Pound him, pound him!"

"Ah, you, over here. There she is, on the branch."

"Grab her by the tail! Grab with your back hand!"

Behind the blue-gray boys hovered a couple: a diminutive, dark-haired girl and a young man with such enormous padded shoulders that he looked like a kiosk. The girl looked rapturously at the monkeys, screaming and laughing, but suddenly caught herself and, looking her companion in the eye, asked gravely:

"Zhenechka, aren't they really one-of-a-kind?"

"Nuts," the fellow condescendingly replied.

And the monkeys lived an independent, tempestuous life, full of work and troubles. They didn't care about the spectators—they were busy; they were all doing something. One disheveled macaque was carefully pushing the water bowl out of the cage. The water bowl was inserted tight, and the macaque tried to shove it first from the right, then from the left. Another macaque squatted alongside, and with great attention observed its friend's work. When it seemed to her that her comrade couldn't manage the proposed task, she heatedly involved herself, but as she was more foolish than the first, she dragged the water bowl backward. Finally the water bowl unexpectedly popped out of the cage. For a moment, both monkeys were dumbfounded—they understood that they'd done something not quite right. Then they began to stick out their thin, childish arms and furtively touch the water bowl, as if trying to make sure—was it the same thing or not? And in the next cage, a gray baboon, bearded and masculine, busily shook the cage: gripping the bars with his strong little fists, he shakes and looks—has anything happened? On the contrary, everything's the same! The gray-bearded baboon's futility was so absurdly human, that I cheered up at last.

"That one's about me; I'm a fool," I thought without any resentment. I laughed and looked at papa.

He looked at me with joy; he himself was in that state of highest contentment and kindness, when a person is left with one desire: to lavish this kindness. He said:

"So, now I'll show you the elephant."

"Ah, of course, the elephant. Let's hurry!"

Playing along was already easy and interesting for me. And, really, I wasn't playing along anymore but living this suddenly appearing joy and this sweet life . . .

"Oh, papa, how big it is, and such ears"—bustling about the fence, my childhood wonder succeeded so well that some haggard uncle, who looked very much like a desert rat, solicitously let me to the front, like a small child.[12] Yet it seemed to me that this was simply a matter of course!

"Papa, and the tail?" I screamed. "What a horribly disproportionate tail. And I'd like to know, what's its name?"

"It's named Betty," the uncle who looked like a desert rat said respectfully. "It's—a lady."

Betty was huge, indifferent, almost eyeless. Only her cracked trunk moved from side to side, and occasionally her legs, column-like and heavy just to look at, took a step.

"If there is a fate, it looks like Betty," I thought, and frightened by this "unchildish" thought, I exclaimed:

"Papa, look, it picked up the nickel!"

"Aha. Now it can buy itself a carrot. It's so smart, I can't believe it!"

"They really work," put in Uncle Desert Rat. "They're conscious."

"Papa, it bought one, it bought one! It's eating! Oh, how interesting."

Digging in his pocket, papa pulled out a coin and handed it to me. It was a dime, all plastered with tobacco rot.

"Here you are," said papa generously, "buy the elephant a carrot."

And with a blissfully stupid face, I threw the elephant a dime. The dime flashed right beneath Betty's trunk, jauntily rolled under her monstrous body, and, turning slightly, came to rest behind the elephant, just under its tail.

"Ah, a miss," exclaimed Uncle Desert Rat. "They won't turn around."

"Won't turn around," spectators in the crowd repeated.

"If the elephant finds my dime—my wish will be fulfilled, everything will be okay," I thought precipitously, and I was thrown into a fever: I was tempting Fate.

"It won't find it!" someone cried, exactly answering my thoughts.

Betty-Fate's enormous trunk probed the concrete enclosure. And in the wrong place, the wrong place! Now it rummaged to the right, then near the bars, then stopped, swaying slightly. It's all over. I dug my nails into my palms. And suddenly my fate, moving slowly on frightening elephants' legs, turned its back on the curious onlookers, extended its trunk and—snap!—found my dime.

"It will be fulfilled!" I shrieked, clutching papa's sleeve. "Everything will be okay—you understand?"

Horror flashed in Uncle Desert Rat's eyes. The spectators gasped. And only papa, my papa—understood everything.

"How could I not understand?!" he cried angrily, but it seemed to me that tears were about to flow from his big eyes. "It'll all be fulfilled! Well, let's go, little girl. Now, we've seen everything. Did you like it?"

"Very much, papa, very much! Especially the elephant."

"Well, well, I'm glad. So, where are you off to? Toward the tram? And I'm off to left. To Uncle. You remember Uncle? Could it be you really don't remember?"

"Wait, wait . . . I seem to remember something . . . Well, yes—Uncle . . ."

"Well, of course Uncle—Minka Volokhin, my Dorpat classmate . . . Hmm . . . And it's really possible you don't remember him—because you weren't even born then. Well of course—we studied together, sang 'Gaudeamus.'"

And papa sang, although he wasn't the least bit tipsy:

"Gaudeamus igitur . . ."

"How far I've come with you today," I thought, looking after the old man, with the military cap familiar from childhood and the short raglan coat that resembled a woman's skirt. And I was very pleased that I had, so cleverly and cunningly, so subtly tricked papa and afforded him joy— strolled with him in his youth. And then an insight flashed: and so papa was now going and rejoicing that he was so clever and cunning and had so adroitly led me from my difficult affairs to childhood. And it turned out that his youth and my childhood—are here beside us, with all their happiness and light—and this after all is life, real life—happiness and light . . . And my affairs . . .

"Well, that's just nothing but nonsense, my affairs," I suddenly marveled—"this is grievous and offensive, but it will pass, and it's not the most important thing. The most important thing is Life. And I have Life; it is with me; I'm delighted with it; I love it . . . And even if there's a Klimanchuk and others of her ilk in the world?! And the editor? How patiently and carefully he clarifies this confusion. He's good . . . And the representative of the district committee is good—yesterday he spent the whole day busy with one issue . . . And my papa—how good and kind he is! There are many kind people! And if there is kindness—there is life. There is, there is!"

And I spent the whole day roaming around the golden, transparent, autumn city and remembering the zoo, childhood, papa, the elephant— laughing, and people thought I was smiling at them, and a few wondered resentfully, and others laughed at me in return.

And during the night I saw my favorite dream. I have two favorite dreams, very similar to each other. My first, the most important and beloved dream—that's about Uglich, about the city where we lived while papa fought in the civil war—I already told about it. And my second favorite dream—is about that forest clearing where our parents on a bright, drizzly day wouldn't let us gather boletus mushrooms. It was in Novgorod province, near the village of Zarucheve, where we went on vacation a few years in a row. And in it I dreamed about how I go to that very clearing—just as we went in adolescence—along a narrow path through a very thick old alder grove, full of anxiety, certain there was something significant about the dusk and the rustling and the muttering of an angry, invisible stream, running along the dark-rusty fallen leaves, between mossy rocks. The black, wet trail twists for a long time in the dusk and the cautious, rustling grove. Going through it was a bit frightening, but as soon as you stepped past the last alder into that forest clearing—a radiant, greenish, soft light immediately pours over you: in the clearing is the most tender green grass, along the sides birch trees with their small leaves, and from the clearing a mighty, bright, quiet, quiet expanse opens up. The clearing is on a cliff, on a slope, and so from the cliff you can see far, far away, all around and down below: the immense trail just described, soft hills, meadows, meadows on them; the dense, deep-blue forest stands in the distance; a narrow blue river winds and shimmers below; a little log hut stands above it—vastness and light, Russian, wise, kind.

And although I never dreamed that I reached the Uglich cathedral, in my dream I always reach that very clearing and stand in it a long time, and long my heart revels in the beauty of the open expanse, and I wake up refreshed, somehow especially calm and confident, because I know: this exists not only in my dream, but in reality—motherland, light, life . . .

3

The Nevsky Gate Campaign
1958–59

Daytime Stars

I learned about them when I was a child, in Novgorod province, and I no longer remember exactly whether I read this in a magazine or heard it from the teacher, Petr Petrovich, who came that evening to the reading-room hut. No, it was probably the village teacher—an old man with deep, small eyes and a long, sparse, luminous beard, who knew a great number of interesting and even mysterious things about the world, about life and people. A July evening, still turning blue, still deepening, the first stars lighting up the reading room's spacious windows, and there Petr Petrovich was saying that the stars never really disappear from the sky: besides night and evening stars there are also daytime stars. They are even brighter and more beautiful than night stars, but they are never visible in the sky: the sun outshines them. Daytime stars can only be seen in very deep and calm wells: standing high above us, inaccessible and invisible to us, they burn in the heart of the earth in small, black mirrors of water, spraying out a halo of short, sharp rays. True, the teacher didn't say anything about the rays, but I immediately pictured them—they had to be there.

And from that evening I was overcome by a frenzied desire—to see daytime stars! I didn't tell anyone, not even my sister Muska, that I knew about them and wanted to see them. I thought—first of all I'll see them *alone, first* and then I'll tell (Muska—right away) and even show—first Muska and then others: look at what I saw, *first.* Not even saw, but spied—which is better than seeing. Daytime stars—this is a miracle, of course, but one that really exists—it's true, I know it! Now you all may know about them, look at them!

The desire to see daytime stars and the whole plan—showing them to others—occurred to me that evening, when I was on my way back from Zarucheve to the nearby hamlet where we had rented a room for the third summer. The road smelled sweetly of a recently passing herd, fresh milk, the cooling dust; small, soft fountains of dust thumped between the toes of my bare feet with a pleasant coolness; glowworms trustingly twinkled in roadside ditches. Wooden and tin bells from unseen horses rattled in the lowlands, in the mist. Occasionally the jingle of a special, very delicate, sad bell could be heard. The road wound from hill to hill, and it was comforting to know that you were walking not simply along a road but through the Valdai heights, where not far from you, bubbling out of the earth, in a wooden chapel was a spring called the Volga. All night the stars were reflected in the Volga spring and the Volga stream and in the Volga river. And in the daytime . . . I would see daytime stars tomorrow! Passing through the garden to the house, I paused and with joyful terror cast a sidelong glance at our old well, covered with grey lichen and moss. It was the same as always: the thin well sweep towered above it, hitting up against the sky and some ordinary star; and huge, thick burdocks (Thumbelina must have sailed away on a leaf from such a burdock), blue evening burdocks smacked and stirred around the well. Everything was like yesterday, and everything—was different! It turned out that this long-familiar well was simply packed with radiant daytime stars, and we, fools, not knowing about this, had purposely aimed to splash the bucket as loudly as possible into its dark, starry water.

"I will see them tomorrow," I thought again, and a pleasant shiver ran down my back. But for some reason for several days I couldn't bring myself to peer into our old well. "No, not today . . . tomorrow . . . or certainly the day after tomorrow—definitely." Unconsciously I put off the happy and somehow frightening moment of witnessing daytime stars, and, strangely, this delay gave me an incomprehensible delight, unlike anything else.

Then, on the eve of youth, I didn't yet know that the expectation of happiness is very often more powerful than happiness itself. Just as the anticipation of big, complex, and much-desired work often brings more joy than the work itself. That's why you sometimes drag it out, put it off, devise reasons why you can't get down to work, so you can relish the possibilities and dream freely—about the process and even about the fruits of your new literary work. How well-constructed and significant it emerges from plans not yet thought out to the end—and it's not necessary, not necessary to know the exact ending—it must come *of itself*, as a discovery, as a reward for labor; from a tangled net of initial incidents, some piercingly bright, some barely flickering images, finally, from naively ambitious dreams of how this work—not yet begun on paper!—will be recognized by the most critical friends, will stir the reader's most sincere emotions and bring you perhaps the highest tribute of tears, tears shed alone and in secret . . .

Poisoned by mustard gas, slowly dying and knowing he was dying, Antoine Thibault, looking back on his youth, wrote in his diary: "I lived in anticipation of life and in active belief in it."[1]

The anticipation of life, that is the ability to live only what will be, only what *can be*, but to really *live* these, is such a generous and cruel gift of being! For a long time, probably too long, I lived in anticipation of only one joy and, perhaps, trusted too actively in it. I now know what it means to live in anticipation of inescapable loss (of love, friend, family), of undeserved accusation, of long and hard trials. But then, in childhood, in Novgorod province, not understanding that I was excessively endowed with the ability to live in the future (as well as the ability to live in the past—a special kind of memory), I simply enjoyed the anticipation of joy, the anticipation of my meeting with the daytime stars.

And then after two or three days, on a sultry, cloudless midday, making sure that no one was in the garden, I rushed headlong to the old well, narrowed my eyes, and, like opening a book, threw open the moss-covered doors, and without blinking stared into its dark depths.

There were no stars in the well.

I couldn't believe it.

I looked into the well for a very long time, for a long time inhaling its coolness and its scent of waterlogged wood, but no stars appeared. From time to time the black square of water began to quiver for some reason, and faint circles rippled out from the center to the walls. That was all.

"Probably, it's impossible to see them the first time," I guessed. After an hour or two languishing in the heat I didn't rush headlong to the well, but approached stealthily, and carefully, quietly opened it and . . . again saw nothing! So I looked into the well until evening, when the first stars, visible to one and all, came out.

The next day there was a persistent rain, then came days when the clear sky suddenly filled with radiant, round storm clouds (those I saw in the well!), then again and again, in different ways, at different times I looked into the well, but I never saw—not even for a moment!—a single daytime star.

I never told anyone, and I was pleased that I hadn't bragged about daytime stars earlier, not even to Muska.

But strange to say, confidence in the existence of daytime stars and of wells that reflected and held them did not leave me. It was probably just that our well wasn't deep enough or dark enough. Maybe some kind of spring bubbled up from the bottom, disturbing the water, depriving it of the stillness necessary to reflect hidden stars. It's embarrassing to admit, but I only recently found out that I had misheard or simply misunderstood Petr Petrovich: daytime stars can be seen not in deep wells, but from a well, that is sitting somewhere in the bowels of the earth. But all the same, despite the fact that in my youth I never once saw a single daytime star, despite the wide distribution of water supply pipes, I even now would like to believe that we live among starry wells, and not only old ones, quietly surrounded by fairy-tale burdocks, but also new ones, popping up recently, well-proportioned, hard concrete walls slashing, reaching so deep into the earth, holding a quiet and dark mirror of water—the likes of which old wells could not even dream. I'm not only certain that such wells exist, but more than that: I want my soul, my books, that is my soul open to all, to be such a well, a well that reflects and holds within itself daytime stars—people's souls, lives, and destinies . . . no, more precisely: my contemporaries', my fellow citizens' souls and destinies.

Invisible to the naked eye and thus seeming not to exist, may they become visible to all, in all their radiance—through me, in my depths and purest twilight. I want to hold them always within me, as my own light and my own mystery, as my own highest essence. I know: without them, without these daytime stars, I am not and cannot be a writer . . . But then they cannot be seen by others—that is, exist—without me, without my life and story about them, without us—writers, and we know that.

And I especially re-remembered this youthful dream of mine, of daytime stars and the wells reflecting them, when I was considering readers' letters and responses to my notes, published in 1954 in the journal *New World* under the title "Last Year's Journey," and now as the opening chapter of this book, "Journey to the Town of My Childhood."[2] I wouldn't risk talking about these letters, if I weren't sure that they relate not only to me but to my professional colleagues, touching on that most important field: our relationship with readers or, speaking more precisely, with the people.

In the first fragment (as we'll agree for now to call these uncertain notes), I told about a journey to the town of my childhood, the ancient Russian city of Uglich; I recalled the distant, difficult years living there during the civil war in a cell in the Novodevichy Monastery, where we had been installed by the city government. I reflected on the Essential Book, which for me, as for many writers, is always ahead, saying how my Essential

Book appears to me—as a "confession of the child of the century." I also wrote about much else.

I received a lot of letters.

Responses came to me from many of my "countrymen" from around Uglich—now soldiers, engineers, boatmen, mothers with families—whose childhood and youth were connected with this unique Russian town, many of whom, it turned out, had gone to school at the same time as me or a little later—at the same school, but as kids we didn't know one another, weren't friends, and only now, thirty years later, we became acquainted in absentia.

People in no way connected to Uglich responded to me.

And—although it may seem unbelievable to some—most of the letters were about the Essential Book.

Among them was a letter from an old female teacher from a village near Moscow, a letter from a Donetsk miner who had been a Red Guard, another from an old forester.

They wrote about how they see my Essential Book; they told about their own lives, adding at the end: "Maybe this will be necessary for your Essential Book."

And reading these valedictory letters and letters of confession, I understood something very important: if I have an Essential Book, still *unwritten*, which always lies ahead, then readers also have an Essential Book, still *unread*, and it too always lies ahead. And just as a writer continuously writes the Essential Book, tirelessly dreaming of it, so that it seems to the writer during his regular work: "Here I'm finally writing the essential one," but later you see that this only approaches the essential one, which still lies ahead; in the same way this feeling exists in the reader: in many books of our truly great Soviet literature, he recognizes his times and himself; he loves many of our books, but somehow the most central, the most all-embracing and expressive of his soul—this book lies ahead, and he seeks, he craves this book. He wants to find in it not only the external movement of events, not only his own external acts, but above all the most profound, secret, intimate, authentic world of his soul. He wants to see his moral path without embellishment and without false modesty, without silences and without idle chatter, without exaggeration, but also without disparagement. Perhaps, the daytime star languishes in its invisibility and "craves detection," craving not only to catch sight of itself, but wanting to know that *others* see and know it, wanting to share with others its cherished, invisible, deep light. The Soviet person, with his titanic biography, wants to share his spiritual experience not only with his contemporary compatriots but with the people of the whole world and their descendants, and not through "silent confession" or patter but through his writer's Essential, Great Book. Above all, he wants, together with the writer, to *create* this book; together with the writer, he wants to be the hero of this book, whose soul is wide open to its very depths, open before the people, that is, he wants to be the hero of the "confession of the child of the century." Craving such a book has nothing in common with the idle vanity of a certain type of demand: "Immortalize us food industry workers," "You've forgotten about us workers in the city finance department," "Get closer to the lives of firefighters and fire extinguishers, comrade writers," and so on.

No, this is not a vain desire to take pleasure in beholding one's own face but the solicitous attitude toward the future of the toiler who is building the future. This is the anticipation of one's own life in the life of those who will come after us, the desire to leave to them not only a material but also a spiritual legacy; to convey with relentless truth the moral experience of the epoch, both the positive and the negative—that's right, do it this way and not that way, don't repeat our mistakes and suffering. This was false. This we for a long time took to be false, fearing and shunning it, but it turned out to be the only true thing.

And there was one more thing I understood from such letter-confessions and letter-autobiographies: the reader worries seriously that we writers, representing, fixing, recording what is visible and known to all, are not rising above the transient and the topical, we are forgetting something very important, perhaps what is most important, most contemporary, both now and forever, in all that has occurred and is occurring in the life and soul of the reader-people. As a daytime star, passing over a well, trembles that the well will not reflect it, will not notice its light in its prophetic depths.

This anxiety is understandable. Yes! We have so far touched upon only superficially and often falsely the many aspects and events of our life that pass though the soul of the Soviet person, agitating it now with bitterness, now with joy, tearing it apart and raising it up; or put differently, the many sides of the soul's history. But we remember all. An ancient poet, lamenting the destruction of Jerusalem, the city of his happiness and his suffering, equally the people's happiness and suffering, cried: "If I forget thee, O Jerusalem, let my right hand forget her cunning. If I do not remember thee, let my tongue cleave to the roof of my mouth; if I prefer not Jerusalem above my chief joy."[3]

The paralysis of the body, eternal muteness—the paralysis of the soul—that is what the ancient poet called down upon his own head if he were to forget that beautiful, dread truth about himself and his people and fail to make it his "chief joy," the foundation of his life, the foundation of his gladness.

No, we forget nothing! We are true to the call of the party: remember, know, and write about our life, about our Soviet person, about his soul—the whole truth and nothing but the truth. We are true to you, reader, who demands this of us, awaiting our—and your!—Essential Books. We will write them with your generous and wise help; we will write, opening our and your heart as the single heart of the people. And I, too, will probably write my Essential Book—no, not probably, but certainly! But today I am still only on the approaches to it, and these notes also only approach it; although it seems to me for some reason—more closely than anything before. Ah, yes, this is only a draft, but the Essential Book is always more plan than embodiment, it is always a dream, the anticipation of itself—the Essential, Great Book. But, I repeat, these notes seem to me today to be closer to the Essential Book than everything else. Thus I resolve to publish them. The Essential Book cannot be created in sterile editorial subsoil, in the safest private study. I think the notes for it must be submitted to the people. This isn't pride; it's the hope of help from the reader as well as from friends in the profession—writers. I go on with my notes as before, not binding myself to a form narrower than the open diary that mixes the past, the present, and the future, the memory of life and the anticipation of it, fallen and living heroes. Here there will be repetitions of the already written, return to the already said. I would like to speak about many things—the present day requires many things. But if I leave something unsaid I know, now more than ever, that the reader, who together with me writes our Essential Book, will understand me to the end.

The present day requires many things, but above all—the defense of peace. So in this fragment I will say much about war—about the defense of Leningrad in the terrible and lofty years of the blockade.

Day of Heights: Childhood

. . . In a previous fragment I left off when I was sitting in an Uglich hotel in front of a window with geraniums on the sill and the gentle silhouette of the "Wondrous" church in the distance, and I was living life fully, for only in that place of my vanished childhood home and unfulfilled dream did I experience the extraordinary state of participating fully in the life of the people, in time and space. But that day in Uglich was preceded by another day, like it in its frenzied incandescence and richness of being, which I still call, perhaps a bit solemnly, the "day of heights." I even wrote verses about it, in which I couldn't express a hundredth part of what I experienced that day. But I have already said that the Essential Book searches for itself in various incarnations.

The "day of heights" was at the beginning of October 1941 in the Nevsky Gate district of Leningrad[4] . . . But first of all I must—if briefly— tell about the Nevsky Gate, about the very beginning of my life—it seems to me that without that nothing will be understood by others or, especially, by myself.

The need to connect the pieces of my life, the need to remember, to compare, to reexamine everything that happened in it, beginning with its sources, to collect myself as something unified, *cut through* by the beginning of the war and then by the events of 1953–57—that, I think, is what this desire to "start from the very beginning" means.

I catch myself very early, at about three years of age. I see myself in our two-story wooden house, among people for some reason very familiar and beloved—this is my plump grandmother Olga Mikhailovna, grandfather Khristofor, beautiful mama and papa, Avdotya, our nanny and servant, my second grandmother—small Marya Ivanna, mama's mama (we called her Baba Masha), many aunts and uncles and finally, mysteriously appearing in the house, my sister Muska.

Actually, it is with the night of her arrival that memory arises in my consciousness, like a silkworm beginning to spin its sticky thread, stitching together separate phenomena into an uninterrupted life.

I see myself first of all in Avdotya's powerful arms as she carries me through the half-dark house, full of indistinct movement, through the glimmering night kitchen, through the hallway, where the smell of the street and frost wafts through the door—to mother's room.

Here a blue hanging lamp burns, and the room is as if filled with glowing blue water. There is an unfamiliar smell, and it's very hot. Under the lamp, in the very center of the room, there stands something unknown to me, some kind of crib with a white pointed canopy that looks like a paper boat. It sways and rustles like a boat. Of course, this is a big toy boat! Withered, all in dark clothes, Grandma Marya Ivanna rocks it. Grandma Olga in a fiery housecoat, crossing her enormous arms on her enormous chest, stands on the other side of the boat. But most of all I see the window. Lit from somewhere in the street, the frozen January window trembles with the most colorful lights—yellow, red, green, blue. The lights run one after the other, flashing, spinning, jumping, streaming, and I can't tear my eyes away from the spectacle of the window.

"Look at you little sister, look, Lyaleshka," Avdotya whispers, and the boat comes to a stop.

I look intently. In the white heart of the boat lies something dark and wrinkled like a walnut that looks a little like a small person. I reach out my hand to touch *it*. I am not allowed to touch it. Avdotya whispers:

"Well, so you like your little sister?"

I answered in a deep bass, impatiently seeking the window:

"No! She's very red."

And both grandmothers laughed, and the aunts laughed, too. It's night, but no one sleeps. Everyone crowded around the cradle-boat, except mama—she for some reason is behind the canopy—they whisper over it, rock it, kiss me, and everyone is so kind—the grannies, father, grandfather, the aunts . . .

I am flesh of the flesh, blood of the blood of all these people, a being born in their faraway Atlantis. They carefully taught me to walk and talk like a human being, as they themselves were taught for thousands of years. I am a witness to the geological destruction of that Atlantis, and I myself, as much as I could, facilitated it. How I sometimes yearn for it now . . .

The first years of my existence, were, as they are for all people, marvelous, filled with secrets and discoveries in a world known to no one.

I remember these years with deep respect, with sad love, envious of myself. I remember those years as a country to which the path has been lost, a wondrous landscape that my soul will never forget.

Everything was alive in the Land of Childhood.

Its vast territory began, of course, with our small, but as it seemed to me then, enormous apartment. Oh, then there was nothing insignificant or dead. On the contrary, each thing lived its own special life, had its own face, voice, and habits.

In the entryway stood a huge barrel with dark, deep water. If you stood on tiptoe, leaned over the barrel and shouted, the barrel answered in a thick, angry voice, like uncle's. Its face was also thick, with puffed-out cheeks. You could drown in the barrel, and fish probably lived in the depths of its water. Winter began with the barrel: in the darkness of its water appeared quick-moving, slippery icicles, like fish fry: Avdotya wouldn't let us catch them with our hands.

Off the entryway was the kitchen, stuffed with small household objects that were also clever living things, and full of forbidden corners where it was possible, all the same, to build a house and live.

The shining, always warm tiled stove had a firebox for stoking the oven and under the oven, another little door, which Avdotya would under no circumstances allow to be opened, and she would shout with fright as soon as I inched up to this door:

"Get out! There's ash there! Don't touch!"

"Why?"

"If you open it, it'll fly out and burn your eye, it will."

I still didn't know what this ash was (the word itself was uttered for the first time!), and I decided it was some evil aunt, who Avdotya had caught and locked underneath the oven. And on winter evenings, when the winds blew—how terrifying it was in the kitchen!—evil Aunt Ash knocked on the little door, quietly whining, and I snuggled up close to Dunya, who was not at all afraid of Ash, but raked her out in the mornings when everyone was asleep.[5]

Over the honey-colored kitchen table that looked good enough to eat hung a shaggy black brush, which was used to clean the lamp glass. When you held it in your hand, the brush's handle squeaked angrily; the brush was alive, he could bite, and I was afraid of him. Avdotya knew this and sometimes, when I was really getting underfoot, she'd grab the brush and exclaim:

"Now I'll hand you over to the Brush!"

And the Brush gave a nasty, angry squeak.

The sugar tongs we called Haha, because they opened wide, like a mouth laughing, baring sharp teeth.

Haha was also alive, and it grinned—it rejoiced when it bit into the sugar.

In the dining room, where the wallpaper looked like oak planks and in the corner stood a gold-embossed metal stove (we were sure it was real gold), and in the center was a big table under a hanging lamp, the most remarkable thing was the wall clock: a small deer's head with antlers adorned it. If you stayed very still, squinted, then quickly rolled your eyes, the deer began to turn its head from side to side, and it seemed that it would now come to life, and small and cute, jump off the clock. "Little deer," I called out in a whisper. But the magic disappeared as soon as I opened my eyes wide.

It was the epoch of the divine need to feel and name things, to breathe a soul into them, to delight in their movement. But at home we weren't allowed to touch or animate things or set them in motion, and they seemed to take some kind of pleasure in diligently destroying our notion of a world filled with little people.

"You'll spoil it! You'll break it! You'll hurt yourself! Get away from that! Don't touch!" Grandmother Olga incessantly cried as soon as I got close to something interesting.

Granny hid from me even toys that she herself or others had given me so that I wouldn't spoil or break them. She hid in a cupboard the beautiful tinware given to me by my grandfather; she buried in the bowels of the dresser my doll Nina with the eyes that opened and closed; she concealed in the depths of a wardrobe that was as big as a house the real little red umbrella given me by Aunt Lisa.

That's why the nicest, most beloved corner of the whole house was the kitchen, and in the kitchen—Dunya's bed. It was pushed right up against the wall, and separated from the kitchen by a ticking curtain the color of bordeaux (Dunya called it "burdo"). Dunya never chased us away from her bed. You could climb onto Dunya's bed, you could hide behind the huge pink pillow, turn somersaults. You could even stand on the pillow and get a close look at Dunya's icon. All of grandmother's icons were the same—with dark, angry, long faces. But Dunya had a very interesting icon: a little old man, holy, awfully like our grandfather, but with a head that was too big and a halo around his head, feeding a brown bear out of his hand and surrounded by a deep, dense forest; a little hut peeped out of the forest, with little windows and a chimney, and smoke even rose out of the chimney—probably all of this was like Dunya's home in Guzhovo. When the green lamp burned before the icon, the forest came to life and moved . . . And under Dunya's bed was a round wicker basket that contained beautiful material covered with roses and butterflies, a bright green silk blouse, and, most importantly, an amazing shawl, gold on one side, silver on the other!

In her free time, Avdotya's favorite occupation was to look through the things in the basket.

She especially valued her shawl and would admire it for a long time, and we would, too, of course. We always scurried to the kitchen the moment Dunya began to go through the basket.

We couldn't tear our eyes away from the gold-silver shawl, which for some reason Dunya called "two-faced."

"Oh, Dunya, it's so beautiful! Let me touch it! What do you think, Dunya, does the tsarina have such a shawl? Dunya, why don't you ever wear it?"

"Why chould I wear it out for nothing?" Dunya objected with dignity. "When I go to Guzhovo, I'll take all this with me. I'll wear it for the first time in Guzhovo."

Dunya was a "Skober," and thus in place of "sh" she said "ch"—and vice versa.[6] The village of Guzhovo, where she was born, was in Skob (Pskov) province, and to go there, in Dunya's words, took a whole three nights, or more.

"And days?" we asked.

"No, you go there only at night," she replied firmly.

Dunya's Guzhovo was very far away—at the other end of the world, at the other end of the night.

The "burdo" curtain by Dunya's bed was usually folded over the cornice; Dunya lowered it only at night when she went to sleep.

But sometimes, she would let it down long before night. This was when all the adults had gone out visiting, and we were left alone in the strangely quiet, half-dark apartment, lit only by icon lamps; the apartment suddenly became a bit alien, scary, as if it weren't inhabited.

Then Avdotya let down the curtain, sat on the bed, carefully extended her hands on her strong legs and, staring fixedly with a blank look, began to fill the whole apartment with a thin, resonating voice, as though weeping:

Oh, my beloved ho-ome . . .

And then she couldn't sing another word: all at once, instantaneously, tears poured down her wide face, and she cried with the same thin, longing voice, without words, without complaint, only from time to time getting out her single phrase:

Oh, my beloved ho-ome . . .

An incomprehensible, painful anxiety began to torment me when Dunya thinly sang-cried in our apartment, deserted for the evening, behind her dark curtain near the smooth, damp wall.

We tugged at her: "Dunya, Dunya, don't sing so scary." But she, motionless, with a stony face corroded by tears and a reddened duck-bill nose seemed not to hear us until we ourselves began to howl at the top of our lungs. Then, as if waking up, she rushed to us.

"Ay, how wretched my woes! But you? What's the matter? You mustn't cry, you have your mama and papa . . ."

"But why are you crying?"

"Just because. I've got no mama. No papa. I'm an orphan. I remember Guzhovo. I feel sorry for my brother. If only I could write—I'd send him a letter."

Her greatest pain and sorrow was her illiteracy. She was uncontrollably ashamed that she was "a dark, illiterate fool." This tormented her even though in the Nevsky district she was surrounded by illiterates—our janitor, the water carrier, the floor polisher, and many residents of our building. But it was all the same to them, while Dunya suffered because she was illiterate. She would look at our books, as a starving person looks at bread, and sometimes ask:

"And what letter is this? And that one? Well, I know the letter 'A,' Lyaleshka, teash me another letter."

Her cherished dream was to learn to write, and not to write just anything, but only so that she could herself write a letter to Guzhovo, to her brother . . . To that very Guzhovo over which she cried and sang, about which we were ready to listen for hours on end.

As soon as she stopped crying, we attached ourselves to her:

"Dunya, tell us about Guzhovo. Tell us, dear Dunechka!"

Her disjointed novellas, sometimes consisting of a single sentence, were full of events, always sad or frightening.

Avdotya told us:

"Our forest in Guzhovo is gigantic. In this forest, the Green Man took a girl and strangled her."[7]

"Dun . . . the Green Man, who's that?"

She whispered, looking around:

"Well, the scariest thing in the world. One mustn't talk about him!"

Overcome with horror, we asked:

"Dun . . . tell us another one."

And, after a pause, she told us:

"Wolves killed my mother. Not real ones, but . . . As she was dying, she kept chouting, 'Oh, wolves came in the house, oh, wolves are coming after me!' My brother felt pity for me."

We cringed and looked around, holding more tightly to her wide, warm arms.

"Tell us another one . . ."

She gazed fixedly ahead, as if peering at something. Her broad, kind face with bright red veins became sad, her lips opened.

"Once, geese almost nipped me to death."

"Oh, Dunya, why?"

"Just because. I was a servant girl for one of the owners of the geese. I was so small, and the geese were big and mean! Evil geese! They all got after me, nipping. I'm howling. My brother came running and beat them off. My brother doesn't have geese. Or horses."

"And your brother isn't afraid of geese?"

"What's he got to fear from geese?"

We sighed with pleasure, and asked for another story about her brother.

After a pause, Avdotya said:

"We once had a cow. It was evil, butting. Always butted everyone. My brother took it by the horns and sawed them off."

Or:

"A farmer had a horse—a biter! It bolted out of the yard and into the forest. My brother went out and caught the horse, and he also collected a ton of muchrooms, enough to feed all of Guzhovo."

"And the Green Man?!"

"What about the Green Man?"

"Your brother really isn't afraid of the Green Man?"

"My brother isn't afraid of anything!"

In Guzhovo, the cows were butters and evil, the geese were huge and evil, and the forest, the abode of the Green Man, was huge and frightening, and wolves came out of it to people in their dying hour; horses were wild and biters, but brother was huge, too, and fearless; he fearlessly walked through the wild Skob forest, drove off raging geese, sawed the horns off butting cows, had no fear of the Green Man, about whom people mustn't even talk, and loudly played on the harmonica the same song that in Peter, Avdotya could never sing to the end.

Oh, the fiercely beautiful Skob village of Guzhovo! Your densely forested countenance gazed implacably from Dunya's icon at the foreign land of the city. And every evening, standing rooted to the ground before the icon, motionless, eyes open wide, Avdotya prayed to the image of the old man calmly feeding the bear, the image of the woeful little hut—the shining image of her three nights' distant Guzhovo. Squatting near the stove, we respectfully watched her wide pleated skirt, the thin plait between her bare, masculine shoulders, her big red hand slowly making the sign of the cross. We strained to listen to her Pskov-accented whisper, and I once thought I heard:

"Lights of God, lights mighty, lights immortal have mercy on me."

Imagination translated the overheard prayer differently,—it was mysterious and beautiful: "Flowers of God, flowers mighty, flowers immortal, have mercy on us."[8]

And right away, easily and gladly, we believed that in God's heaven grew such flowers—huge, growing on trees, unfading, mighty, and good; they glowed like lamps and did everything that you asked of them. And we believed in God's flowers, in their wonderful power, peacefully and joyously and with great confidence we asked:

"Flowers of God, flowers mighty, flowers immortal, have mercy on us!"

I hid this prayer from the adults, instinctively feeling that they would forbid it, that they, praying to their boring, dark icons wouldn't believe in the cheerful and good holy flowers.

Many, many years went by—there was the revolution and the civil war; we lived almost three years in Uglich, and then returned to Petrograd, where all the little people had disappeared from our apartment, and even the Uglich "little old man" had disappeared. Nine years later, I left the house forever, left Nevsky Gate, and was already a Komsomol and even a candidate member of the party.[9] I had long since stopped believing in God, and had entirely forgotten about his almighty flowers—when I saw them with my own eyes, alive! This was in the summer, the first time I went to the south, to the sea, and while waiting for the bus to Gagra I wandered alone in the Sochi arboretum.[10] It seemed my heart could accommodate no further rapturous amazement in the face of the first sight of the beauty of the south; it seemed it was filled to overflowing only yesterday by the open sea, the sea, the sea—a quivering, moist, infinite silver. But now I turned down an avenue with some tall, dark green trees, completely motionless in the mysteriously fragrant dusk, and—I froze: on the branches of these trees, among the dark green leaves, shining like lamps, sat huge, motionless milky-pearl flowers. They were magnolias. I didn't yet know their name. But when I went into this avenue and saw these glowing, huge flowers, so mighty, seemingly immortal, so calmly beautiful, I suddenly remembered the dream-prayer of early childhood. And I laughed—lord, I'm really in *heaven*! And in cheerful happiness, I whispered, not praying and not blaspheming: "Flowers of God, flowers mighty, flowers immortal, have mercy on us," just like so long ago, in Nevsky Gate.

But I was in Nevsky Gate less and less frequently. I lived now in "the city," at 7 Rubinstein Street, in a strange building constructed at the very beginning of the thirties—I wrote about it in the first fragment.

In Nevsky Gate, in our old building, there was now only papa (he and mother had separated, and mother lived with her sister), Aunt Varya, Granny Marya Ivanovna—Baba Masha—and our nanny Avdotya.

Papa's wavy blond hair had started to turn gray and to thin; although he still occasionally tousled it jauntily and sang the old neighborhood song:

> And Alesha wore golden curls!
> He sang perfectly the city's songs!
> And here is how he didn't fall in love with Marusya . . .[11]

He still worked there as a doctor at the clinic of the former Thornton Mill, now the Thälmann Red Weaver factory, which he entered after the civil war, after the Kronstadt ice, on which his war service was completed.[12]

He now and then stopped by my place, the improbably small, somehow "make believe," model apartment in the "house-commune," but I could never snatch the time to drop in on him—neither at his neglected room in our old house, nor at the factory, at his dilapidated wooden clinic with a front garden, papa's second home, in fact, where for many years he grew roses unusual for Leningrad.

Granny Olga and grandfather had died a long time ago, but Baba Masha kept on living and worked incessantly around the house; she had become quite tiny and withered, barely rustling, but all the same she was lively and had quick black eyes. She thoughtfully looked after her former son-in-law—papa, when he was at home—and the only daughter remaining with her—Aunt Varya (a nurse at the Alexandrovsky Hospital)—while incessantly chiding her. Aunt Varya began to work as a nurse at the hospital in the first months of the war with Wilhelm, when her fiancé was called up.[13] He was an ensign, and when in the evenings my aunt quietly sang the romance "Martial Seagull,"[14] it seemed to me that it was about Aunt Varya's fiancé:

> Here is a young ensign with an infantry section
> Endeavoring to defend the regiment's flag
> Of all his company
> > he alone remains . . .
> But no! He will not retreat!

Aunt Varya's fiancé, the ensign, was killed in battle, and perhaps, too, as in the romance:

> The night flew by, the dawn rose,
> The enemy we drove back from the river.
> The next morning the fallen ensign we found,
> Still holding the flag in his stiffening hand.

Aunt Varya never got married, and quietly, meekly, even in some ways willingly, she faded; and this was her third decade weeping over her fiancé-ensign; she worked in the same hospital, which after the civil war became a workers' hospital, wearing the same white headscarf with the small red cross in the center. Although such headscarves are not supposed to be worn now, Aunt Varya, as a very experienced, skilled surgical nurse, was allowed to wear it, with the cross.

And our Dunya had long worked at the "Kartontol" factory as a charwoman, where she had studied in the "liquidate illiteracy" campaign since the twenties, but in all that time she never became literate—she couldn't write or even read.

"I just can't get the letter 'sha,' she complained to me on the rare occasions when I stopped by our Nevsky house. Lyaleshka, I understand 'k,' 'n,' 'r,' 'l,' 'm'—those I read, but the letter 'sha' (she said 'cha') and the ones like it I just can't read!"[15]

Then she would begin to cry and wipe her eyes with the corner of her headscarf, whispering:

"I was a dark fool under the tsar—and a dark fool I'll remain under Soviet power. I'll leave for my brother in the country; I'll help him."

Her brother was seriously crippled in the war against Germany.

But Dunya never did leave for Guzhovo—the city still held her.

The years went by: the thirties began, the first Five-Year Plan, the ardent storming nights at the Elektrosila factory, where I worked; the end of the thirties, my daughters' deaths, one after the other, then immediately the grave trial of 1937–39, which left an indelible trace in my consciousness, and then there was, almost immediately—the Great Fatherland War.[16] More and more, life fell, caved in, piled up between me and my old home, and so different were my sorrows and joys, especially the sorrows, from the fixed, as it seemed to me, sorrows and joys of my relatives in Nevsky Gate, that the thread connecting me with them became thinner and thinner and was just about ready to snap.

I didn't regret this—strictly speaking, I didn't even think about it. I rarely met my father; Nevsky Gate lived somewhere far away in my subconscious; I hardly remembered Avdotya, my grandmother, or Aunt Varya until the time at the beginning of October 1941, when Leningrad was already surrounded by a solid ring of Germans and the assault on the city did not cease for a minute—until that time, early in the morning when Aunt Varya's voice came through the telephone.

"Lyalechka, come say goodbye to grandmother."

I didn't understand her, and was surprised, but by something else.

"Aunt Varya, how can you think about evacuating her? There's no more road out."

"She's not evacuating, Lyalechka. She's dying."

"Yes, what of it?" I almost said; something didn't get through to me.

"She's dying, Lyalechka, and wants to say goodbye to you."

"Aunt Varya," I mumbled, getting quite confused. "Today we've got an emergency meeting of political organizers at the Regional Committee. And I'm a political organizer, you know . . ." But suddenly a thought obliquely flashed by, interrupting me, and I spluttered, "How many years has it been since I've seen Baba Masha? Wait, what is it? . . . more than two years . . . Living nearby . . . And she's about to die."

And suddenly she rose before my eyes, just as she was in my childhood: small, ever and efficiently working, gently grumbling, so good and kind . . . My grandmother! My good, old, last granny . . .

"Aunt Varya!" I shouted. "I'm coming right now. I'll . . . I'll be in time?"

"I think you'll be in time."

"I'm coming, Aunt Varya!"

Day of Heights: Flanders Chain

This was a few days after a regular air-raid alarm during which we, like many Leningraders, picked up the famous German leaflet "Wait for the silver night" in the courtyard. And this morning, the residents brought me a few new leaflets. We found them slipped under the door, so these weren't German leaflets: they were written on small pieces of square-ruled paper, apparently torn from a notebook, written by hand, in pencil, in the uncertain, shaky handwriting of a child or an old person, and above the penciled text there was an image of something like a spiral or a chain, also somehow naïve, childlike. However, there wasn't a single grammatical or stylistic error in the text. Here is the text, which I already knew almost by heart, as I myself, early in the morning, had found the exact same leaflet on the floor near the door:

"Someone sent the Flanders Chain of Good Luck to me. I am passing it on to you. Hurry! Send it within twenty-four hours to four people to whom you wish good luck. This chain was started in Flanders in 1729 by a certain scholar and should go around the world three times. Whoever breaks the chain will have great misfortune. Pay attention to what happens to you on the fourth day after receiving the chain. On that day you can expect great good luck if you do not set aside this letter."

While that same number tram on which I had traveled to the "city" while I was still living in Nevsky carried me to my half-forgotten homeland,

I thought not about seeing the Gate, not about saying goodbye to my grandmother, but precisely about today's leaflet, its naïvely hypnotizing text. I involuntarily repeated: "The Flanders Chain of Good Luck . . . should go around the world three times . . . whoever breaks the chain will have great misfortune . . ." And just then a disturbing thought occurred to me: who, who put it together, who was spreading these words, this "Flanders Chain of Good Luck"? It wasn't dropped from German airplanes, but something worse—it was made by enemies living among us. Enemies? Or maybe a person hoping that in these days when everything all around was breaking and collapsing, people would give one another a hand? Would link themselves in an unbreakable chain? Yes, but why this fog instead of simple, ordinary, heartfelt words, why intimidation: "Whoever breaks the chain will have great misfortune . . ." No, even if a confused person copied and slipped this leaflet to me, it was made and set in motion by enemy hands. And this enemy lived somewhere nearby . . . maybe in my own house . . . because last night or at dawn someone passed through the corridors of our house and slipped this leaflet under the door—the enemy or the enemy's envoy or someone intimidated by him breathed at my door, listening for my footsteps, someone threatened me: "Whoever breaks the chain will have great misfortune." The enemy is clever, literate; he understands that in days full of unexpected shocks and horrors, foggy words full of vague threats and vague promises are the most dependable—so who is he, the author of this leaflet? Today I was given four such pages, plus mine—that's five . . . Five people broke the "Flanders Chain of Good Luck," but how many people were sitting now and copying and sending out this piece of paper, stupefying in its mystery. And not only in my establishment but in other houses, in all of Leningrad—because this "chain" was long-running, we had information about it, and this morning it arrived at my house, clanking at my door with its rusty iron. No doubt this will be discussed today at the regional committee. I would say that it makes no sense to keep silent about this leaflet—on the contrary, it's necessary to talk about it at meetings or in bomb shelters during alarms, even read it aloud and . . . ridicule it. Posters and appeals plastered around the city say "The enemy is at the gates." This needs to be sharpened to say "The enemy is at the door." We must grab his hand at the moment he slips this written proclamation under the door or surreptitiously drops it into the mailbox . . . If it's not an enemy, but a confused, bewildered person it must be explained to him.

I was so deep in thought about all this that I didn't notice that the tram had been standing for a long time. The conductor angrily and impatiently shouted at me:

"Citizen! Citizen, what are you doing? Get off!"

I glanced out the window. We were stopped near the Lenin factory, the former Semyannikov.[17]

"I'm one more stop," I said.

"What's with you? Have you gone deaf? Artillery shelling. Get off. The shelter is just opposite, in that house over there."

I jumped off the platform. Indeed shells were crying high overhead and exploding somewhere ahead—there, where Palevsky Prospect was. Huge, dense, round silver clouds stood like a wall at the end of the straight line of Shlisselburg Prospect, and in these clouds something rumbled and rolled, just as though a huge cast-iron potato were boiling in a huge pot. "The battle is there . . . Probably for the Murzinka.[18] But maybe already for papa's factory?" A prolonged howl, a shell flying very low overhead, and then a few seconds later an explosion could be heard—and again there, in the direction of Shlisselburg, where my house was. And suddenly an icy thought hit me: "What if that was—our house?!" I so passionately longed to see *one more time* our house and my grandmother and my family, my heart so tightened, that, without feeling fear, I almost ran down the avenue to Palevsky, on the fly pulling out of my gas mask my two passes, just in case: a pass to be on the streets during an air raid and a "pass for travel to the front from the city of Leningrad and back."

Holding tight the two passes in my right hand, the left holding my heart, I ran toward the house where I was born, where the world opened before me, first love and the irresistible call of the revolution, to the house that I had left at age twenty, despising it and its inhabitants for their "philistine essence," to the house, which I had almost forgotten—I ran to it under the noxious howling of shells, choking, grief-stricken that I might never see it again. Oh, just once! Just one more time . . .

It was intact!

Flowers Immortal

For a moment I stopped in front of it, in front of the mighty poplar, which through my whole youth looked in at me through the window and turned blue toward morning, in front of the front garden's crooked wicket gate. My house was intact, but how small it had become! Even smaller than when we came from Uglich. But it was intact. True, a similar little wooden house opposite was totally destroyed, but that had clearly not happened today or even recently, because there was no fire, and the ruins gave off a smell of cold ash. But the shells were falling, and falling nearby; suddenly the earth shuddered—this was a bomb dropping, also somewhere nearby—and immediately a siren sounded, repulsive and wild, like witches, and another bomb hit, whistling a deadly warning and the thick, round, silver clouds started to rumble louder. Taking a breath and remembering that I had to say goodbye to my grandmother who was dying I went into our house.

. . . In that room that I remembered from childhood, the long, tall mirror between the windows was completely dead—it was as if shrouded in eternal fog, and it no longer reflected anything. The room was light—those silver, mortally rumbling clouds illuminated it. The only thing that was dark was the tremendous icon of Nicholas the Wonderworker in the corner, which had scared us as children and with which my "iconoclasm" had started before joining the Komsomol. A red lamp burned in front of Nicholas the Wonderworker, and so the brown haughty-stern face of the old man with a miter that looked like a chapel stood out from the solid black field and seemed more implacable and deathly. The rubber plant, for which I had a frenzied loathing at the time of my "iconoclasm," had spread horribly, so that it had become like some kind of impudent living creature.[19] And the room smelled of one of the most forgotten scents—the sad and pure smell of incense. I took this in and grasped it in an instant, before in the next moment grasping the most striking thing: the extraordinary, almost solemn calm that reigned here, and the proud, incredible simplicity of my dying grandmother. Aunt Varya in her nurse's headscarf with the red cross in the center stood at the foot of her bed; Aunt Varya worked in the same Alexandrovsky—actually Proletarsky—Hospital, which was once again a war hospital, and a war hospital in the sense of proximity; it was considered a frontline hospital.

Seeing me, she calmly approached, kissed me gently and calmly and quietly said:

"She's still conscious. She'll be glad to see you."

I for some reason pulled the shawl from my head and approached granny's bed. At that moment, a strong explosion shook our house, and the red lamp in front of the impassive face of the saint swayed from side to side; Aunt Varya, standing on tiptoe, stopped it with her hand. And grandmother was lying on pillows, a white shawl tied around her, peasant-fashion; her face had become very small and wrinkled, her eyes sunk very deep, but they looked out of their hollows with wisdom and enlightenment, glimmering with something especially alive. But most of all I was struck by her hands folded across her chest. They seemed inordinately huge—so many nodules and calluses on her fingers, so swollen, twined with prominent, blue veins. These were the hands of a woman who had worked exactly eighty of her eighty-seven years, the hands of a mother who gave birth to, nursed, swaddled, and raised fourteen children and many grandchildren and even great-grandchildren, and survived and buried many of them, and closed their eyes with these hands, and threw the first handful of earth into their graves. I looked at her tiny, almost glimmering face, at her alive, shimmering eyes and at her enormous hands with unprecedented trembling, almost with fear, and suddenly thought that through my whole life I had never once done anything nice for my grandmother—or even said anything nice to her—with her living eyes, with these hands . . . How had I let this happen? I also suddenly remembered how she took me to the bathhouse, set me in the tub with "cooled down" water, drawing the stinging soap away from my eyes, and afterward by the bathhouse gate bought me black, deliriously sweet locust bean or gave me slightly sour kvass to drink.[20] And I? What good had I done for her, Aunt Varya, father? Nothing. I wasn't in the mood for them, had no time: the First Five-Year Plan, shock construction projects, mastering theory, my life—building my own new family—oh, I wasn't in the mood for them, not for them! I was building a new society, and here was a grandmother and aunt, with their "name days" and still more philistine fuss . . .

When I sat down nearby, my grandmother seemed to be in some kind of half-conscious state.

"Mama," Aunt Varya called out to her, "Lyalya came to say goodbye."

Her eyes became more lively, and she began to move her huge hands.

"Varka," she said sternly, "how could you leave the hospital at such a time?"

"Someone's taking my place there, mama," Aunt Varya answered submissively and repeated, "Lyalechka has come to you, do you see?"

Grandmother turned her head to me, and looked at me long and silently, with indescribable tenderness and love.

"Lyalechka . . . my first granddaughter . . . You're an atheist . . . a Komsomolka . . . Well, all the same I will bless you. You won't be angry?"

"No, grandmother," I answered.

Another violent explosion shook our old house, as she, with her gnarled hands, looking like cast iron, but weightless, slowly blessed me. I pressed my lips to her already cool hand.

"Well," she rustled faintly but distinctly, "well, at least I've seen one granddaughter . . . And that Muska, that Muska, where's she?"

"She's in Moscow, grandmother . . ."

"That Moscow . . . also being bombed?"

"Also, grandmother . . ."

"And where is it, Moscow? Well, in which direction?"

Not completely understanding her question, I randomly indicated the wall against which she was lying.

"It's in this direction, grandmother."

She turned slightly toward the wall and again raised her hand making a small sign of the cross—she no longer had the strength for a big one—and blessed her, rustling:

"Lord, save thy servant Maria and the thy red capital Moscow . . ."

And suddenly a hitherto unknown feeling, like a glow flaring up, began to rise in me.

"This is how she dies: slowly, solemnly . . . How she says goodbye, gives her blessing . . . This is all she can do to participate in the war . . . This is her last labor in life. Not death—the last act. She dies in the Russian way, or rather, departs—devoutly, understanding all. And it doesn't have to do with God for her, absolutely nothing to do with God. They say that when Pavlov died, he observed his own state and dictated his sensations to an assistant sitting nearby.[21] And when somebody knocked, wanting to come in, he answered: 'Pavlov is busy—Pavlov is dying.' The genius of humanity—and my ignorant grandmother . . . But why call her ignorant? To work, to love, to love without end, so that in your last hour you remember your loved ones, your native land—isn't this the soul's purest height? And so the genius Pavlov and my grandmother died in the same way— fearless and all the time thinking of life and in its name performing their last acts . . . But this isn't death, it's a challenge. A challenge to death raging all around us. This is a military death. But aren't we dying in the same way? We, those who are under artillery attack, and those who fight there in that rumbling cloud? In the same way! Not noticing death, keeping in mind only life. And so that means . . . means that death simply doesn't exist, and we needn't fear it. Can this be true, that it doesn't exist?"

My thoughts flew, just like this, one following another, repeating. And involuntarily I withdrew my hand from my grandmother's palm, which was growing cold, and glanced at my watch. "I have to go to my post and then to the regional committee and the radio . . ." She caught my gesture and affectionately, almost indulgently smiled, as an adult smiles at a blundering child.

"Go on, Lyalechka," she whispered tenderly, "go, dear one, don't wait . . . for me . . ."

"Grandmother, forgive me," I answered, exactly as if I said goodbye to her not forever but until tomorrow, "I really have to run, you understand . . ."

"I understand everything, little granddaughter, my child, go . . . Go!"

Day of Heights: "Guzhovo Will Not Be Taken"

I went out into our yard, looking at the garden—it was lovely in its dusky-golden dress, thick, sprawling again after having been almost entirely cut down during the civil war. Shells whistled overhead almost continuously—the fire now directed further away. My thoughts flew, ever more urgent and weighty.

"Lyaleshka," a familiar voice called to me, and I saw Avdotya, our Dunya, approaching me. In one hand she held a spade, in the other a bundle with food, a snow-white scarf tied around her head.

"Dunya, Dunechka!" I rushed to her, rejoicing. "Oh, how glad I am to see you . . . Well, how are you? Where are you working?"

"On the trenches, of course," she answered, also smiling. "I'm heading there now. Wearing a white cloth, you see?"

"I see. And why white?"

She whispered mysteriously and significantly, looking around the golden garden:

"For three days they've been dropping leaflets: 'Go out in white scarves—then there'll be no bombin'.' We decided among ourselves at the factory—well, we'll go out in white scarves."

"Dunya, what are you thinking?! Well that means that you surrender, you understand?!"

"Well, what's with you! Surrender! We want to *outsmart* them. As soon as they see women came out in white scarves, they'll quit bombin', and we'll keep on digging. What do white scarves matter? What do you think you can get up to under bombin'? And we need to dig out some pits there, so that the devil'll break both his legs in them."

She adjusted with dignity the scarf with which she wanted to "outsmart" the Germans, and sighing, added:

"And as soon as we beat those Germans, I'll go to Guzhovo, wearing that kerchief, you remember, the two-faced one? I've never worn it once—still like new. I'll wear it in Guzhovo for the first time."

"Dunya," I couldn't help saying, "the Germans have taken Guzhovo . . . and Pskov, too."

She looked at me, almost contemptuously, even haughtily, as at a disorderly drunk spouting nonsense.

"No," she said absolutely calmly. "Fools have lied to you, Lyaleshka. The Germans couldn't take our Guzhovo in a hundred years. How could brother let that happen?"

And with growing enthusiasm, fearlessness, and resistance, I understood at once. "Of course! How would it be possible to take Dunya's Guzhovo?

That is, take it forever? With its savage forests, biting horses, evil geese, and especially with brother—with cheerful, good, and fearless brother? No, Guzhovo cannot be taken. And Leningrad will not be taken . . . Not taken, not taken! . . . All this *now*, it's some kind of delirium, nonsense, we will stand our ground, of course . . . And if death—for me . . . Well, let it be death—since it doesn't exist!"

"Olga," my father suddenly called out to me.

Happily I turned toward his call. He ran into the courtyard, in his plain, worn raglan coat, like a woman's skirt, in an old military cap, probably from the last war—and something about his merry blue eyes, something youthful in his voice, made me realize that he, like I, was possessed by a cheerful feeling of resistance to an almost inevitable death . . .

"Did you see granny?" he asked quickly. "Well, that's good. I just escaped for a moment from the office. Wait for me—I'll be back soon. We'll walk down Shlisselburg together. But why are you standing there like fools," he suddenly and angrily cried. Go into the shed. If a shell gets you—we won't be able to collect the bones."

But it was all the same to me whether I got hit or not; although before today, every bombardment and shelling—I, as a political organizer, did not take cover—cost me such deadly, such devouring fear, that after the all clear I felt that I existed only somewhere far below in my freezing cold feet and high up in my ice-cold face. I couldn't feel my body or my hands.

But today I was calm.

"Well, Lyaleshka," said Avdotya, pressing her kind, doughy face against mine, kissing me. "Now you look here, be clever; don't believe enemies; under bombin', don't come out, and if it comes—quickly put on your gas mask—you understand, gas mask! The chief explained it to us."

She moved away a few steps, then turned around and sadly added:

"And I never learned to read 'n' write. Well, I'll learn after this war. Holy God, I'll learn!"

She shook her spade threateningly at someone and went out of the yard, swinging her mighty hips, her life-saving gas mask smacking against them.

I laughed because I suddenly remembered how one instructor at Elektrosila taught us air defense and how he shouted: "In the event of an emergency air-gas alarm—what do we do? Put on the gas mask! Put on the boots of a rubbery nature!"

Father came out, looking serious, with his cap in his hand.

"My mother-in-law is departing with dignity," he said quietly. "Eternal memory . . ." And with a stubborn shake of his head, as if throwing off some weight that had suddenly fallen on it, he smiled and said sternly, with a defiance I so well understood: "Well, let's go, little girl. It seems to have gotten quieter."

So papa and I started running down Palevsky, down its ancient wooden footbridges, and both of us, possessed by cheerful resistance to death, spoke quickly, telegraphically, almost irreproducibly.

Glancing at me, father asked:

"So, you a commissar?"

"Kind of . . . Political organizer. And I still work at the radio. In various departments. Including counter-propaganda. And also in 'TASS Windows.'"[22]

I spoke as casually as possible, but it wasn't in my power to contain either my happiness or my pride: after all, for me he was still *papa*, who I was a little afraid of, and here I was walking with him, a participant in two tough wars, under artillery fire, as an equal.

Yes, he participated in two wars! At first he fought against Emperor Wilhelm. We saw Wilhelm's portrait in *Niva*: with bulging eyes and a horrible mustache, the points of which somehow almost reached his eyes, with a helmet on his head.[23] And the top of the helmet ended in a point, too, like the mustache, a spike. Once, when the hospital train was not far away, some place called Suvalki, papa came from the war for a few days; he brought just such a helmet and gave it to us to play with. It had a spike on top and a repulsive eagle with its tongue thrust out, rapaciously splaying its clawed feet. The helmet gave off some kind of unbearable, sour, suffocating smell—we figured it out: it smelled of . . . war! We didn't play with the helmet . . . neither I nor Muska, we didn't even try it on, but having turned it over in our hands, quietly and with disgust stuck it behind the stove . . .

Later papa fought against the Whites in the south—against Wrangel and Kaledin and Krasnov.[24] He was the chief of the hospital train "Red Eagles"; later, already after he brought us back from Uglich to Petrograd, he went with our units putting down the counterrevolutionary rebellion across the Kronstadt ice and provided aid to the wounded—he was an excellent military field surgeon—and here I was, for the first time in my life walking with him as an equal, more than that, as a soldier alongside a soldier, and that's why I told him so much, so casually about all my war work.

"They also wanted to take me on at the military newspaper, but I refused—too much to deal with."

Papa snorted and furrowed his eyebrows, which signified the highest degree of chagrin or annoyance.

"Hmm, yes . . . So a girl like you they take into the army, but me they refuse!"

"How's that?"

After a pause he said, "I applied to join the Home Guard." He spoke with such a plaintive, guilty, boyish voice that my rampaging heart came to a stop: I realized that my papa, who had fought in two wars, *envied* me.

"You're just crazy!" I said to him as dryly as possible. "At your age, with your heart—you're going off to the Home Guard?"

"Was about to," he crossly confirmed, "your comrades told me the same thing: doctor, your job is to select people for the army and the militia, that's it. But I wanted to be in the Home Guard myself . . . I'm a military field surgeon—how would I be superfluous? And your comrades are bureaucrats! Yes, yes!"

Here it needs to be said, that from the time that I, against my father's will, left Nevsky Gate, papa considered the party, everything that was happening, all our triumphs, and all our shortcomings to be "mine." He said, "Well, it seems that something will come of your Five-Year Plan after all . . ." or "So, your comrades have overdone it again." Yes, on the whole everything was "mine," and I answered to papa for absolutely everything—ugh, it was difficult!

And here he was again accusing me of something, precisely me, and envying me, and, grumbling on simply ridiculous grounds: why hadn't he, already an old man, been taken into the Home Guard? But his envy and his grumbling added to that reckless joy, that frenzied freedom and light, that was growing and growing inside of me.

We quickly reached the intersection of Palevsky and Shlisselburg and stopped on the corner. There, on the right, not so long ago had stood a public lavatory made of corrugated iron in such a way that the feet of the citizens using it could be seen below the wall, and the roof was constructed in the exact shape of a German helmet, with an eagle in front and a spike on top. The lavatory was constructed by the Gate's patriotic merchants in the second year of the first imperialist war,[25] and I remembered it from that time. And opposite it, on the left, also not long ago, was situated another commercial structure: a wobbly wooden stall, or, more accurately, a hawker's stand over which a wooden canopy on two rails trembled; under this unsteady shelter stood an old man, Uncle Grisha, who, at the very beginning of the NEP, built this "shop" and began selling fudge and toffee.[26] Every morning, on the way to school, I approached Uncle Grisha and asked:

"Uncle Grisha, how much is toffee today?"

"Today, two hundred and eighty million apiece," he imperturbably answered.

That was during the time of inflation, when the ruble fell uncontrollably, and it was so nice and at first surprising when suddenly billions and millions were converted into rubles and even kopeks, and the first coins appeared: real silver rubles, fifty-kopek pieces, twenty-kopek pieces, big, weighty copper fivers, tiny quarter-kopek pieces. On the silver coins were images of peasants and workers: arm in arm, they looked into the distance, and behind them, the sun rose.

Now both Uncle Grisha's stall and the lavatory with the roof in the shape of a Wilhelmine helmet were gone, but I remembered them as though I saw them before me . . .

"Well," papa said, "bye, little girl!" And after a pause, he asked quietly: "How's Nikolai?"

"At first, when he received the white card, he was quite grief-stricken.[27] It meant nothing that his company covered the retreat all the way from Kingisepp . . . Now he's over it, working for the civil antiaircraft defenses. He writes for the military newspaper. And, you know, he's even continuing with his article 'Lermontov and Mayakovsky.'"[28]

"I don't like your Mayakovsky," said papa. "Esenin—that one, yes."[29]

"You'll fall in love with him when you read Kolya's work. And right after the war he'll undertake a big book: 'Five Poets: Pushkin, Lermontov, Nekrasov, Blok, Mayakovsky.'[30] He's thought it out so splendidly; he's already got lots of drafts! And even now, when he's not on duty . . ."

"You should get out," father interrupted me, with a sidelong glance. "You definitely should go. By any means necessary."

"Well, you're not leaving? You're trying to join the Home Guard . . ."

"Well, so what!" he shouted angrily. "In the ancient books it's written: 'Woe to him who leaves the besieged city.'"[31]

"Fair enough. And here we are . . ."

"He won't be able to withstand it, with his illness," father said almost through his teeth, and immediately interrupting himself, shaking his head, he called out almost cheerfully: "We've gotten caught up in conversation! And work awaits us. Take care, little girl."

He gave my shoulder a slight nudge but didn't kiss me, or squeeze my hand, or embrace me; he almost ran off, to the right, along Shlisselburg, without stopping or looking back.

This wasn't a pose or self-restraint, simply that he, like I myself, knew that we couldn't die. I looked after him for a full minute, at his funny, billowing coat. I looked into the depths of the Nevsky Gate, there, where dad's factory was, and Aunt Varya's hospital, and the ironworks, the largest in the Nevsky Gate—the Obukhov. And there round clouds, biblically beautiful, primordial, formed a wall, roaring and rumbling, louder and louder. I looked in that direction, and suddenly my whole life spread before me. With an incredible swiftness, for which I can't find the words, pictures of my whole life, and the life of my homeland, and recollections of things that had taken place even before my memory rolled through my soul.

No, I wasn't recalling, I *was living* that which was, is, and will be. These resurrected feelings were sudden, fragmentary, scattered, and at the same time they merged into a single, unbroken stream—no, into something like a strong southern tide that surged with unbearable, almost painful happiness.

It was once said: time will cease to exist.[32] You can believe this or not—but I know it, I know what it's like when time doesn't exist! On that day, it didn't exist—all of it contracted into a single radiant bundle inside of me, all time, all being. And the partitions between life and death, between art and life, between the past, the present, and the future merrily collapsed. Oh, how brittle they turned out to be, how conditional, how easy it was for me to take pleasure in *all of life at once*, all its poetry and all its tragedy, at its very edge, the edge of life, at the corner of Palevsky and Shlisselburg, among the ghosts of absurd structures past, during a lull in the artillery fire.

> Like an ethereal stream
> Through my veins the heavens flowed . . .[33]

My whole life was contained in an instant, in just a few instants, but I need pages for them. These moments of my whole life flared up suddenly, and in hindsight I will not look for other explanations. I don't know why, looking at the figure of my father disappearing into the distance, I thought: there he is going to his factory, and at that factory my first *published* verses appeared, and they were about Lenin. Lenin! And a frenzied wave of warmth and light poured over me . . .

Lenin

He came into my consciousness in earliest childhood—at the time of the avid dream about Dunya's Guzhovo, at the time of my first contact with Lermontov's poems about the oak leaf and the lonely cliff, at that dim, as it were predawn time, when fairy tale and reality are still inseparable from one another and a hint is enough to create a legend and believe in it.

Papa was in the war—the war with Wilhelm was still going on and seemed it would never end—and papa didn't come to us after that single time when he brought us the helmet, and we were already beginning to forget him, how he really was. It was summer, and we lived in Finland; the hot breath of pine needles and resin filled the air, and at the seaside the most delicate smell of warm sand flowed, and the adults whispered anxiously:

"There was a huge manifestation of factory workers in Petrograd."

"They say something unbelievable happened on Nevsky, especially near Sadovaya . . . And everyone—with red flags! Thousands and thousands of people . . ."

"That Lenin stirred them up . . ."

"All the factory workers are solidly behind Lenin. And the ironworks rose up . . ."

"Yes, but he came from Germany in a sealed train?!"

"God, what a risk! To go now through Germany . . . Horrible!"

"But think about it, even that didn't stop him! He was impatient to join the Petersburg workers."

And so in my imagination a fabulously strong and fearless Lenin arose—a person "all the factory workers are going out for." I had often seen how they came out in a vast, unbroken stream when the gates of the factory where my grandfather worked opened, how many of them there were, what a rumble rose over them—and now *all* are coming out for one Lenin! And still going, going, going . . . And the ironworks also somehow rise up for Lenin—the flickering, gloomy glow above them was always visible in the evenings from the windows of our house. Something so heavy and huge screeched and roared there that it could be heard in our rooms, and now all of that rose up for Lenin—all that roars and that gives off trembling crimson light . . . And he, Lenin, traveled across Germany, where Tsar Wilhelm, with his horrible mustache and wearing a helmet with an eagle and a spike, ruled, and where there lived a million such mustachioed, horrible Germans, against whom our father and all the soldiers fought, but Lenin was in no way afraid to travel across this country, even in some kind of special "sealed" car—he had to go to the workers from our Nevsky Gate, from grandfather's factory, from Uncle Shura's Obukhov works.

In my memory flashed the night when I clung to Dunya in frenzied fear, because the window of our room was full of bright pink light—which

Дни революціи. Разгромлен. полиц. архив.

A police archive destroyed during the "days of revolution" in Petrograd, 1917. As concrete reminders of tsarist power, police archives and police stations were often targets of revolutionary violence. (Library of Congress, lot 2398, https://www.loc.gov/item/2009631825/)

meant that somewhere nearby there was a fire, and more than anything in the world, I was afraid of fires . . . A small, cold tremor shook me, and Avdotya, never taking her eyes off the pink window, held me to herself, whispering:

"It's nothing, Lyaleshka, nothing . . . It's the police station burning—your grandfather's factory workers are revoltin' again . . . Not enough for them that they threw over the sovereign-emperor, now they've set the police station on fire . . . It's nothing, it's far away, the embers won't fly to us, don't be afraid."

The police station on the corner of Palevsky and Shlisselburg, where later the petty Nepman Uncle Grisha stood with his toffees, for some reason burned not in February but in October 1917.[34] In the morning we walked with mama along the avenue and saw the still-smoking ruins of the police station, while along Shlisselburg raced trucks in the back of which stood workers in leather jackets leaning on rifles and sailors crisscrossed with machine-gun belts, the wind blowing the huge red ribbons on their chests.

And once again the name Lenin was on the lips of everyone in the Nevsky Gate, and along with his name sounded the awesome, beautiful words: "decree," "Sovnarkom,"[35] "revolution," and he became more legendary, more mighty in my childhood.

Troops on Liteiny Prospect during the "days of revolution" in Petrograd, 1917. Their banner, not visible in full, appears to call for the end of the monarchy. (Library of Congress, lot 2398, https://www.loc.gov /item/2009631819/)

Then we left for Uglich, and there I entered school and grew, and studied, and like all schoolchildren, already knew that this Vladimir Ilich Ulyanov-Lenin was the chairman of the Council of People's Commissars, our leader, and that this Lenin gave instructions for defeating Kolchak and all the other damned Whites, whose fault it was that we were so terribly hungry and freezing, and living so long without our fathers. He was thinking all the time, worrying about us all the time, Vladimir Ilich Lenin—and how we relied on him!

Then, on the way from Uglich to Petrograd, at night in a miserable train car in which half the occupants were infected with typhus, waking up at dawn, I overheard some old man telling about Volkhovstroy, which would "flood all Russia with light," and that Lenin ordered the Volkhov-stroy dam built. Then, at the beginning of the twenties, our old wooden house in Nevsky Gate was lit with electric bulbs, which we called "Ilich's bulbs" . . . As a great, sometimes formidable force, as a great good light— that's how Lenin entered into the heart of my generation from earliest childhood. As we grew, his image became more human, closer to the soul, and our love for him was deeply human—it was constant, natural, and calm, like a healthy person's breathing. But how frightened we were when he fell ill! Following the poet we repeated, muttered, entreated:

A shadow darkens the spring day,
ungluing the government bulletin.
No!
Don't! . . .
We refuse! . . .[36]

At school we prepared an evening in honor of the nineteenth anniversary of Bloody Sunday in 1905; we created a dramatization, rehearsed a collective recitation, conducted choir practice—the choir sang "Hostile Whirlwinds," "Tormented by a Lack of Freedom"—we prepared for the evening as if we really had to fight on the barricades.[37]

"To the barricades—no mercy to the bourgeoisie!"—we didn't sing, we shouted. Oh, how we wanted to really go to the barricades, how we wanted to die for the revolution! The carts carrying machine guns had only just stopped rumbling; the fires, campfires, and stinking *burzhuiki* stoves had only just gone out;[38] the delirium of typhus only just thrown off, yet the civil war, when we had been so cold and hungry, already seemed to us like a legendary, beautiful time, and, forgetting that we ourselves had in a way been participants, we envied those who had been born in time to fight for the revolution with weapons in their hands.

But it was during the demonstration against Lord Curzon,[39] when intervention again suddenly threatened—that meant again hunger, the freezing Uglich winter, war—at that demonstration we gave ourselves free rein! We ran out of school with a placard inscribed in sloping black letters with the cry that was already sounding around the Nevsky Gate: "Slug the lord's mug," and with a flourish we very successfully poured into the stream of workers—ardent, loud, banging feet on the cobblestones, howling with trumpets, blazing with banners and red kerchiefs—weavers, metalworkers, spinners . . . And we immediately fell in step and went with them as equals; moreover, we were fortunately situated, because just ahead of us moved a truck that carried a long black coffin and a very handsome young worker—alive—in blue overalls holding a huge stake thrust at an angle into the lid of the coffin, and on the body of the truck was stretched a banner: "We'll drive an aspen stake into the grave of the world bourgeoisie."

We walked swiftly—not walked, but really rolled in the general stream along Shlisselburg, past the old, gloomy shops of the Semyannikov, past the board and log houses of the Gate—heading to the city. Anger and courage blazed on the faces of unwashed, sweaty, dusty, sooty people—they came out into the street directly from their machines. The boulevard smelled of machine oil, woolen dust, and the reeking fat of the Stearin factory. Near the Semyannikov, someone shouted from a truck: "Down with the sharks of imperialism!" and we vehemently joined in: "Do-oooown with them!" and we sang, sang at the top of our lungs, trying to outshout one another:

> White army, black baron
> Trying to restore the tsarist throne.
> But from the taiga to the British seas
> The Red Army is the strongest of all!
> So let the Red
> Powerfully grasp
> His bayonet in calloused hand,
> And we must all
> Irrepressibly
> Go into the last fight to the death![40]

We also sang "Boldly, Comrades, In Step" and "Tears Fill the Boundless World . . . ," the song with the piercing refrain about the banner:

> Our blood burns with fire,
> Our comrades' blood upon it . . . [41]

And we sang still other songs, and endlessly "The Internationale," "The Internationale," "The Internationale"—"the last fight let us face."[42] And here's what's astonishing: that day every song wasn't a song at all, but simply the absolute truth—about the British seas and our readiness to go into battle—we didn't sing songs at all, we only articulated, exhaled what was in our hearts, all of us—workers, schoolchildren, and the teachers striding beside us.

Returning from my dying grandmother's in the fall of forty-one, just as I approached the Semyannikov works, passing by our old brick school, this recollection—no, more searingly alive, the desire to die for the revolution, this holy adolescent trembling, first experienced at the demonstration against Lord Curzon—overtook me like a wave, and at once merged with today's state of resistance, fearlessness, and limitless freedom. It seemed impossible to be more free, but freedom kept growing in me and around me, and new recollections (reexperiences?) arose, link by link, link by link . . .

Yes, the demonstration (then they were still referred to in the old way—manifestation) against Lord Curzon was in May 1923, and Lenin then was already ill, but when January 1924 came, we were getting ready for the evening in honor of Bloody Sunday on the ninth, he was still sick, and there was no good news . . .

No!
Don't!
We refuse!

. . . For our generation, Lenin's death was the border we crossed from childhood directly into young adulthood, almost passing by that anxious, uncertain time called adolescence . . . We grew up and matured several years on that brutally cold day, when covered in snowdrifts, covered in hoarfrost, the workers' district, Nevsky Gate wept over Ilich with all the whistles of all its ironworks, all its spinning and weaving factories—the ones that rose up for him, the ones that came out for him in 1917—it wept with the resonant, intermittent whistles of locomotives. It keened like a Russian widow or a mother who has lost her son, it sobbed loudly, recklessly, self-lessly, endlessly—the orphaned, log-and-plank, piled-with-evening-snow Nevsky Gate.

Still, after thirty-five years, I hear that inimitable rumble of mourning. Probably, in the city, where there were sweet shops with fancy pastries and Nepmen strolling along Nevsky Prospect, you couldn't hear it as we did in the Nevsky Gate, because there the factories and works were close by, side by side. They roared completely differently than they whistled every morning—every whistle in turn, one after the other—now they somehow roared all at once, although at the beginning I could distinguish the mighty whistle of the Semyannikov and the high-pitched voice of grandfather's factory, but later they merged into one unbroken roar. My friend Valya and I stood right in the middle of our snow-covered yard, and the mournful rumble became louder and louder, and suddenly it seemed to me that my chest opened wide, icy air poured in, and there was nothing to breathe, as if I, too, had begun to rumble, to disappear and soar upward, as if I, our yard, the snowdrifts, the shed—the whole earth—were drawn up a giant chimney.

"Yes. It's everywhere on earth. Everything rumbles. But people stay put. Like Valya and I: we don't move,"—and again, as at the Volga Station on the way to Petrograd, I felt that I am not separate; there is something huge, frenzied, that with all its might screams in grief, and I am all—only this communal, all-consuming cry. There is a universal numbness—and I am frozen together with everyone. We are a single piece of ice. But that cry, that universal numbness—it's also a call to the whole world. Yes, a call. Because the Nevsky Gate's weeping achieved such force that it sounded like a threat—no, like a triumph.

And the tragic roar lasted a long time, it seemed a very long time, and gradually subsided, only a nearby plant still sobbed piercingly, like a "cuckoo," for a full half minute, but then it, too, fell silent, and absolute quiet crashed down on our dusky yard, deafening Valya and me. We nonetheless remained motionless, standing at attention, and we were silent. We kept silent a long time.

"Valya," I finally said, "I'm going to join the Komsomol. Immediately. I'm not old enough, but I'll prevail upon them . . . Grandmother's against it because of God, and mama—because of the boys. But all the same, I'll join."

"Me, too," dark, thin Valya Balkina softly replied . . .

We talked, still standing motionless, at attention.

"Valya, I have to tell you a terrible secret. I haven't believed in God for a long time already. You know, Valya, he doesn't exist."

"I know," answered Valya. "I will also join the Komsomol."

"Valya," I said, almost suffocating with a strange new happiness, "I will join the Komsomol, and I will be a professional revolutionary. Like Lenin."

And it wasn't the frost all around, but an inner cold—a chill of delight, a chill of self-abnegation—that ran down my spine: not with my head—with my whole being, with all my flesh and spirit, I understood that I *gave an oath* that I wouldn't be able to break, because at the moment of that oath, an entirely new life began for me, and to abandon it—would be to stop living . . .

. . . And since then, this has given me the strength, despite all the misfortunes, to live fully, to live with all my being—this belief that I didn't break my sworn adolescent oath, the consciousness that I belong to the party, fused with Lenin's name.

"You're Published at Our Factory"

. . . And, silent, Valya and I continued standing motionless, at attention, among the snowdrifts, until my Grandma Olga called out to me from the window:

"Lyalka! Do you want to freeze out there, fool! I'm gonna pull you by your braids . . ."

She shouted angrily, even viciously—but what did I care now about Grandma Olga and her threats? Or kind Baba Masha? Or even mama and papa? Or Muska? Or generally our whole house? Not the slightest bit.

After the oath among the snow-covered wooden sheds, total alienation and a weighty silence descending into my soul, I went silently into the kitchen, to Dunya's corner, and began to write verses about Lenin. I wrote about what had just been:

> How our whistles sang today!
> As though all the factories
> > got on their knees.
> Because they are now orphaned.
> Lenin died . . .
> Dear Lenin . . .

And when "dear Lenin" sounded within me and I wrote the words on paper—it made me so sad, so unbearably sad that tears rolled from my eyes. I wasn't sobbing, I just brushed them away with my index finger, and still writing, writing, trying to make every stanza end, like the first, with the words "dear Lenin . . ."

I deliberately sat in the kitchen and not the dining room so that no one would see that I was writing, but father, passing through, noticed all the same that I was sitting over a notebook. Smiling at his own thoughts, seeing me he immediately became serious and quietly approached.

"What's doing? . . . Inspiration struck?" he asked cautiously.

"Yes."

"Well, then . . . Write, little girl. I won't interfere. Then you'll show it?"

"If it turns out."

In the family, my poetry writing was treated in different ways. Avdotya—usually the first listener of my poems—reverently marveled:

"Lyaleshka! You did this all yourself—out of your own head?!"

"My own, Dunya."

"Oh, clever girl! And I'm an illiterate fool, there's no way I'll master reading and writing. I wouldn't write verses but a letter to Guzhovo, at least one little letter, with kind regards, at least a single one—yes, that'd be it!"

Mama liked literally everything; no matter what I wrote, she went into raptures, but in such a way that I felt ashamed, and the main thing—she was always taking drafts of my verses and hiding them in the chest of drawers in order to read them later to acquaintances and guests and endlessly say how I'm a "gifted girl," and this made me want to moan quietly . . .

Papa liked some—but not others. When I read him a verse about our garden, he shook his head, ruffled his hair, and said: "Splendid . . . Like

Pushkin's!"—and all evening, pacing around the apartment, as was his habit, and ruffling his hair, he hummed the first line:

You doze, old garden, strewn with frost . . .

But when I fell in love with a boy from Ninth Parallel Street and wrote the poem:

Lilies of the valley! Fragrant,
Wonderful flowers!
Silvery tears
Of a maidenly dream,—

he said: "m-yes . . ." and softly, but very annoyingly, sang to the jaunty tune of "It's a Long Way to Tipperary . . ."

Sentimentality! Sentimentality!
Sentimentality, gentlemen!

And since I knew that for papa the word "sentimentality" was worse than any swear word, I burst into tears of grief and grievance. Mama quietly consoled me, saying that the poem was "wonderful, wonderful" and that papa didn't understand it, just as he didn't understand her. But I knew that papa understood everything.

That's why, when I wrote my very first poem about the revolution, about Lenin, I read it to papa—without mama, without Muska, without Avdotya, to him alone. My heart was pounding terribly when I read, and pounding even harder when I finished reading, and papa said nothing, only looked at me a long time with a new expression, then stretched out his hand, silently read the verses and said sternly:

"Write a clean copy, more neatly. I'll show it to the editors of our wall newspaper. Maybe they'll even print it . . . It seems to me, they can print it."

Two days later he came home from work looking important, even somehow puffed up, and at the same time obviously elated—he absolutely couldn't conceal his joy, or even cover it up for a while with importance or indifference, he was impatient to share it with others. At the same time he did not know how to complain about adversity—he was ashamed when he was unhappy, as if he himself were to blame . . .

"Well, Lyalka, as things stand . . ." he began pompously and then immediately exclaimed, clapping his hands: "They've printed it! You understand, they printed it in our wall newspaper! They said it's excellent. Congratulations. Now, it seems, you're a real poet: in print!"

I became awfully pleased and even frightened. I blushed, ran into another room, and eyes closed, arms outstretched, I circled a little, but very quickly, like when I was little. Then I looked at myself in the pier glass: well, how did I look after having my poem printed? Because I was now . . . a real poet! Alas, I was still the same—snub-nosed with long blonde braids. I so wanted to have cropped hair, like a real Komsomolka, and wear a long, belted Tolstoy blouse! I could only dream about a leather jacket, as about a long "classical" nose . . . But all the same my verses were printed and I . . . I'll ask papa to let me come to the factory tomorrow to look at my verses in the wall newspaper!

And the next day—frosty, smoky-pink, crisp—I took the horse-drawn tram to the Farforov plant, and then I ran across the Neva River, along the hard, ringing path, to the right bank, where near the squat brick buildings of the paper mill, the former Vargunin factory, stood my father's textile mill. I went to his clinic—a cozy log cabin with a front garden surrounded by a low wooden fence—and he led me into the factory committee office, where the wall newspaper was. My poem was actually printed by a real typewriter in large violet letters, not entirely straight—one letter was below, another above, but it was glued right in the center of the wall news-paper, and above it were drawings of mourning banners, and under the poem in very large letters was my family name, and, the main thing, my *full* "adult" name. It said "Olga" . . . and not "Lyalya," as they called me at home.

I stood a very long time in front of the wall newspaper, reading all the notes in which the weavers of the former Thornton factory, men and women, remembered Ilich—they knew him informally, when he was still alive, quite young, and coming by horse-drawn tram to the Nevsky Gate to visit the first workers in the revolutionary underground.[43] And here, in the middle of these notes—inarticulate, awkward, full of inexpressibly austere tenderness and love for Lenin—was my poem. The pride of the first-time author (incredible!) mixing with the first (the sharpest!) embarrass-ment in the face of a not-yet-deserved honor was causing my heart to burst.

"I will be a professional revolutionary." I repeated the words that for four days already had not left me, "I will be a professional revolutionary poet. I will even be the equal of the worker correspondents."[44]

. . . Returning to the city through the deserted, ominously hushed Nevsky Gate and visually remembering that wall newspaper with uneven violet letters and naïve drawings, I once again felt the embarrassment and pain of not having become "the equal of the worker correspondents."

The present moved further and further away, was more and more rapidly and irrevocably forgotten, while the most faraway days and even what had never been, approached me, caught, and carried me to a distant spot I didn't know. With the memory of my first printed poem, a wave of poetry caught me . . .

Day of Heights: Lermontov

Poetry also became part of my life from earliest childhood. I had scarcely learned to write, was writing in large printed letters, not yet separating one word from another, writing like people spoke—after all they spoke without commas or periods, run together—and then one day, a long winter's evening, in an old anthology with a cover the color of Zhukovsky soap, a little poem caught my eye. It began:

> Now, driving clouds along, the North
> has blown, has howled, and now herself
> Winter the sorceress comes.[45]

I froze: it was winter, the street and our garden were covered in wispy hoarfrost, in fluffy snow, and everything in the verse was said as if about this very thing, ours, which I could easily see, but in the verse everything was so wonderful that I at once understood that Winter was something *living*, because she *arrived*, that she was after all a real sorceress, and the North was alive—he "howled"; that the verse and our winter in the Nevsky Gate—were one, but how beautiful this all was in the verse!

I read the poem again and again, and suddenly I so wanted that this terribly right and amazingly beautiful verse about winter had been said—by me!

No, I have no way now to convey this primordial rapture in the face of the life-giving, spiritualizing miracle of poetry. Yes, as a rule it is impossible to convey, retell, or explain this rapture. In this is the secret of poetry and in this secret—its power.

Furtively looking around, I rewrote the poem from the anthology in large printed letters, without breaks between the words, on a large sheet of paper; stuffed the anthology deep, deep under the couch, so that no one would find it ever again; and ran to Baba Masha: I was at her place; they all lived in the same house as us, downstairs.

"Grandma!" I shouted, trembling with excitement. "Grandma, listen to what I wrote *myself*!"

"Ah, well done," said my grandmother, "how fluent!"

And I no longer had any doubt that I had composed it myself.

All the same, my first conscious love in poetry was Lermontov. A thick book in a shabby gray binding with a portrait of a sad, big-eyed Hussar drawn with "threads" (it was an engraving) lay under my pillow at night; I didn't let it out of my hands during the day unless I had to darn socks or do something to help out around the house—this was right before we left for Uglich, I was seven, then eight years old . . .

The beauty and humanity of Lermontov's verses, unconscious, and thus all the more powerful, captivated me with all their strength. And if through Pushkin's lines I discovered, found out, that winter is *alive* and the north—wind—is alive, then Lermontov's verses revealed to me that not only was everything around me alive, but that everything was about me! I read and immediately memorized the verses about the solitary pine, about the little oak leaf, about the cliff and the little golden cloud. I felt so sorry for the pine, the cliff, the oak leaf! Since then, for me, in the fall all the Nevsky Gate's leaves whirled away only to the south, and all the pearly clouds floated only to the south, and every tree in our dusty and smoky garden dreamed of another—distant, beautiful—which it would never ever meet. But why was all of this about me?! Because—together with the pine and the cliff—I was so agonizingly sorry for myself, because I was alone, completely alone in the world, and so lonely that I wanted to cry, because no one loved me (they all only pretended to love me). What is it with me—plane tree, proud plane tree why do you not want to shelter the oak leaf—me? Why?!

Withered and faded from the cold, the heat, and sorrow.[46]

No, I can't bear it . . . I can't take it any longer! If only I could set off into the sea like the solitary sail! In the huge sea—alone, alone, but at sea being alone isn't frightening, after all the sail is not afraid of storms—and neither am I!

Oh, how sweet was this torment, this yearning for an unprecedented, desired other—a beautiful palm tree, this dream of fearlessness before the storm—before death; how happy I am that even at the dawn of consciousness it was given to me to know this ecstasy, this enchantment, this power of poetry, this communion with the whole world through its magical melodies, beyond understanding; how happy I am that since that time it has exercised the most powerful dominion over my heart and over my life.

Among the many crafts and arts influencing the human soul, there is no force kinder or more ruthless than poetry. It is capable of everything. I affirm: poetry is stronger than the atomic bomb—the most destructive and creative word, sustaining the loving heart with blood, the seeking spirit with light, inspiring our greatest ideas. There is no subordination more voluntary or irresistible than the subordination to poetry. There is no love more rewarding than the love of poetry: loving poetry one is twice a poet. There is no trust simpler or more enriching than trust in poetry. But that trust must be boundless and reckless—unconditional, because poetry is selfless, she trusts you completely, she is ready to give you all her vastness, all her dusk, all the daytime stars—yours and others', burning and visible only in her depths. Trusting poetry is endowed by destiny, as they said in olden times—it is blessed. Again and again I repeat: I am happy that from earliest childhood I was given the gift of unconditional trust in poetry.

I was captivated not only by those verses that were "about me" but also by many of Lermontov's other verses. True, many of the verses in the thick Lermontov book were for some reason incomprehensible, and embarrassed for myself and the poet, I skipped them, but the verses "not about me" that were understandable agitated me no less, and perhaps even more—as if, in the evening, from a high bridge, through another's window, I peeped into someone else's life, not mine, hidden from all, and finding out about it, I became its accomplice, the owner of another's important secret . . . The craving for the mysterious, the thirst to discover and unravel the secret, and having unraveled it, to hold it inviolable or, even sweeter, to share it with a friend: "Valya, Valya, I know something! But not a word, it's a secret . . ."—how much pure joy there is in this, and how good it is if, at least in some small measure, this craving remains in maturity, and how poor, how piteous the person for whom everything is absolutely clear and for whom there is nothing mysterious, even in art . . . It was this gloomy secret that captivated and amazed me in the poem "In the midday heat, in a Dagestan valley . . ."[47] Oh, why does the slain Hussar lying in the valley with a smoking wound in his chest dream of the faraway beauty? Why does she dream of him? How did she sense that he was killed; how did he, dying, know that she was thinking of him? But it's all true, it is so, and the slain Hussar is like Lermontov with his big, sad eyes, and the knight sleeping on the bottom of the river, about whom the mermaid sings so wonderfully, is like the slain Hussar and Lermontov himself . . .[48] Charmed by this poem, I repeated it to myself, by heart, all day long, exhausted with the enjoyment of a beautiful sadness, not my own.

But I—like father, I don't have the strength to carry the burden of joy *alone*, I need to share it with others, to boast about it. Perhaps this is a selfish feeling; while grief shared shrivels and diminishes, joy shared grows, strengthens, flares up in you, and you become richer, happier. No, I simply couldn't possess this blue river, this magical mermaid song *alone*! Taking the book—to authenticate that this was written—I almost forcibly sat Muska down in the corner of the sofa and began to read her the poem from the book. She, the fool (no wonder, she was all of six!), at first said:

"I don't want you reading from that book. It doesn't have pictures!"

"Well, just you listen, listen, it's better than one with pictures . . ." And I, hurrying before she got away, in a voice choked with emotion—I for the first time read these verses *aloud, to another*:

> The mermaid swam along the blue river,
> Illuminated by the full moon;
> And she tried to splash as far as the moon
> The silver foam of the wave.

I read, and right away someone splashed me behind the collar with the same silvery, moonlit, mermaid water! And it ran along my body in a glistening, cool trickle, and I, almost breathless with it, was finishing:

> But to the passionate kisses, I do not know why,
> He remains cold and mute;
> He sleeps—and, bending to my breast,
> He does not breathe, does not whisper in sleep . . .[49]

"Well? Good, isn't it?" I impatiently asked Muska upon finishing the reading.

"Uh-huh," she answered in a deep voice, and after a pause, sternly asked: "Lyalka! But passionate kisses and breast—what are they?"

I was confused, but only for a moment.

"Well, fool . . . How can't you understand? These are some kind of unusual underwater flowers . . . wonders of the sea . . . or some kind of, you know, big goldfish . . ."

On that day, going from the Nevsky Gate to the city, I began to laugh and even paused out of joy, remembering the mermaid and Muska's question . . . That was the Lermontov of my childhood. Then there was the Lermontov of my brief adolescence and my sudden, early young adulthood, when his verses simply and powerfully merged with the thirst for exploits in the name of the revolution, fed the stormy denial of God—Demon!—gave birth to dreams of a future, definitely unusual, and frightening love—again, Demon!—and the decision to become a real professional revolutionary-poet certainly relying on Lermontov's image of the poet/lover-of-freedom/dagger/bell.[50] Oh, most importantly—the bell! Despite the first rapture of atheism, lines about "God's spirit" didn't trouble me a bit—they seemed not about God, but wind, a storm, the elements.

> Your verse, like God's spirit, floated over the crowd.
> And the echo of noble thoughts,
> Sounded, like the bell in the tower calling the assembly
> On days of the people's triumphs and misfortunes.[51]

And I was ashamed even to think about this, but all the same these verses, like the verses about the sail, the cliff, and the oak leaf, were also about me—but about the me that I had to become, joining the Russian Leninist Communist Union of Youth . . .

Was it surprising that, without ceasing to love Lermontov, I, we, our generation wholeheartedly adopted Mayakovsky and spoke—of ourselves—with his verses at the decisive moments in our lives?

And there was also the piercing Esenin and Blok—his blizzard, his "Twelve,"[52] and all the majestic revelations of Pushkin, and then alongside them in our hearts sounded the Komsomol poets, who had been "born in time" and had fought for the revolution with weapons in their hands, especially Mikhail Svetlov and his astonishing "Granada," where everything was actually already about us![53] Not about me, but *about us*, even though we hadn't been born in time, when we should have been.

※

"Poetry accompanied us from the dawn of consciousness until today," I thought, walking along the cobblestones to the city, "until these days of the assault and defense of Leningrad; and now it walks beside me." And again I smiled broadly from joy: good heavens, who can take Lermontov from me? No one and never. Who can destroy him, even if they destroy me? No one and nothing. He can't be destroyed—he is immortal. Lermontov is immortal and eternal, and our Russian poetry is eternal and immortal. But Lermontov and all our poetry—has long been an integral part of my soul, all of me, which means that I . . . I was frightened—out of happiness—to *think this through*! But if I, which means also you, my dear, my only, with your warm, big, dark gold eyes, you are also . . . immortal? That's why during the alarm I didn't give a single thought to the possibility of your death! I've been out of the city two hours already, the shelling started two hours ago, then the air-raid warning—the air raid covers the whole city, and you, of course, are now standing on the roof, or more precisely—in the solarium of our "teardrop"—whether or not you're on duty, you always substitute for those who are afraid of the bombing, and on the opposite roof, across the street, sit the same boys, they're probably, as always, whistling and whooping at the "Messers" rushing by . . . No, a bomb didn't fall on our house, and you and our boys are alive—how can you die, when there is no death, when we are immortal?! I will come and tell you about this. However, you know this all yourself. Reexperiencing almost my whole life, I didn't remember you. I didn't remember "our" Islands, the first declaration to one another and that early, early morning on the deserted and ancient Tuchkov Embankment,[54] where overturned boats smelled of resin, and seagulls floated over the pink water, pink from the dawn—I didn't remember this until now, because I don't need to think about you as something particular, separate; everything that happens to me, happens to you at precisely the same time . . . So I remembered Lermontov, not yours, tragic, disastrous, rebellious as he lives in your planned work "Lermontov and Mayakovsky"—two miracles, two originals, two poets, so different and yet in contact across the centuries. How directly Mayakovsky spoke about his relationship with Lermontov when he stood, barely keeping his balance, on Ivan the Great's church tower, and an unruly crowed of philistines tormented him to death:

> And so it's by love's sickness I'm a cripple.
> Keep a slop bucket for your own kind.
> I don't interfere with you.
>   What's the point of insults!
> I'm only poetry.
>   I'm only soul.
> But down below:
>   "No!
>   You're our age-old enemy.
> One like that was already caught—
>   a Hussar!"[55]

My dear, I remembered the Lermontov of my childhood, with "underwater wonders"—breasts and kisses, but we have the same one, because for a long time there's been no separate you and I, there is one—*we*, because time doesn't exist and life, we now know, is a single moment, but it contains *all*, and it is infinite.

So the border between life and death, between art and life collapsed. They merged into one—into full, triumphant freedom.

Day of Heights: "Defend the Revolution!"

But the Nevsky Gate was strangely, ominously silent: no whistling of bombs or howling of shells could be heard, but the all clear didn't sound—the artillery and air-raid warning continued. And even the enormous round clouds no longer roared, they just moved slowly, rolling over one another, swirling and swelling, and it seemed they themselves gave off that barely ringing, measured quiet, or rather—silence.

"Why so quiet? Or did I miss the all clear? But then there would be people on the street . . . and there are almost none . . . and the trams are stopped . . . It's very quiet! Oh, it would be better to have the damned shells whistling . . ."

But it was deathly quiet, as if all were hidden, preparing for the last terrible leap that would decide the outcome of the death match.

I walked alone between two rows of brick warehouses, squat, bulky, blind—without windows. There were no other buildings besides these here along Shlisselburg—only warehouses. A brick and rather hostile world . . . I remembered that in the days of the October Revolution revolutionary slogans were painted in crooked capital letters on the pediments of these warehouses: "He who does not work shall not eat!" "He who is not with us is against us!" "The mind cannot bear bondage!" "Defend the Revolution!" And many, many others—on every warehouse slogans were inscribed on the pediment in a half circle.

The revolution screamed like a newborn baby. No, better, the revolution had to speak out, cry out all the essential things that she wanted to establish and make law, everything with which she wanted to make the people happy. She endlessly, at any time of the day sang "The Internationale"; she compelled even the stones to cry out with her slogans and the words of "The Internationale."

And in the days of the Great Fatherland War this happened again! She also compelled the stones to cry out about her path and victories and sorrows. Oh, inscriptions on the ruins of Sevastopol, already liberated, inscriptions, especially frightening in the days of the blockade, on the walls of Leningrad—sisters of the fiery inscriptions of the revolution!

Revolutionary slogans were inscribed everywhere, on all the city's stones, buildings, and fences; they were especially plentiful in the outlying districts: on mill and factory gates, on the works themselves, on the wreckage of police stations, and—with all the menace and naïveté of the newborn revolution—even on these squat brick warehouses. I distinctly remembered these slogans; they were still clearly visible in the years of the NEP and the First Five-Year Plan; I always read them when I went from the Nevsky Gate to the city, to the university, all of eleven years ago. But now they have completely disappeared—only barely visible brushstrokes remain on the brick semicircles. I walked between the rows of warehouses, along the tram's route—after all the trams were stopped—looking from one side to the other, eagerly searching for the ancient inscriptions, but they were all gone, gone . . . And suddenly I detected—on one of the brick pediments, narrow, crooked letters appeared as a barely perceptible shadow. I stopped, stared, and made it out: "Defend the Revolution!" And sobs choked me—happy sobs!

. . . I too often repeat the word "happy" in these pages, but on that day I recalled nothing of my countless sorrows, not for a moment did they take possession of my soul—not my daughters' deaths, nor the unjust accusation of 1937, whose apparition before the war had been invincible . . . I recalled none of this, nothing wounded me, nothing tormented me. No, I walked along the heights, only the loftiness and beauty of our times possessed me, only happiness and the ecstasy of life. And I knew, I knew that it wasn't this way only for me, but for Nikolai, and for papa, and for Dunya, and for my friend Galina, for the workers at Elektrosila, for my new friends at the Radio Committee. Soon Old Nevsky. Soon the warehouses ended. What a pity that they didn't retain all the inscriptions, only the barely visible shadow of one . . . But you know, I remember them all! It was in my time that they were written on these brick buildings, when I was repeating Lermontov's verses, when I heard that Lenin arrived in Petrograd and the Gate's factories and plants rose up for him and went to meet him at the Finland Station . . . Good heavens, wait—yes you know they went to the Finland Station by this same route, past these gloomy warehouses! There probably weren't inscriptions on the warehouses yet. But to meet Lenin they walked here, where I am walking now!

And it was by this same road that, during a blizzard in February 1918, the workers from our Obukhov factory went to Lenin. They had decided to build the world's first workers' commune in the Altai, a beautiful, just, real commune, the likes of which had, before them, only been dreamed of and written about in books—for centuries, for millennia. They called it "Pervorossiisky," which meant "First Russian Society of Agricultural Worker-Communards." They went to Ilich for advice about how best to construct their commune, and above all—with the request that he help them go to the Altai. Yes, yes, they walked between these same warehouses, everything was the same as now, except that then the inscriptions on the pediments were bright white, recently applied to the red bricks. "The mind cannot bear bondage!"—they asserted. "We are not slaves!"—they exclaimed. "Defend the Revolution!"—they ordered. And now—this girl in military uniform and forage cap, and some guy, and I—we are walking on the same path, their path, and the same inscriptions burn on the same walls, and even if they've been erased by time, we remember them, yes, and not only do we remember—we in fact *are defending the revolution*. We are walking their path, step by step, we are their contemporaries, and they are our contemporaries, because we live in the same time—at the time of the revolution, we will not be broken, we will not be separated, we are a single chain, link by link . . .

Chain, chain . . . Wait, where did that word come from? Why did it so suddenly scratch my consciousness? Chain, chain! That's it! "The Flanders Chain of Good Luck" . . . The leaflet that the residents of my building and I myself found this morning . . . So, it really exists, only *not their chain, but ours*. It is going around the world, it will go around it not three times but thirty-three times three, not as a symbol of slavery, constraint, and bondage but as a symbol of indestructible unity, eternal continuity, the indissolubility of our lives and actions,—link by link, step by step, century by century, life by life, generation by generation, people after people, revolution after revolution. *Our* chain will not break because this is the chain of life. I am a link in it, and all of it, from its unknown origins stretching into infinity, is mine!

And as if in answer to this thought, suddenly clear, high-pitched bugles sang out from the loudspeakers along the street: it was the all-clear signal!

And right away, people poured out onto Old Nevsky; the trams jingled, rattled, flooded with bells and scraping, breaking into a run, signaling loudly; the buses all came to life, started talking, began to ring; it seemed even the piercingly golden rays of the autumn sun began to chatter above Old Nevsky, even the glass in the houses, turning blue with the sky, even the asphalt under our feet—everything was filled with frenzied-cheerful ringing and humming, and above everything flew the silver, slightly sad voice of the bugles: they heralded the end of bombing, horror, death; they heralded the return of the usual bustle and of life—what could be better?! This was the most ordinary, everyday *city* noise—how is it that what used to vex us now gives us such joy?

"When victory is declared, we will demand that the all-clear signal plays for a full hour," I thought, jumping into the tram, and it seemed to me that victory was not very far off. How I loved the scraping, ringing tram, the angry conductor, the citizens pushing one another, but happily exhilarated—it was all so sweet, dear, and most of all, mine! But as I'm finishing the story of the "day of heights," the day, so similar to the feeling in Uglich of connection to the world, with the word "mine," I must fulfill the promise given in the first fragment, in the chapter "That's mine!"—to tell about the Valdai shaft-bow.

The Valdai *Duga*[56]

I heard it in Uglich, where we lived with mama while father fought against the Whites in the south. It was in a museum, in the former palace of Tsarevich Dmitry,[57] a dark-red brick palace on the steep, sheer bank of the Volga that was surrounded by a small but very dense garden with ancient, brooding trees and huge, dark lilac bushes, so huge that there were real, small caves inside them. And under the weeping branches of ancient birch trees, between the swirling lilac bushes, wound sandy, bright yellow little paths, and beyond the palace was a real sundial, which was there during the time of Tsarevich Dmitry. He gazed at it and probably already understood what time it showed—after all, he was then fully seven years old. He also looked out from this garden, from the cliff toward that shore of the Volga where there stood an astonishing pine forest: very straight and dense, trunk to trunk, at attention, dark blue, motionless, it stood along the bank in three large, regular, descending steps, somewhat staggered,—it seemed as if three regiments of giant Red Army soldiers in pointed Budenny helmets were standing shoulder to shoulder across from our Uglich, defending it.[58] The forest echelons looked most like Red Army soldiers on early winter evenings, when a very red sun set into the frosty lilac haze behind the forest, and the Budenny tops of the pines glowed and dripped with red.

But you couldn't walk in the palace garden during the winter—large, also somehow ancient, very cozy, but absolutely impenetrable snowdrifts filled it. So we loved to run in the dark little garden in the summer, on hot days, when a pleasantly cool breeze came from the Volga and a fragrant wood dampness wafted from the hollow depths of the lilac bushes. It was very nice here, and it was somehow pleasant to know that we were walking along the same paths that Tsarevich Dmitry walked—just like in the icon: in a long white shirt, with pink palms that he held like wings above his shoulders, and a neat golden halo relentlessly spinning above his head.

We already knew how the tsarevich was killed: on just such a hot spring day he strolled along these same paths, raising his palms, with the spinning

Г. УГЛИЧЪ. - Дворецъ Св. Царевича Димитрія.

A postcard view of the Tsarevich Dmitry Palace in Uglich, c. 1913 (Library of Congress, Winokur-Munblit Collection of the Russian Empire Postcards, https://www.loc.gov/item/2012648284/)

halo above his head, and Danil Bityagovsky jumped out from the thick, luxuriantly flowering lilac bushes with a long, gleaming, sharp knife and murdered the tsarevich—with a knife to the throat.

And we deliberately avoided the lilac bushes—imagining: Bityagovsky will suddenly jump out and throw himself on us! . . . True, we hadn't done anything to him; but what had the tsarevich done?! Why would he kill him—even though he was the tsarevich, which of course was not exactly good, as we learned after the overthrow of our Petrograd tsar, but all the same he was still little, he still didn't understand that it's not good to be the tsarevich; he even wore beads, like a girl—Bityagovsky tricked him with beads to get the tsarevich to come closer to him and slashed his throat.

It was a while, almost a year, before we went to the museum itself, the chamber where the tsarevich lived—mama could never manage it: first getting settled at the school, then always migrating from apartment to apartment, then having to plant potatoes and to go on unpaid Saturdays collecting pinecones for the electric plant and lilies of the valley for the pharmacy.[59] But finally we managed it, and washed, with bows in our braids, we headed to the museum with mama and a couple of her friends from Petrograd. The lean, noble-looking, gray director of the museum met us very courteously and first took us around the museum, explaining what was there, and then led us to the basement, displaying a very interesting lantern that resembled a whole chapel and a large, ugly wooden cart that looked like a coffin on huge wheels. This turned out to be the wagon that carried the coffin with Kutuzov's body to Russia.[60] The director explained why it ended up in the Uglich museum—but it went in one ear and out the other, because my eyes were fixed on a different object behind the coffin-wagon. And our mama, it's true, very politely listening to the whole story about Kutuzov's body, also asked about that same object— what is that, could it be a duga? She probably asked because she and our aunts, getting together in the evenings in the Nevsky, loved to sing songs about the coachmen who in winter raced along the Mother Volga and, to the ringing of bells and chimes, grieved for abandoned or dead brides or who themselves froze to death on the steppe, whispering the name of a beloved wife, praying for her happiness. Many people in the Nevsky sang songs about troikas and coachmen.[61] They were by turns piercingly sad and recklessly cheerful; I knew almost all of them and most of all loved the song about a coachman who froze to death on the distant steppe . . .

> Tell my wife,
> that on the steppe I froze
> and that her love
> I carried out of this world . . .
> And also say—
> don't be sad.
> Let her with another
> remarry . . .[62]

"Ah . . . This is an antique Valdai duga," said the curator of the museum, and his dry, gray face warmed up.

We got closer. Huge, smooth, sloping, it shined faintly, flickering in the fading semidarkness that magnified its authentic fairy-tale beauty— blue, crimson, and green roses on a pale matte gold, it looked like a small, but absolutely real, wooden rainbow. And at the center of the rainbow-duga hung a large tarnished bell, and to its left and right were smaller round bells, and ornamented jingle bells: yes, this was the very duga— from the song!

> And the bell, gift of Valdai
> Rings and weeps beneath the duga . . .[63]

Horses harnessed with a *duga*, a wooden shaft-bow, often decorated and hung with bells, that arches over the horse's neck and joins the vehicle's two shafts, c. 1900–1923. (Library of Congress, Frank and Frances Carpenter Collection, lot 11469, https://www.loc.gov/item/2001705701/)

And the curator, smiling slightly, reached his hand toward it, and two or three times gently rocked it from side to side, shaking it. Oh, how it sang out, began to ring, began to sob, began to laugh, as if alive, and this was all at once: both sharp, piercing sadness and soaring merriment, this crazy silvery ringing, striking the stone vaults and crashing down in them like a sparkling downpour, filling everything—the basement, my heart, life!

I was no longer listening and didn't hear anything the curator said, I only whispered threateningly to Muska: "That's mine," and continued looking at the Valdai duga . . . And when the curator said that now we could go to the chamber, upstairs, my heart sank, and I said despairingly:

"Mister . . . shake *it* one more time . . . please!"

He smiled and shook my—my singing-duga, fairy-tale-duga. I still remember its brief, fiery, residue . . .

> One time, one more time resounding,
> in life, in song, finally in lament

oh, Valdai duga, my love,
my heart, a lifeless bell . . .

. . . But when I was in Uglich in 1953 and went to the museum, to Tsarevich Dmitry's palace, neither Kutuzov's cart nor my Valdai duga were still in the basement. And only the famous Uglich crop-eared bell was in the palace, in exactly the same place, and it is precisely with a short story about this bell that I will end my "day of heights."

The Crop-Eared Bell

It had this name because it was dishonored and stripped of one ear for a crime against tsarist power:[64] At the moment when Tsarevich Dmitry was killed, people struck this very bell, and it rang out a warning. And at its sound, the people of Uglich came running, and saw the child, lying in blood on the sandy path, his throat slit . . . It is not my task, as you know, to investigate whether the tsarevich himself cut his throat in an epileptic fit or whether the Nagoys provoked the people[65]—what mattered to them, to the people, in my opinion, was that in the name of some obscure noble intrigue "they hurt a child," and not simply hurt but killed. But this is an age-old anguish, this is an immutable law for the Russian person, later formulated by Fedor Dostoevsky: "so that the babe should weep no more."[66] And here—they hurt, they killed a small, defenseless child. And the people of Uglich, coming together at the sound of the bell, exacted their own justice on those who murdered the child. They tore the murderers to pieces.

On that day, with the murder of a child guilty of nothing, the Time of Troubles began, ushered in by the tocsin.[67]

"Oh city, you, city, blessed city of Uglich! A bitter cup you drank for the Russian land . . ."—so it is told in the chronicle.

The history that began in Uglich after the lynching of the Bityagovskys constituted perhaps the greatest draft of bitterness in this cup. Boris Godunov dealt ruthlessly with the people of Uglich. Two hundred people were put to death as traitors and murderers. Many others had their tongues cut out for bold speech; sixty families were condemned to exile in Siberia, in Pelym.

The bell that announced the spilling of the child's blood and the beginning of the great people's tragedy did not escape punishment: it was taken down from the bell tower, stripped of the sign of the cross, had one of its ears cut off, its tongue pulled out, and in the public square, before the people, was given 120 lashes. After that, the crop-eared bell (as it was called henceforth) was sentenced to exile—to the same place that the sixty Uglich families were sent, to Siberia. The exiled people of Uglich had to pull it after them to the place of exile.

They walked to Siberia, pulling the bell after them on a special carrier like a sled.

They walked a whole year—summer and winter, spring and fall; taking turns in the harness, they pulled the very heavy bell through swamps, along the high roads and where there were no roads, through forests and over hills. More than once the crop-eared bell fell from the carrier—its edge got jagged, and the whole thing darkened, but it didn't crack. Many of the people from Uglich did not make it to Pelym, they died along the way, not a few—harnessed to the bell. But none of them murmured against the bell: they pulled their herald after them; they dragged their singer and poet with them. Yes, so it was, although, of course, no one from Uglich realized it, and a full two hundred and fifty years had to pass, before Lermontov said the poet:

> Sounded, like the bell in the tower calling the assembly
> On days of the people's triumphs and misfortunes.

. . . At last, the bell arrived in Tobolsk with the first party of exiled rebels. The then-military governor of Tobolsk, Prince Lobanov-Rostovsky, ordered it surrendered to the clerk's hut, where it was recorded as the "first inanimate exile from Uglich."

And the crop-eared bell passed a full three hundred years in exile. More than once, educated Russian people, loving the motherland's history, asked the government to return the bell to its motherland—to Uglich. Tsars—one after the other—stubbornly refused, more than a century of refusals. And only in 1892, when it was *legally* demonstrated that the "first inanimate exile" had fully served the term of punishment, was the bell allowed to return to Uglich.

. . . The bell returned ceremoniously, it sailed along the Volga in a special steamship designed especially for it; along the way its ear and tongue were restored, and it was met ceremoniously—especially by the clergy, the people, the intelligentsia. And in Uglich, where the bell arrived late in the evening, a kind of low belfry was constructed for it, not far from the palace, and there it was hung for the night; all night an honor guard stood watch around the bell-rebel. In the morning, before a huge gathering of people, there was a solemn prayer, and then instead of a religious procession, all

The "exiled bell" displayed in the Uglich museum, c. 1910. (Library of Congress, Prokudin-Gorskii collection, lot 10340)

the people of Uglich passed under the bell, and each one pulled the rope tied to the bell's tongue, and the tongue beat ceaselessly against its chipped edge, and the bell boomed and sang, just as it did 301 years before, only for many hours.

However, the crop-eared bell was not raised: even the clergy understood that it was not a religious but a rebellious people's relic that been returned and solemnly welcomed. The clergy and the government were forced to return the bell to its motherland and receive it honorably, but this bell couldn't call the people to church services, it couldn't be trusted with that! Thus the bell was hung in the Dmitry museum-chamber but also in such a way that it was possible to pass under it. And so I remember how, when we lived with mama in Uglich, and I still believed in God, we went every year on 15 May — on Tsarevich Dmitry day — to Mass in the Church of Dmitry-on-the-Blood, and then, like all the people of Uglich, went through the museum, under the bell, and struck it, and its dense, groaning, threatening, somehow *dark* sound resounded right overhead, coming from somewhere far away, from the fathomless past and at the same time as if from your own chest. And if the Valdai duga spoke to and rang in my heart with snowy, sparkling, frenzied sorrow and joy, then the bell rumbled through my soul like a gloomy rapture, almost fatal, but desired.

. . . Arriving in the city of childhood, I didn't find there the Valdai duga and didn't hear its silver sobs . . . And the little garden around the museum was sort of plucked, and in the museum itself, much was missing. A young, and as they say, "not hardly educated" museum director, with a round indifferent face, capable of explaining almost nothing, led me indifferently around the museum, and I had only one wish: that he would be quiet so as not to interfere with my heeding the surging sounds, smells, and memories of my sweet and severe childhood. And when we entered the Dmitry chamber and I saw the bell in the same place, I heard its boom within me . . . But I wanted to test myself: How would I hear it after so many years and such a life, after the Great Fatherland War, after the Leningrad blockade? I knew that the custom of passing under the bell hadn't existed for a long time and, probably, was simply forgotten . . . And suddenly a strange, irresistible desire overcame me. I was alone in the chamber with the museum director.

"May I strike the bell?" I asked him.

He glanced at me as at a lunatic—he didn't know about the old custom, probably didn't know the history of the bell.

"Please," he said anxiously.

And I stood under the bell, and I vigorously pulled the rope. And it began to sing and boom over my head as it did *then*, but the sound for me was nevertheless now full of a new power and new meaning: this was a voice warning all those who might think again of harming a child with war, famine, or loss of parents that retribution was on guard, that the bell-poet would be the first to summon it.

Touching the chipped edge of the deeply and threateningly singing bell, I said to myself, not as in childhood but powerfully and deliberately, "That's mine!"

That's how I walked from the Nevsky Gate at the beginning of the dry, golden October of 1941, immeasurably fearless and joyful, intoxicated with the consciousness of my immortality and the immortality of everything that surrounded me or that had surrounded me earlier, and even of that which was before my memory.

But neither I nor any, any of us knew that we Leningraders would walk that same ecstatic, lofty, illuminated path in a different way, and very soon . . .

The Path to My Father's House

Then, only four months later, I traveled the same path, but in reverse: I went from the city to the Nevsky Gate. I walked to my father's in the early days of February 1942.

> I walked to my father's, and did not wipe away the tears:
> It was hard to raise my hands.
> An icy crust hardened
> on my swollen face.
> It was difficult to walk between the snowdrifts:
> You stumble, you barely drag yourself along.
> You meet a coffin, you can't get past it.
> You clench your teeth—and step over it.
> My friend, I, like you, have met
> hundreds of them, crawling over the snow.
> I, like you, have stepped over coffins . . .
> May the memory of such steps live forever.
> May the memory live forever in silent glory,
> The easy luminous journey . . .
>
> Those who then could step over
> a coffin—have a right to life . . .

These verses are among those that are written or, more accurately, inscribed in diaries, on the margins of the Essential Book. But I rarely write them down; I don't know why. They are written down somewhere, not on paper, but perhaps on the heart? That's pompous . . . Let's say: they are memorized. From time to time you murmur them to yourself, only for yourself. Sometimes for those closest to you—out of the blue.

I don't write down most of these—diary—verses. And this poem, like most of them, had been forgotten and then came to mind, unexpectedly and distinctly. Something has been added, something dropped, not voluntarily—and then finally written down. As in all of these verses, here everything is true, except one line: I didn't cry that day, when I went to my father's. I cried once during the entire blockade: when I left the hospital where Nikolai lay dying . . .

Setting off for the Nevsky Gate, I equipped myself thoroughly. Comrades at the Radio Committee, where I had already been living for some time in a sort of barracks situation, equipped me as best they could. They filled a segmented bottle that appeared from somewhere or other (the kind of bottle in which children's clinics dispense formula) with weak, slightly sweet tea. Someone gave me two cigarettes. I took my bread ration. At that time, it was a full 250 grams of bread.[68] I decided to eat it little by little and under no circumstances to eat it all at once, even though all I could think about was that in my gas mask there was a whole 250 grams of bread with the makeweight pieces . . .

Yes, at my side hung a gas mask, the same gas mask that in October still seemed to our Avdotya the thing that would save us from all the horrors of the war. "You, Lyaleshka, at the first hint of trouble, put on your gas mask," she admonished me . . . In those days it still seemed that paper crosses on the glass might save us. In the summer of 1941—was it really only seven months ago?—how assiduously we had glued these crosses on the windows! A few eccentrics overdid it: They didn't just put up a barrier on the window; they cut complicated fretwork and whole scenes out of paper. One of the windows of an apartment on the Fontanka was still decorated with palm trees, and under the palms sat paper monkeys. Perhaps the inhabitants of this apartment wanted to recover somehow, to laugh off the war, and thought this would help?

Nothing helped! Nothing kept death out of our homes: not paper crosses, not fanciful fretwork and pictures on the glass, not carefully calibrated gas masks, which at the sound of the air-raid signal we quickly opened and set to the "ready" position. We didn't need to wear them once; death didn't blow in our faces, suffocating us with gases. It simply entered each of us as extreme bodily weakness, as gnawing hunger, as a constant icy chill . . .

Instead of gas masks, people wore on their faces wool masks and half-masks of all colors—either knitted or a wool rag they'd found. Red, black, green, blue masks with narrow slits for the eyes came toward me.

But the rubber mask had long ago been thrown out of the gas mask bag. The bag most often held the "mini starvation kit": one or two half-liter jars, a spoon, food, if the person had some.

When I began my journey, I had in my gas mask an empty jar, a bottle with tea, and bread, bread—250 grams of bread!

I knew that it would be a long trip. I had to reach the Lenin factory, then go a long ways down Shlisselburg Prospect. I had to cross the Neva, and climb up the steep right bank. This was roughly fifteen to seventeen kilometers from the Radio Committee. I very gravely collected myself for the journey and overall I was filled with some kind of strange zeal, and a surprising calm. Well, not exactly calm, more like deathly indifference, or better, a novel quietness, a strange meekness. I was not sure that I would make it to my father's, and I decided not to take such a long view. I decided: During the trip, I would set myself micro-goals: now I'm at this lamppost. I must get to the next. Then to the next. Then to the Moscow Station. And then, we shall see! I must put one foot in front of the other, not hurrying, there is no hurry, trying to stay on the path and not stumble in the snow.

And so I went. First down Nevsky Prospect, from one lamppost to the next. From one to the next . . .

Anton Ivanovich Is Angry

In Leningrad before the war a musical comedy of that name was scheduled to open, and thus on almost every lamppost there was a heavy plywood sign on which was written in large, garish letters: *Anton Ivanovich Is Angry.* Nothing more. We didn't manage to see the film comedy, and we didn't manage in the first days of the war to take down these posters. So there they remained, under extinguished street lamps, until the end of the blockade.

And so, walking along Nevsky Prospect, whenever you raised your eyes, there were the posters, which, because of the way the war, the assault, the blockade, and the city's disaster had unfolded, had turned into a kind of warning, a reminder, a loud reproach: "So, Anton Ivanovich is angry!" And the idea unwittingly arose of a real, living person, very kindhearted, who, not understanding everything and fiercely desiring people to be happy and good, with anguish was becoming angry at people for all the needless, absurd, and awful suffering to which, for some reason or other, they were subject.

After artillery attacks, the citizens' maimed corpses were dragged under the lampposts. The starving grasped the lampposts, trying to keep their balance, and slowly sank to the pedestals, so as not to stand up any longer. Anton Ivanovich was angry. Oh, how he fumed, sadly fumed about all this! And so one sometimes felt ashamed before Anton Ivanovich—*the person.* One wanted to say for oneself and on behalf of all the people of the earth: "Anton Ivanovich, dear, kind, Anton Ivanovich, don't be angry at us! We are not to blame. We are still good people. We'll come to our senses somehow. We'll fix this ugliness. We will live humanely."

But on that day I did not address Anton Ivanovich with this silent tirade or entreaty. He was beyond my mental power. Even before him I could not explain myself. And in any case I wasn't thinking about him. I wasn't able to think about anything, concentrating on carefully putting one foot in front of the other, advancing from lamppost to lamppost.

But Anton Ivanovich was angry, and became sadder and sadder . . .

And so I reached the Moscow Station. I glanced at my watch: stopped.

I reached Old Nevsky. There again from lamppost to lamppost. To the left from the Moscow Station all the way to the Alexander Nevsky Monastery a chain of trolleybuses, iced-over, snow-covered, dead—like dead people. One after the other, rows, dozens. Also stopped. And on the tracks near the monastery, rows of trams, with the glass broken out, with snowdrifts on the seats. Also stopped. They would probably stand there forever. It was impossible to imagine that they would ever move, clanging and swishing along the asphalt. Did we really once travel on these? Strange! I walked past the dead trams and trolleybuses in some other century, in another life. Whether I was living one hundred years before the present or one hundred years after, I had no idea. It was all the same to me.

The path snaked down the middle of the street. But it was already quite wide here. I heard behind me the scrape of runners. I stopped and looked over my shoulder: a woman pulling a man on a sled. He was tethered to the sled with a towel, but he sat and was clearly still alive. I dully thought: "Where is she taking him?" Because I had come to the beginning of the warehouses, the scene, some four months before, of the last, exultant, high-altitude section of my journey on "the day of heights." I didn't recall it for a moment. Instead, looking at the warehouses, I thought: "This is a granary. A warehouse for grain. Yes, well, at some time there was grain in all these warehouses—rye—and even between the warehouses, in the sheds, there were piles of rye grain. I remember that. When I drove down Nevsky I saw piles of rye."

At the thought of rye, my mouth filled with cold saliva. I recalled how we ground the ripe rye ears in our hands in the summers, when we lived in Zarucheve, where I learned about daytime stars. At that moment I could smell the field of rye. If there had suddenly been a single ear of rye to grind, to put in my mouth and grind for a long time with my teeth—oh, how living on soup had made us long for "solid food"!

"Now I'll get out my bread and eat it all," I thought, and everything went black before my eyes. I stopped, jerked open the gas mask bag, but then I suddenly managed to suppress the living thought that had flared up so quickly, the only one I had on the whole journey. I said to myself quietly, but aloud:

"No, at the Lenin factory. I'll sit down. Have a taste of tea. Eat a bit of bread."

And once again, after a moment of disturbance, the unhealthy, submissive quiet was restored. I began to move forward and I still remember that the whole journey I was amazingly meek, calm, and somehow very ready to die. Not even to die, but to melt into the snow, into those enormous snowdrifts, into the frosted red-brick warehouses, into the low slate sky.

This meekness, as we understood later, was really the beginning of death. In this condition a person started to talk always in diminutives: "a tiny bit of bread," "a little crust," "a drop of water," and to become boundlessly polite and quiet.

True, there were those who became brutal. Somehow I will return to them later . . .

Cigarette Break

My path down Nevsky intersected with another. And it happened that as I reached this small crossroads, I encountered a woman, wrapped in a mountain of shawls, dragging a sled with a coffin, or more properly speaking, not a coffin but something like a bureau drawer. Maybe it really was a bureau drawer covered with a piece of plywood. She was dragging it, her whole body leaning forward, about to topple over. I stopped in order to let the coffin pass, and she stopped to let me pass, straightening up and sighing deeply. I took a step, and at the same time she yanked the sled. I stopped again. And she couldn't budge the sled: it had probably run against a pothole or a bump in the path, and it stopped right near my feet. From under her shawls, she peered at me with abhorrence and shouted, barely audibly:

"Go ahead, then."

And I stepped over the coffin, but as I had to take a very long step, I almost fell backward and involuntarily sat down on the drawer. She sighed and sat down beside me.

"From the city?" she asked.

"Yes."

"A long ways?"

"A long ways. About three hours."

"Well, what's going on there? People dying?"

"Yes."

"Bombs?"

"Not now. Artillery."

"Same with us. Dying and artillery."

I opened the gas mask and took out my treasure: a "sprig," a thin cigarette. I've already mentioned that I had two: I was bringing one to papa, and one I decided to smoke on the way, near the Lenin factory. But I had no more patience, and I lit up.

The woman looked at me with frantic greed. In the deep caves on her face, where her eyes were, something seemed to flash.

"Leave some?" she said, or more like whistled, and gulped down some air.

I nodded. While I smoked, she didn't take her eyes off the "sprig" and, when she saw that it had been smoked halfway down, she held out her hand. There was enough for her to take two drags.

Then we stood up. We both took up the rope attached to the sled and dragged the coffin across the bump on which it had gotten stuck. She silently nodded at me, and I at her. And once again, from lamppost to lamppost, I set off for father's. The meeting with the women dragging the drawer-coffin, the cigarette break with her, didn't stir anything in me then. I only thought: "Now I won't sit down again until I reach the Lenin factory. And at the factory, I'll eat a little piece of bread."

Little Steps in the Ice

I walked on steadily and unthinkingly, and along the way met more and more coffins and corpses, carried on sleds, wrapped in sheets or quilts, and corpses lying in the snow, their feet toward the path. Almost all of them were barefoot—well, that's as it should be. The shoes were needed by those still alive who walked along the paths of the dead, frozen, and steadfast city.

At the Lenin factory, where, a long, long time ago, in my childhood and youth, the "city" began—because the horse-drawn tram went as far as the factory and the streetcar left from the factory—at the Lenin factory, the former Semyannikov factory, I sat down on a concrete bench, alongside a concrete control tower (constructed, of course, in the style of Le Corbusier[69]), and carefully ate "a tiny bit of bread" and set off further along Shlisselburg Prospect. Our school did not trigger any memories. I didn't look to the right, on Palevsky, where five months before, my grandmother, blessing the four corners of the earth and praying for the salvation of Moscow, unhurriedly and ceremoniously died under the howls and thunder of shells. I didn't glance at the intersection, where under biblical silver clouds I stood with father and hurrying along, talked about Nikolai, about his work "Lermontov and Mayakovsky," about poetry, about the future . . .

I'm writing this *now*, and *now* I am remembering that icy journey, but then I absolutely did not register what was there—didn't glance in the direction of our house, did not think of who had lived there. I repeat, I had almost no feeling then, no human reactions. More accurately, they were all constricted, elemental reactions.

I stopped only when I reached the Neva, the crossing to papa's factory, because it was already getting dark and the first, soft, almost lilac shadows settled over the earth. The snow-covered Neva was a smoky lavender-rose, and it seemed a vast, savage, snowy desert. Father's seemed far away, although I could see his factory across the Neva, and I knew that to the left of the main buildings stood his old log clinic.

I still had a very small piece of bread, 100 grams, in the gas mask bag. I thought that father would probably give me a mug of hot water, and we would share this little piece and eat it. That we would eat it as soon as I arrived. This thought gave me strength, and I set off across the Neva.

"Soon, now; soon now, but my God, how far away!"

The very narrow path across the Neva was solidly packed down, but by some unsteady, extremely light steps: it was jagged and faltering. The right bank towered above, a forbidding ice mountain, its summit lost in the rose-gray shadows. At the base of the mountain were women wrapped in shawls, hardly resembling people, drawing water from a hole in the ice.

"I won't be able to climb that hill," I dully thought, feeling that my whole awful journey had been in vain.

All the same, I approached the hill, and suddenly saw that there were steps cut out of the ice.

A woman, unbelievably resembling the one who was pulling the coffin, with the same shawls, with the same brown parchment face, approached me. In her right hand she carried a can with a liter or two of water, not large, but nonetheless she leaned over to the right.

"Shall we crawl up, friend?" she asked.

"Let's crawl!"

And on all fours, side by side, holding one another tightly, supporting one another with our shoulders, we crept up, clinging to the high notches in the ice while raising our legs from step to step with difficulty, stopping every two or three paces.

"The doctor carved out the steps," said the woman, gasping, when we stopped for the fourth time. "God bless him . . . it's easier . . . to fetch water . . ."

But I didn't understand that she was talking about my papa. It was harder for her than for me, because I held on to the higher steps with two hands, and she with one—with her other hand she moved the can of water from one step to the next. On the second half of the trip, we took turns moving the can, first me, then her, and so we got to the top and reached the factory gate.

The factory courtyard, the log clinic, the front garden, fenced with carved balusters, where papa had endeavored for years to grow roses—I recognized nothing, absolutely nothing. I stood for a long time in front of the clinic's little porch, trying to fathom: where had I gotten to? Maybe I had ended up at the neighboring Vargunin factory, or the wrong place entirely? What was this strange wooden hut and the half-disassembled little fence? I had never in my life seen it . . . but I'd known it since childhood, and it was almost identical. On a clear-rose day, ecstatically wintry, sparkling, I arrived there many years ago in order to look at my first published verses, commemorating Lenin's death, that appeared in the wall newspaper of papa's factory.

I didn't recall that then.

Looking around, I convinced myself that this was papa's hospital, and noticed with indifference that everything inanimate—the buildings, the fence, the snowbanks—can also die. Everything here was dead. Or more accurately, it was as if everything had crossed over to the "other world," where everything is, of course, different: the same, but without a soul. In the silent, uninhabited, frosty forest, even in the snowy, empty steppe there is life and there is soul, but not there. Everything was there, and it seemed that nothing was alive.

The Secret of the Earth

In the small entryway of the clinic, dimly lit from the next room, a woman lay on a wooden bench with a high back—the sort of bench one finds in a railway station. She wore a quilted jacket and was carefully wrapped up in a shawl. She lay on her side, resting her folded palms under her right cheek. The way passengers waiting for long-distance trains sleep at the station. But she wasn't sleeping. She was dead. I saw that right away.

"Papa probably has a lot of these," I thought, walking into the next room. There, behind a wooden screen of rounded columns, sat my papa at a table. A low, wide tower of a candle ("oh, he has such candles!") lit his face from below. He was very swollen and even in the candlelight it was evident that his face had a greenish-blue tinge . . . But the hair on his temples and at the nape of his neck, light blond hair with a trace of gray, was still full and curly. And his eyes, big, bulging, and blue, seemed in the flickering candle especially big and blue.

I stood silently before the screen, in front of papa. He lifted up his swollen face, looked me over intently, and politely asked:

"Who are you looking for, citizen?"

And for some reason I answered in a wooden voice that only I could hear:

"I'm looking for Dr. Berggolts."

"I'm he. What's the problem?"

I looked at him and was silent. Something overcame me, not sobbing, not fear, something unfamiliar—something that even now I can't define—but also something deathly, callous. He warmheartedly repeated:

"What's wrong?"

"Papa," I said, "don't you see, it's me, Lyalya!"

He was silent for what seemed to me a long time, but was probably just a few seconds. He understood why I had come to him. He knew that Nikolai was in the hospital. And papa came out from behind the screen, stood in front of me and, bowing his head, silently kissed my hand. Then, raising up my head in his hand, with a firm and as it were gentle glance looked me in the eye and quietly said, "Well, let's have a glass of hot water, daughter. Maybe rustle up something to eat!" And he added, smiling slightly, "After all, the cabbage soup is salted . . ."[70]

I understood his quotation and sensed the grief with which he uttered it. He had loved Nikolai very much. But we said not one more word about him and his death.

We went into the clinic's small, poorly lit kitchen. Papa brought the candle with him and immediately put it out. It was valuable state property, and papa only used it when seeing patients.

Two women in white smocks over padded jackets—one short with black eyes, the other very tall with a face sharply accentuated by malnutrition—clasped their hands when they saw me.

"Lyalechka," the short, black-eyed one practically sang, "how . . . how you've grown!"

"It's Matresha," said papa. "You didn't recognize her? Matresha, my best nurse. And this is Alexandra Ivanovna. You didn't recognize her either?"

"Papa, it has been five years since the last time I was here."

"It's possible," he remarked and gently clapped his hands. "Well, ladies, what riches are there? A little hot water for me and my daughter!"

Matresha bustled about near the small stove, frying something in a pan. A disgusting smell pervaded the tiny little kitchen. I guessed that it was some kind of machine oil. It smelled awful—but how warm it was here!

I took off my shawl and coat, my knitted hat, and the head scarf under the hat. I sat in my ski suit, bareheaded.

"How warm it is here, papa!"

Matresha chimed in:

"Warm! We're slowly taking apart the fence. The doctor regrets it, but what can you do? You need to stay warm, right?"

"Right."

"Lyalechka!" she exclaimed. "Maybe you'd like to wash yourself? You can undress to the waist. And you can wash your feet. I'll bring water."

But I remembered the icy, nearly vertical staircase that I had just scrambled up, and I waved my hands.

"No, no, no, I'm not dirty. At the Radio Committee we look after ourselves. There are no lice in our room. In the mornings, we carry up water from the basement, from the old boiler room, some kind of strange, alkaline water drips from a broken pipe and is almost warm. No, we look after ourselves. We even require that the women wear a little lipstick. And check in the mirror to make sure there's no soot in our nostrils, the corners of our eyes, or our ears. Well, if the woman of the house doesn't look in a mirror—that means the mirrors are covered, it means a death in the house. So we require the women to look in the mirror, to look after themselves."

Some kind of unhealthy talkativeness came over me. I had been quiet for a long time in the past few days, and here the heat from the stove, the people surrounding me made me drunk. I suddenly became sleepy, swaying, and at the same time I wanted to talk, to talk about anything.

I pulled out the remaining "sprig" cigarette. Father was thrilled.

"There you go!" he said, reverentially taking the "sprig" in his big, clever surgeon's hands. "You know how to live!"

Something stinking and strange was brought to the table in a frying pan. We divided my sliver of bread among all four of us with pharmaceutical exactness and poured the hot water into mugs—also in exactly equal portions. Sitting at the small table it was so tight that we squeezed up against one another as in a jam-packed railroad car . . . The small flame of the oil lamp flickered from side to side. Our shadows, monstrous and terrible, swayed on the walls of the room, and this added to the sense that we were going somewhere—very far away—on a long-distance train. And the woman in the entryway was just waiting for her train . . .

The door scraped, and in the gap appeared a brown-parchment face, it wasn't clear whether male or female, all bundled up, in a gigantic fur hat pulled over a woman's scarf.

Glowing dark yellow eyes peeped out from under the hat.

"Doctor, we are here . . ."

"Don't let in the cold!" shouted father. "Come all the way in."

A person squeezed through the door (it turned out to be a man); he handed father something wrapped in paper.

Papa flared his nostrils and furrowed his brow.

"Well, well, don't play the fool! Again?"

"Doctor," the person drawled in a trembling voice, "don't offend me!"

Snorting angrily, father took the small parcel.

"Well, okay, thank you, but this is the last time! . . . How's by you? Everything alright?"

"For now," wheezed the person. "Today, thank the lord, it's quiet; yesterday, tormented by incendiaries."

"I'll look in on you in an hour," said father. "Go on. And don't stick your neck out, take it easy. If there's anything, come for me immediately!"

Backing up, the person opened the door a crack and squeezed through, without a smile, but with a friendly nod to us.

"Fire department," said papa, and, raising his index finger, sternly looked at me, as if waiting for an objection. "Heroes! Lions! People! On their last legs, but they haven't allowed any fires to spread. They love our place, the Thälmann factory."

"What did he bring you? Is it edible?"

"A delicacy! Near the Vena factory—a brewery, you remember?— we're now undertaking a massive excavation, digging up the brewery mash from years past. They're excavating with Egyptian labor, they warm it up and bake flat cakes. This 'delicacy' causes monstrous stomatitis.[71] So many people with stomatitis come to the clinic each day! Well, how can you convince people to not gobble up the stuff? Matresha, heat us up a flat cake!"

The flat cake seemed very tasty to me.

"And by us, at Kuznechny they sell Badaev earth," I said. "When the Badaev warehouses burned, huge amounts of melted sugar seeped into the ground. The first meter is one hundred rubles a glass, the second, fifty. You dissolve it with water, filter, and drink . . ."

When we'd finished eating, Alexandra Ivanovna went off somewhere, but Matresha again proposed that I wash myself, and I again refused, remembering the Neva and the staircase, and remembering it, not out of necessity, but driven by something spiritual and half-forgotten, I said:

"Father, you really don't take care of yourself . . ."

"How's that?" he asked, surprised.

"Well . . . you're cutting steps in the ice . . ."

He looked at me almost with compassion.

"You fool, daughter of mine and celebrated poetess of the city of Lenin," he said mildly. "For pronouncing it all in vain, without faith . . ."

We were silent for a while, and as if continuing the conversation without a break, he quietly and pensively began to speak:

". . . I was told that here at the Nevsky, in one plant, perhaps the Alexandrov, there was an old man in the foundry, a molder. Well, he was one of those old wizards, who don't know their letters, but know their work so well that even foreign engineers throw up their hands. At the Obukhov, for example, there was at one time such a foundry worker . . . They're casting, say, gun barrels—well, you have to process it further: drilling there and all that—I don't understand it. On the whole, it takes a lot of work. And suddenly, something defective is cast, with these, what are they, well, air pockets? Then they call this old man: 'Gramps, listen, is there an air pocket in the barrel or not?' He knocks with a little hammer, ear pressed to the metal and says: 'There are no air pockets, it can be finished.' Or the reverse. And what do you think—he's never wrong! They used a number of current scientific methods to test him, and they verified everything the old man said. Well, that's exactly how our molder was. He knew the special secret of the earth. Its special composition, such that nothing defective was ever cast—as the fault of the molders, of course. And he never, not once had a reject. They ask him: 'Gramps, how come you never have a reject?' And he only chuckles, 'I know the magic word.' And he is silent.

"Well, last November the factory of course came to a stop. The people dispersed, only security, like here. But the old man feels he's dying: he refuses to be evacuated. And then he says to his old wife, 'I'm an old skinflint, they say, and a miser, a great sinner, they say, though I don't even believe in God. Until now, I haven't told my secret of the earth to anyone. But now—there's no one. Except you. Yes you, wife, though you're no longer young and have no connection to the work of the foundry. Well, it can't be helped—last resort. I will not die until you have mastered my secret. Let's go.' Her: 'Where?' 'To the factory, the foundry.' She took him by the hand and led him to the foundry—and he began to teach her his secret of the earth. The composition, the proportions . . . Imagine—a couple of starving, half-dying old people alone in the bitter cold foundry . . . But every single day, both, exhausted, trudged to the foundry—and worked, digging in the cold earth. Moreover, the old man made the old woman eat half his evening soup, saying, 'I will die, but you must survive, so that when the factory is up and running, the secret of the earth will be disclosed to all the molders.' And he taught her! And when she had made this composition with him a few times, reproduced his secret, the old man lays down and says: 'Thank the lord, I can leave this world with a clear conscience.' And the next day he died. Eternal is his memory—I will find out his name. And they say the old woman is alive, even, they say, evacuated and being cared for: well, such a secret—that's important . . ."

He paused and said more pensively, really talking only to himself:

"And perhaps, when the plant is up and running, the old man's secret won't be needed. They'll have invented something more accurate, scientific. No matter. Not in this case . . ." He paused, shrugged. "And maybe they won't invent anything. Above human love—of different kinds . . . for one's native soil, for a person, for a woman, or of a woman for a man—nothing higher than this can be invented, Lyalka . . . No, they won't invent anything . . . 'This is a great mystery':[72] the secret of the earth . . ."

He probably wanted to have a talk, to philosophize, even, with a person close to him, and he talked a lot that evening, and, you know, we spoke very little at that time—instinctively saving our strength.

Papa told how he's organizing the hospital at his factory.

"Well I go to the Nevsky Gate with our factory authorities, and bring onto the hospital staff our male and female weavers. Of course I know them all—praise God, twenty years at the factory . . . At my place they won't die! Well, damn, the factory has to start up some day! People will need cloth, during the war threads get frayed, right?"

"Certainly," I said.

For some reason, thinking about cloth made me sick, I even felt nauseous when I imagined it—gray, tough, and for some reason it had still to be chewed . . .

I was quite drunk from the stinking food, from the boiling water, from the heat, slumped to one side, not quite falling asleep, not quite dying. Black-eyed Matresha was the first to notice my condition.

"Doctor," she said, "it's time for your daughter to sleep."

And in a tone of command added:

"Take off your boots, I'll help you wash your feet. I melted some of that snow, warmed it up."

"I can't get them off, Matresha."

"Come, have a drink," said my father, and gave me something bitter.

And Matresha, adroitly, albeit with difficulty, pulled the boots off my swollen feet and plunged them into a bucket of warm water. Oh, what bliss, clear infantile bliss! Warm water and someone's tender, motherly, powerful hands, quickly sliding along my aching feet—that nurse Matresha, kneeling, rubbing soap on my feet, and somehow I was not ashamed, that I, a grown person, was having my feet washed, and she was glancing up at me with her sweet, round eyes, talking in a little sing-song voice, as though telling a fairy tale, and I listened to her as if through a dream:

"... And she came from afar, from the city, what's more through snow and through ice ... Clever one, to daddy she came, thought it through correctly ... And she looks so much like daddy, so similar, so similar, the spitting image ..."

I started, as if startled awake, and I looked straight into Matreshka's eyes: the nurse looked at me with such love, that it became clear to me: this woman also loves my father ...

Princess Barbara

"Well, now I'll put you to bed," said papa, and he led me though his small log clinic to some cubby. I lay down on the bed, and he sat alongside on a low stool and even lit that turret candle—it was brighter than the wick lamp, and seemed warmer.

"Father, why do you burn the official light?" I murmured with a nod to the candle.

"It's nothing, I'll be a moment. Go to sleep now, and I'll stop by the hospital to see my firefighters and dystrophics[73] ... I want all the same to make our hospital a showcase ... What do you think, little girl, is it?"

"Of course. You have a good staff."

"Ah, good!" father selflessly, almost ecstatically sang out, and embarrassed, added, "They don't steal!"

He so loved people—and not humanity in general, which is easy, but precisely ordinary people, sinners—that he felt too shy to speak of his love for them, as if it were the most intimate thing. Because of this, he sometimes—out of jealous love—cursed people, got angry at them, like Anton Ivanovich, or deliberately spoke rudely of them, like now. He didn't understand that people saw right through this passionate and pure-hearted sage, always a big kid ... He considered himself ... a cynic!

"No, truly, they're good women," he corrected himself. "People! After all, Matresha here, she washes everyone we take in, like you just now ... No, working with them is possible ... but ... but ... oh, little girl! Would that I had Princess Barbara here!"

. . . I've already said that I have very early memories, from even before the first imperialist war. I remember the day when papa—incredibly handsome in his uniform with shining buttons, an enormous sword at his side, and his magnificent golden mane—went off to war. I remember how violently our maples and poplars rustled under the windows on that sunny and windy day, how Grandma Olga cried out, and the aunts wept, and Dunya wailed, and mama, pale and also very beautiful, stood silent alongside papa. Or can it be that I don't remember this, but only imagined it all later? No, I remember, I remember, because when the picture of that farewell appears before me, with my handsome papa, almost unfamiliar in his new beauty, there arises in me that confused feeling of alarm, fear, trouble, because the lush summer foliage, loudly, gleefully, triumphantly murmuring, rustling, mixes with the women's hoarse cries. And mama stays silent, and father is so splendid . . .

. . . He began to work as a military surgeon on a frontline hospital train, the very hospital train that, also in the first days of the war, received sister of mercy Princess Barbara Nikolaevna B–va. She wore the same scarf with the red cross as our aunt Varya, but, as mama told us later, she came from a very noble and ancient family, she was a real Russian princess. And here it needs to be said that in childhood for me and Muska, among all the fairy-tale heroes there was none as wonderful and beloved as the Russian princess. Of course, we still very much loved Little Sister Fox and the Gray Wolf, but—of animals and of people the dearest of all to us was the Snow Maiden and the most beautiful and important of all—the Russian princess, the Swan Princess. Well perhaps you could compare her to some princess from Grimm or Hans Christian Anderson—or even the sad little mermaid? No, the best of all was our Russian Swan Princess.

> In her braids a crescent beams,
> On her brow, a bright star gleams.
> She herself is sweet of face.
> Full of majesty and grace.[74]

That was just how we imagined Princess Barbara.

We never saw her in life, never even saw a photograph. We knew about her from mother's fugitive stories, from accidently overhead conversations about the princess between family and friends.

Princess Barbara worked the whole time together with father on the fronts of the imperialist war, and after the October Revolution, when father immediately moved to the Red Army, Princess Barbara went with him

ПЕТРОГРАДЪ
ВО ВРЕМЯ
ВОЙНЫ.

*Дамы, работающія, какъ
сестры милосердія.*

Ал. Пав. Гартвигъ, рожд. Кар-
цова. Вдова бывш. русскаго по-
сланника въ Бѣлградѣ.

Княгиня Тат. Фед. Шаховская, уѣхавшая
въ санитарномъ поѣздѣ на войну.

Е. Н. Тимашева, рожд. Евреи-
нова. Работаетъ въ лазаретѣ
княгини З. И. Юсуповой.

А. В. Кожевинасъ, рожд. Ореусъ,
учред. лазарета на Каменноостр. пр.,
№ 22. Помощн. предсѣд. благотв.
комитета Греческой колоніи въ Петроградѣ.

Барон. Зоя. Ром. Мейен-
дорфъ, рожд. Вишау.

Фрейлина И. И. В. Государынь Импе-
ратрицъ Ольга Ник. Хвостова, сестра
милосердія Юсуповскаго лазарета въ
Петроградѣ.

14

During World War I, many aristocratic "ladies," like Princess Barbara, worked as "sisters of mercy."
(New York Public Library, Slavic and East European Collections, photo 53043, http://digitalcollections
.nypl.org/items/ff352850-e8fe-0131-12d4-58d385a7bbd0)

and through the whole civil war worked as a senior surgical nurse on the hospital train "Red Eagles," which my father commanded. Hospital train "Red Eagles" fought in the south against Wrangel, Kaledin, and other Whites.[75] Twice the train miraculously escaped White Guard encirclement; many times it came under fire; it participated in short but fierce battles and skirmishes—and not for a minute did Princess Barbara leave father; she was never scared of anything, never took a leave.

Four times papa felt the death grip of fever—typhus, typhoid, relapsing, paratyphoid—four times Princess Barbara pulled him back from death.

We lived in those years in the ancient town of Uglich, and we learned about this from mama: on four occasions a long time passed without any sort of news from father, and then suddenly a very short letter arrived. Mama cried long and bitterly over it, and then led us to the Church of Dmitry-on-the-Blood, made us kneel before the scary, dark icons, and in a strange, tinny voice that wasn't mama's said:

"Children pray for Princess Barbara. She again saved the life of your father."

For a long time, for three years, there had been neither tsars, nor princes, nor nobles in Russia, all were simply people, citizens and comrades, and the tsars, princes, and princesses remained only in fairy tales, but mama still spoke of red nurse Varvara Nikolaevna as "Princess Barbara."

Perhaps by so referring to the woman, who by the will of destiny took her place in the life and heart of the man she loved, she found some small measure of relief for her jealousy—the balm of vanity? After all, none other than a well-born princess saved the life of her husband, the father of her children.

Then father came to Uglich and brought us to Petrograd, to grandfather and the grannies, to the Nevsky Gate, and our new Petrograd life; Petrograd school began. I never ever saw Princess Barbara, and the child's imagined picture remained deep, deep in my soul, like the barely visible crescent moon at sunrise.

. . . And that was the first time father spoke to me about Princess Barbara, on the day when I, widowed, came to him from the city.

"And where is she now, papa?" I asked.

"I don't know," he answered after a pause. "I hardly met her after bringing you from Uglich."

And I understood that he broke up with her because of us, when after the civil war he gathered his family and returned to it, most of all to us—to me and Muska . . . I asked him nothing more about Princess Barbara, but the image of an ageless, graceful, captivating woman momentarily flashed before me in the cold darkness of the blockade dwelling . . .

I saw her three years after the Great Fatherland War, in the hospital where papa lay. Civil war typhus, the famine, and the misery of the blockade finally caught up with him, and hypertension finished him off. He was an excellent doctor and knew he was dying, and how it anguished him to part with life, with everything that he loved in it—and he loved much: work, people, open spaces, animals, roses . . . He did not fear death but sometimes simply couldn't hide his anguish in leaving life. He even told me once, in the boyish, plaintive voice in which he once complained that he wasn't accepted into the Home Guard:

"Lyalka, little girl . . . You're famous—write someone, let them send me some real ginseng? Say your papa, an old doctor, asks for it."

"Okay, papa," I answered submissively. "I'll write Samuil Yakovlevich Marshak. He will try . . ."

"I know! I know that he will try . . ."

It needs to be said that at the very beginning of the thirties—in 1931 or 1932, when Samuil Yakovlevich Marshak edited my first children's books, papa came running all excited to my place. How young he still was then! How often and happily he guffawed—precisely guffawed, not laughed!

"Lyalka!" He cried practically from the threshold. "I read in our paper that your Marshak is going to Germany."

"Yes. And why are you so excited about that?"

"What is that—why? Here are prescriptions. One, for Mercusal, the other for Luminal.[76] You know, the Germans are famous for their pharmacopeia—Bayer—we still haven't learned how to make those medicines. Understand?"

"Not yet."

"Oh, lord! You have to be spoon-fed. Well, I have one weaver, a good woman, swells up terribly—she needs Mercusal. And another weaver, a good, diligent man—needs Luminal. He has some sort of seizures, like an epileptic. I want to see if Luminal will help. Well, that's it. Let Marshak send me Mercusal and Luminal from Germany. Must be Bayer."

"Papa, you must . . . you must understand—it's not proper, not convenient. He has to pay hard currency for all that. It's awkward for me!"

"Quite proper. Say your papa, an old doctor, asks for it. Marshak's clever, he understands everything, he writes well: 'Crocodile, crocodile, crocodilovich!'"

"That's not Marshak, it's Chukovsky."[77]

"True. I mixed them up. Marshak's good, too. When he talks about all you writers:

> The pike's mouth may open wide
> But you hear no song inside.

"Samuil Yakovlevich did not write that about us! You're just a demagogue."

"About you! I'm a reader, I know better. In any case, I know that he's a good man. Kids love his verses . . . Take the prescriptions. And ask Samuil Yakovlevich. Say it's for your papa, an old doctor. For his weavers."

And I, dying of shame, all the same asked Samuil Yakovlevich, and he so simply and readily took papa's prescriptions that my shame disappeared. Two or three times he brought what father asked for . . . Samuil Yakovlevich probably still doesn't know how many of papa's weavers he helped papa to put on their feet, to save from death . . .

"I will write, papa, to be sure," I repeated. And I didn't write, because I already knew from the doctors that his days were numbered, that he had a week, at most two. I knew I had to send telegrams to Muska and mother, so that they would come, but I was afraid that papa would understand why we'd all gathered around him, and simply did not know what to do.

On one of those evenings, when he was especially depressed and was already breathing with difficulty, I was asked to go out to the lobby—where someone had come for me.

I went out. An unfamiliar woman rose from the sofa and came to meet me. She was tall, overweight, with graying hair, parted in the middle and drawn into a small, old-fashioned bun at the nape of her neck, a broad folksy face. She looked a lot like our Dunya, but Dunya's nose was a duck-bill, and hers was more aquiline, and her eyes were different—soft gray, with full lashes, a gaze intelligent and sad.

"Hello, Lyalechka," she said, stretching out her hand.

"Hello," I answered, wondering who this old woman was.

She took my right hand in both of hers, and held it for a long while, gazing intently at me with a faint smile in the corners of her large, probably once beautiful, mouth and her sad, intelligent eyes.

"You look so much like your father, Lyalechka," she said quietly and as an afterthought added, "Excuse me, we know each other only in absentia, and that was long ago. I'm Varvara Nikolaevna B–va."

I shuddered involuntarily, jerking my head; my face probably showed surprise, maybe fright, because with a brief, sad grin she added,

"Yes, it is I. I came to ask you to let me help you care for your papa. I heard that he's in serious condition."

So this was the red nurse, Princess Barbara, the Swan Princess of our childhood?

Before me stood an old, sad woman in a simple cotton dress, even a little clumsy, swollen, nothing, absolutely nothing, like the Princess Barbara imagined in ancient Uglich, in the years of the civil war and our disastrous childhood. And all the same, there was something of the Swan Princess in her. What exactly I still couldn't understand; I eagerly listened to her voice, and she said:

"I've already come to an understanding with the doctors; they've trusted me with a post near your papa. Let's go to him, Lyalechka. Excuse me, I can't call you anything else."

"Let's go," I answered almost mechanically, and we went.

Father lay breathing with difficulty, his eyes closed, but I could see he wasn't asleep.

"Papa," I called out to him, "someone has come to see you."

He turned, saw Varvara Nikolaevna, and his face was transfigured, lit from within and rejuvenated with a selfless, happy smile.

"Varyusha," he said slowly with indescribable tenderness, "my dear. You're with me?"

"With you, my little doctor, my dear," she answered, bending over him and kissing his hand just as he pressed his lips to her palm, "Of course with you. Where else would I be?"

"Well . . . just like on the train 'Red Eagles,' comrade princess . . . to-gether looking death in the eye . . ."

"Like on the train 'Red Eagles,' comrade commander," she answered and suddenly she let out a short, happy laugh, "like on the train 'Red Eagles'—not afraid of anything."

I started. This was the voice of the Valdai duga—the voice of love, the voice of life.

. . . This time Princess Barbara didn't succeed in snatching father from death. But with her arrival he became lucid and calm; he wasn't delirious and depressed as before but was confident of his recovery; he never asked me again whether I'd asked Marshak to bring him ginseng; he didn't fear mama and Musya's arrival, and even joked with them. He died under the Valdai duga, in the arms of the red nurse from his combat hospital train.

Glory of the World

On that evening, when I was lying down in papa's office, he sat beside me, stroking my hand and head, as he'd sometimes done in my early childhood, when we'd had measles or a sore throat.

And because he was stroking my hand and forehead, because we'd had a conversation about Princess Barbara, and her fairy-tale image momentarily lit the cold gloom of the blockade dwelling, a breath of childhood brushed my face, and I remembered Palevsky.

"Papa, how is everything at Palevsky? How is Aunt Varya? Dunya?"

He was silent for a long while, staring fixedly at the candle.

"They died of starvation. Auntie Varya, on the way to the hospital. Avdotya at her factory, on duty. And a shell hit the house."

"That means . . . no one is living there?"

"No. No one. Only snowdrifts now."

He got quiet again, and so did I. And suddenly with the clarity and certainty of a hallucination I heard Dunya sing (sang?):

Oh, my beloved ho-ome

Dunya would always get out this line in her thin, resonating voice, then copious tears would choke her up and she couldn't continue singing. And now Aunt Varya had died, "on the way to the hospital," that is along the same path by which I had come today. Dunya had died, never having sung her cherished lament to the end, never having worn her golden and silver shawl in Guzhovo; her Pskov province, with its dense forests and fearless brother, was occupied by the Germans and covered with impenetrable, cold, silvery snow, and our dead, half-ruined house was also covered with snow, snow spreading over all of Russia—only snow, snow, and snow, and such endless, silent sorrow, like mine. Slowly, slowly pain awakened in my heart—that meant life, but I didn't yet understand that.

"Papa," I said aloud, "I think I'm already no longer alive . . ."

"Lies," my father said angrily. "You're alive. If you were dead, you would have lain there and not have come here."

"No, that's true. I don't want to live. Or rather, it's all the same . . ."

He answered sadly and tenderly:

"Foolish child! And I, for instance, want very much to live . . . You know, I've even become a collector."

"A collector . . . of what?"

He got embarrassed.

"Any sort of junk . . . Perhaps it's some kind of psychosis. I collect whatever I can: postcards, buttons, rose seeds."

"Buttons? Why?"

From behind the candle, out of the twilight, I don't know, from some other time, some other century, future or past, he looked at me with his unbelievably clear blue eyes and confessed with distress:

"You know, maybe it's unseemly, especially among us, in Leningrad, but I have acquired such a thirst for life! Inconceivable—like first love—a thirst. Not, not even thirst, no, greed . . . that's it. And so I want to preserve everything, save, simply that . . . to press it to my heart! Everything there is in the world: buttons and postcards and rose seeds. Press everything to my heart to the last button, so that nothing would disappear . . ."

So trustingly he looked at me, confiding all this nonsense, the "great absurdity" of our times. How enthusiastically, even conspiratorially he added:

"You know, I've been promised the seeds of some very special roses. They're called 'Glory of the World.' These are, you know, huge, slowly blooming golden roses with a tinge of orange around the rim. They actually grow in the south, and they don't grow everywhere even there. But I'm going to plant them here, alongside my office. It's a pity, of course, that Matreshka will burn the garden fence this winter, but no matter, we'll build another. In the spring, I'll put these roses in the ground. And after a few years they ought to bloom. You'll come see them? What do you think, it'll be nice?"

"Nice," I answered, noting with amazement how, alongside the growing pain in my heart, yet another feeling was arising.

Perhaps because Matresha washed my feet like a mother or older sister, or because the firefighter brought cake made of earth—the generous gift of the hungry to the hungry—or because papa told the story of the old molder, and now spoke of roses called "Glory of the World," and of my traveling to see them—"that means even the trams will be running?"—from all that and much more of which I was not conscious, yes, alongside the pain there rose in me a sense of calm and steadfastness. It was perhaps something like pride, but it was not pride. I repeat, I now understand that this was all the return of life. "Of course father is right," I thought, "I'm alive, I can walk, and I made it to him. To hell with it, don't listen to yourself, just do everything that you can! Lord! I've still got two radio programs to do—one for the city and one for broadcast—they must be done right . . . Now I'll sleep, and tomorrow—or at the latest the day after tomorrow—I'll go to the Radio Committee and work. Better to die on the run and at work. But I won't die. I will survive in spite of everything that has been done to me and to her . . . to my native land. She lives, and she, too, will survive. And now she and I will sleep. She and I. We are tired. It's night. We will sleep."

"Papa, I think I'll sleep well tonight," I stated. "Put out the state candle . . ."

He laid his large doctor's hand on my face, and I kissed it, as in childhood.

"Well, sleep, sleep, that's best of all . . . And then you'll see 'Glory of the World' roses in my front garden."

He got up and before putting out the candle, encircled its yellow flame with his palms and made a circular motion to show how big the roses would be, how they would bloom.

"Like that, you see, like that—huuuge, golden," he said, moving his fingers. "That's how big they can be! Magnificent, eh?!"

And I looked at his hands: lit from within, translucent pink at the edges, almost as if they themselves gave off a golden-rosy light—

the hands of a Russian doctor, a surgeon, which had saved the lives of thousands of soldiers, and others, too, had hewed steps to the water hole in the ice, now really looked like a huge, wonderful flower;

as beautiful as my grandmother's hands that looked like cast iron, intertwined with dark veins, nodules, and calluses, hands with which she blessed me and our whole country in the days of the attack on the city;

as powerful and good as Matresha's hands;

as big and skillful and fearless as the old molder's hands;

hands, exuding light and strength, knowing and communicating to each other and the future the secret of the earth, working hands—the highest, most real, eternal glory of the world.

"Yes, I will see papa's flowers in the summer," I thought firmly and simply, as about something ordinary and self-evident, "just as father said they'd be . . ."

The Path of Return

Two mornings later, with the same feeling of calm assurance I returned to the city along the same path by which I had come, the day before yesterday, almost dead, and along which I had returned, four months earlier, immensely happy, ecstatic, immortal. I didn't think about my journey two days earlier and didn't experience anything like the "day of heights."

I now knew that my grief was permanent, that my widowhood would never pass, even if I fell in love with someone else. But all the same, I would live. I was as weak as the day before yesterday, but I knew that I had to go, I had to live and work, because people needed my work. I did not experience, I repeat, this consciousness as pride or happiness. I just walked and got on with business: I was thinking about my upcoming radio programs, interspersing them with quietly muttered lines of verses that suddenly occurred to me and that I had to write for Red Army Day—also a Radio Committee assignment . . .

I already knew what they would be about: about today in Leningrad, about myself as a Leningrad woman, about what was most important to us through eight months of war, about what we felt, how we were fighting now, about how starving, losing those closest to us, ourselves dying, we loved life and therefore must be victorious.

I couldn't wait to write about this, to write the whole truth, sparing neither myself nor the reader, hoping that it would come out right, worthy of my fellow citizens, wanting to quickly give this to them. To that woman, pulling a sled with a corpse wrapped in a sheet, to the officer I met—he was going toward the Nevsky Gate, probably to the front, to the Fifty-First[78]—and to Matresha and papa and the women who crawled up the icy mountain from the water hole . . .

Now, when I think about all three campaigns—the first from the Nevsky Gate, then to the Nevsky and back—I remember a piece of Indian wisdom that became known to me after our victory, as recounted by Ivan Bunin. I describe it with less complexity and nuance than him, but I'm sure that I accurately convey the essence.

That Indian wisdom says that a person must travel two paths in life: the path of departure and the path of return.[79] On the path of departure a person stands within his personal boundaries, where *part* of the unified life lies. A person lives mostly for himself, lives purely by personal greed, by a lust for "capturing," a lust for "taking"—for himself, for his tribe, for his people. On the path of return the boundaries of the personal and social "I" fall away, the desire to "take" ends, giving way to a growing desire to "give back"—what was taken from nature, from people, from the world. In this way the individual's life and consciousness merges with the unified life, with the unified "I"—and true spiritual existence begins.

I repeat, I am summarizing another's account, and this position, this wisdom of course cannot coincide at all points with our—with my—life.

All the same, it seems to me that my dizzyingly happy and terrifying journey from the Nevsky Gate in October 1941, despite the feeling of merging with universal life, was still in some measure the "path of departure," but the way back from father, when my main desire was to give back as much as it was possible to give, to give my fellow citizens and my country the strength and words they needed, this likely was my entry onto the "path of return."

No, the "desire to take" even from the past did not cease and die out in me, but the "desire to give back what was taken" prevails.

To give not only what you have taken, but to give it transfigured into the word that has passed through the soul, becoming its essence.

I spoke about this—only with different words—at the beginning of my notes, in the chapter "Daytime Stars," and with this I break off, as always unexpectedly for myself. And, having read these notes, some may ask: "Yes, indeed! After all you promised us daytime stars—where are they?"

To this I reply: "I opened my soul to you like lifting the cover of a well, with all its darkness and light. Look into it! And if you see some part of yourself, some part of your journey, that means you have seen the daytime stars; that means they have been lit in me. They will glow more brightly in the Essential Book, which is always ahead, that you and I are continuously and tirelessly writing."

Part II

4

Good Morning, People!
June 1960

"Our Fritz Is Dying"

And I returned to the city and went to the Radio Committee. Near the entrance, the artist Yosif Gorin was carefully winding a rope around his hand, the other end of which was tied to a child's sled.

"Going to the fire, Osya?"

"To the fire."

Three days earlier his sister's house, somewhere on Liteiny, had burned, and Osya went every day to the fire, as if to work, collecting himself slowly, carefully, and unhurriedly.

That winter our fires in Leningrad were long and slow—and there was no way to put them out; there was no water. People just carried out of the house whatever they had the strength to carry.

"Still burning?"

"Yes, third floor."

We were silent for a bit.

"And what's new at the Radio Committee?

"Same old . . . well, our Fritz is dying."

"Our Fritz is dying? Can't be!!"

Just yesterday I'd learned about the deaths of Aunt Varya and my old nanny Avdotya, that is about the death of a part of my soul, a part of my life and childhood, and it already seemed that there could be no greater shock. But still, the news that our Fritz was dying staggered me, so incompatible were Fritz's figure and the notion of death.

The Radio Committee's foreign department, which engaged in propagandizing the enemy and which we grandly called the "counterpropaganda department," employed, in addition to the department head Nikolai Verkhovsky and his assistant Nikolai Rimsky-Korsakov, two Germans, really—Austrians, the brothers Fritz and Ernst. Ernst was thin, almost miniature, with deep-set eyes, and Fritz was the typical prewar literary "Fritz": ruddy, with light brown hair and pale blue eyes, thickset, and exceedingly good-natured. Not infrequently I wrote short appeals directed to the Germans as an assignment from this department. Fritz or Ernst would record them, and Kolya Rimsky-Korsakov would bring the records to the front line near the Izhorsky or Putilov factories, and there broadcast them from the radio center, so that the enemy could hear them . . .

I will never forget one October night, when hunger had already imperiously entered Leningrad, and the Germans were assaulting the city and were on the near approaches to Moscow. All five of us listened to a broadcast from Hitler's headquarters. One of our Germans noted it down in shorthand.[1]

At first we heard roaring bugles, although they didn't really roar—they growled some kind of crude, arrogant, solemn march. A well-fed and at the same time tinny voice intoned: "Now the Fuhrer's headquarters will speak." After that the bugles roared for another five minutes.

We sat around the receiver, clenching our fists, gritting our teeth. And then after the bugles' hideous growling and march, the tinny, well-fed, self-satisfied voice said almost lazily that Moscow was reportedly surrounded and that incalculable numbers of our troops had been destroyed, that the days of the Bolshevik capital were reportedly numbered, that Leningrad was also doomed.

And after this bulletin the bugles once again roared, growled, thundered—crudely and for a long time—and then all of a sudden, without a pause, this wild, terrible march changed into a careless, crooning foxtrot.

Foxtrot followed foxtrot, tango followed languid tango, without a break, while in our dark city, cut off from the whole country, the metronome sounded. It sounded more rapidly, like a straining heart, when there was an air-raid warning.[2] And in fascist Berlin, the plunderers' lair, they were making merry. They danced and rejoiced because rivers of blood were frothing in Russia; thousands of Russian villages were burning, and on the streets of Leningrad women and children were already beginning to fall from hunger.

And the head of the department Nikolai Verkhovsky said through his teeth:

"When the time comes, their metronome won't beat after two months!"

Lean Ernst added: "Less."

Fritz smiled an uncharacteristically unkind smile.

Afterward, we each devoted ourselves to our own affairs . . .

But only quite recently, on the eve of the New Year, or rather, on the eve of Christmas, I was assigned to write a broadcast to the enemy in connection with the arrival of Christmas. Already heavily swollen with hunger, I wrote it in my icy apartment. I wrote:

"German soldier, you are freezing and starving in your trenches outside Leningrad. But just remember, not so long ago, how cozy it was in your home on Christmas Eve. Remember how the Christmas tree glowed and wood crackled in the stove . . . Has all this really left you forever? In the name of what?! For what are you freezing outside of Leningrad? You're getting frostbitten, you may become a cripple . . ."

And I was suddenly chilled by the thought that this was really all true, that living people were freezing in the cold earth outside of our city, and they were freezing just as I was now freezing, that they were also people. I immediately pushed away this incorrect, unnecessary thought. But all the same the thought, or more accurately, not thought but feeling, returned to me like a boomerang: however firmly I threw away this sure statement, it returned to my soul more strongly.

"They are enemies, and not people," I told myself and began to write further: "Could it be that you don't want to return to the warmth and joy of your hearth . . ." Oh, *I* want to, I want to, I so want to! And I remember the fir tree from childhood in the Nevsky Gate, and the recent sweet and cheerful New Year's gatherings at our Elektrosila factory club—oh, where is all this, why is it gone, where is simple, peaceful *life*, how it is offended, cruelly offended . . .

"What nonsense! I'm beginning to get hunger psychosis," I whispered to myself. "They are enemies, aggressors, invaders, and that's all . . ." How could I be sorry for them? No! But I'm sorry . . . I'm sorry for *us*. I'm sorry for us all together, as something that once existed in beautiful human unity, as something living, whole, that was ruthlessly and senselessly cut through by some "Third"—not human, someone alien to humanity. Yes, this "Third" someone cut through us, the united Person, Humanity, and threw the cleaved halves at one another, so that we tormented and hated one another, and it rose between us. By the evil will of this "Third Wheel," one half of the united Person devours, torments, and hates the other half. I hate this "Third Wheel" with all the strength of my soul and life. This "Third" is a fascist. He torments me; he bombed out Fritz's house, from which Fritz miraculously escaped. And the Germans Fritz and Ernst are starving just as I am. They have the same enemy as I have. It's the "Third Wheel"—fascism, Nazism.

There is no greater crime against the person, against life than the crime of this "Third Wheel." And I wrote the broadcast, pouring into it all my thirst for peace and happiness and all my hatred for fascism.

"And if you, German soldier, don't turn your guns against Hitler you will not get out of Leningrad alive!"

This is how I ended the leaflet, and I completed it with a fully tranquil soul, convinced that I was right. Our Fritz recorded it, and on Christmas Eve Kolya Rimsky-Korsakov took the record to the front line—to the Izhorsky factory. He returned frozen stiff but satisfied: they broadcast from very close to the lines—so close that you could hear the Germans singing Christmas hymns. But they undoubtedly heard the broadcast because when it began the hymns ceased, and they did not fire at the voice.

"And God grant—your voice sounded there!" said Kolya to Fritz. "Well done, Fritz."

And our Fritz smiled with satisfaction.

And now our Fritz was dying, just as my Dunya and Aunt Varya, and many, many other Leningraders had died.

"Okay, Osya," I said. "Go to your fire."

"Bye," he answered. And he quietly trudged to the fire.

For some time already all the essential workers at the Radio Committee had been living in a barracks right there where they worked. I stopped by the foreign department, and although I had only been away for two days, the changes in Verkhovsky and Rimsky-Korsakov's faces surprised me. They were almost black, dried up; Ernst looked positively charred.

Fritz was lying on a cot, behind a screen. He wasn't black but absolutely transparent and very meek. Seeing me, he tried to smile.

"How you doing, Fritz old man," I said. "What is it you've invented to loaf about?"

"It's nothing," he answered with a barely noticeable accent. "I'll get up soon."

And he didn't die. Not him, and not Ernst. Fritz now works in Austria. And a few days later, our comrades took Nikolai Verkhovsky—before the war a tall, healthy fellow, brash, smart, a talented literary scholar—and mild, extraordinarily charming Nikolai Rimsky-Korsakov by sled to the Astoria Hotel, to the clinic. But nothing could save them, and they died there. They were already gone when I did the broadcast "Berlin Fell." Ernst turned out to be right: Berlin didn't hold out two weeks. And three years after the victory, in a hall at the Astoria Hotel, we, a group of Leningrad writers, met with a delegation of German intellectuals arriving from Germany, from Berlin.

Meeting at the Astoria

The delegation was made up almost entirely of communists or antifascists close to the party.[3] Among them were: the remarkable writer Anna Seghers;[4] the venerable Bernhard Kellermann and his wife;[5] Stephan Hermlin, poet, novelist, critic, in the past an old member of the Komsomol, now—that is, already then, 1948—a communist;[6] Wolfgang Langhoff, actor, director, member of the party since the days of the Spartacus League, author of the book *Peat Bog Soldiers*, had been in a Nazi camp, and in those days and even now is the director of the Max Reinhardt Theater.[7] There was professor Jürgen Kuczynski, a famous economist, author of many important books on political economy, an old party member;[8] and Eduard Claudius, a novelist, old antifascist, who fought in Spain and during World War II with the partisans in northern Italy against Hitler.[9] Günther Weisenborn, poet and playwright, a member of the Resistance group Red Orchestra, was liberated from prison by our troops;[10] Michael Tschesno-Hell, an old party member, who was in emigration in Switzerland, was a supporter of Thälmann, one of the writers of the screenplay about Thälmann; and others.[11]

And here we were seated around a table heaped with food and good wines in a banquet hall, in the same hall where, during the blockade, there was a morgue.

And the first glass was raised, the first toast made. Loud but cold applause rang out. We sat alongside antifascists, communists, and all the same literally every one of us (I'm speaking of the Leningrad writers) felt that between us and *Germans* stood an invisible but unbreakable wall, as if there were a wall of special glass or ice, through which we saw each other, tried to explain, but did not hear each other. They were Germans, they came from that country, from that city from which, a few years ago, the most brutal, clanking iron had surged at us, at our motherland, under the roar of cannibalistic bugles, from which impenetrable darkness, arctic cold, thirst, and the plague of hunger came to our city and irrevocably carried away thousands and thousands of Leningraders, among whom were people of such spiritual purity and courage and selflessness, people like my late husband Nikolai, like the Radio Committee's Yakov Babushkin,[12] like my old nanny Avdotya and Aunt Varya, like Nikolai Verkhovsky and Nikolai Rimsky-Korsakov, who died in this building.

I remembered that Hitler was going to organize a gala banquet for officers in these same halls in the event that Leningrad was taken, that invitations to the banquet and medals for taking Leningrad had already been prepared. I proposed a toast to the fact that we were feasting at the Astoria with different Germans on a different occasion. The toast was applauded with satisfaction, coolly.

And we were smiling at one another, but a sense of alienation—more than that, a sense of profound weariness and irreversible loss—couldn't pass from my soul. This sense of loss—huge, universal—even seemed to sprout anew here in the Astoria during the meeting with the Germans. I felt some kind of raw dryness in my eye sockets, a dryness in my mouth, a dryness in my soul.

The master of ceremonies on our side was Yevgeny Lvovich Shvarts, a marvelous playwright and, without a doubt, the world's last real storyteller, a person with enormous, generous, pure, true storytelling talent.[13] It was impossible not to succumb to Yevgeny Lvovich's charm . . . But I will speak more about him and his wondrous work . . . later . . .

And here he stood up, and in a mashed-up Russo-German began to introduce us, the Leningrad writers, to the German delegates.

"Ich bin der Shvarts," he said importantly, pointing at himself. And we all began to laugh because both Yevgeny Lvovich's manner of speaking and his intonation could not but elicit soul-gladdening smiles.

"Ich schreibe du plays," he continued. "Das ist the poetess Olga Berggolts, she schreiben eine verses . . ."

He introduced all the Leningrad writers in this dear, merry, ingenious way, and raised a toast to our friendship, and standing, we drank to it.

And once again came such alienation, like someone breathing cold air on us.

After Evgeny Shvarts, Professor Jürgen Kuczynski spoke. He spoke about how walking around springtime Leningrad today, admiring this inimitable city, they saw its still unhealed wounds . . .

"And it seemed strange to me," he said, "that no one in this city threw rocks at us. Sitting here, we are not guilty of that which occurred, but the feeling of the shame and guilt of our people does not leave us. And you, instead of throwing rocks at us, meet us with warmth and friendship."

He spoke, and tears ran down his cheeks. We saw that the Germans were agitated and stunned by the reception given them in a city that suffered so grievously in the days of the Great Fatherland War. But the "Third

Wheel"—or its accursed shadow?—continued to stand between us; a painful bewilderment divided us, and something very simple had to be said and done in order to make everything clear and make it possible to live and breathe once again. But what?

And suddenly, unexpectedly someone from among the Leningrad writers began to sing "The Reds from Wedding," one of those songs that Ernst Busch brought to Leningrad in the early thirties, singing it at the Philharmonic, in factories, and even at our place, in our luckless Engineers' and Writers' House-Commune, better known by the facetious nickname the Teardrop of Socialism.

And suddenly everyone sitting at the table picked up this song:

> Left . . . Left . . .
> Join us, comrade,
> Join our workers' united front,
> Because you are a worker, too.[14]

And suddenly the whole of our youth soared above us, like two gigantic wings, like blazing red banners, like an ocean wave, soaring and pouring down on us all its freshness, all its light, and all its belief in the revolution, pouring down and even washing away the "Third Wheel" that wanted to cause us to quarrel.

Oh, lord, here were young Spartacists, and Thälmann, and members of the Red Jungsturm raising clenched fists with the cry, "Rot front!"—this had also come to us from Germany, from its revolution, from its working class![15]

And we sang song after song: "Peat Bog Soldiers," and other songs by Ernst Busch, and then "Bandiera Rossa" and "Warsawian," and—standing—the "Internationale," and enjoyed the feeling of indestructible human love that only the socialist revolution brings to humanity.[16]

And later, after the banquet, at dawn, a few Leningrad and German writers—among them Michael Tschesno-Hell, me, Langhoff, Lev Levin,[17] and others—walked for a long time around Leningrad and we reached the Neva when it was already almost light.

The white nights were approaching, and it got light very early. The Neva and the university on the other side and the Rostral Columns were indescribably beautiful, and the young sun cast on them the first, transparent-golden patches of light . . . And suddenly, remembering a beloved and wondrous Leningrad story, I turned to the German comrades, and boundlessly happy, said:

"Guten morgen, Fritz!"

I repeated this phrase a few times, and someone asked me what it was about, but I didn't say anything about this then — I will tell about it now.

"Guten Morgen, Fritz!"

And so here in Leningrad my friend had a daughter, Galya. When the blockade began, she was about four years old, and her older brother, Vadik, was ten. The children were clever and inquisitive, everything interested them, and like all blockade kids, they understood and thought beyond their years. They bore hunger with a courage and patience that an adult would have envied. They never whined or cried or begged their mother for food. They understood — that could not be done. All bundled up, in fur coats and hats with earflaps, they sat silently and still, side by side on the bed in the big, very cold room; they sat and remained silent . . . waiting for the next feeding.

And Galka never asked to eat ahead of time. But, having eaten no more than a tablespoon of soy kasha or a saucer of yeast soup with a tiny piece of bread, she inevitably sighed, smiled and, looking with her sweet eyes at her mother's gloomy face, full of tightly controlled despair, would say conspiratorially:

"And the next time the Fritzes come near us in Leningrad, we'll hide all the rolls in suitcases. So they won't take them away from us."

She already knew that these Fritzes — Germans — took food from her, that it was because of them that she and Vadik couldn't play or enjoy themselves, but could only sit, silently huddled together.

It must be said that Galka very often returned to the idea of Fritzes, of enemies — more frequently with every year of the blockade. If they went out walking with their mother and passed a bombed-out house, she would always ask:

"Mama, and who did Fritz kill in this house?"

Her mother answered tersely and morosely:

"A boy."

They walked further.

"Mama, and who did Fritz kill here in this house?"

"An old woman."

But although Galka didn't cry and didn't ask for food, understanding that this was impossible, when air raids or artillery fire began, she began to thrash about, grieving not at all like a child, big, silent tears running down her cheeks, and looking up at her mother with pleading eyes, she would ask:

"Mama, why does Fritz always want to kill me?"

"Because he's Fritz. A German."

Galka continued crying silently.

"What are you crying for, Galochka," her mother comforted her. "We're on the first floor. It won't fall here. You're my brave little girl; don't be afraid."

"I'm not afraid," answered Galya, when she was already almost seven years old. "No, I'm not afraid. I'm offended . . ."

"The babe should weep no more," but the babe wept, offended that for some reason they wanted to kill her . . .

The roar of planes in the sky, the whistling of bombs pierced Galka with frantic fear, and she didn't even like to look up at the sky.

A small, stunted person, walking along the streets at moments of clam, she looked mostly down at her feet, and hearing a plane flying, ran into the gateway.

And then the day came when Leningrad saluted the full lifting of the blockade. Their mother brought Galya and Vadik outside, and they stood next to their entryway, on the corner opposite the Gostiny Dvor shopping arcade. And on the corner of Gostiny Dvor hung an enormous poster depicting a gorilla-like fascist wearing a helmet with horns, carrying a bloody woman in his outstretched hand.

The first solemn, celebratory, triumphant volley was heard. Millions of sparkling lights flew into the sky, and the children raised their eyes, following the unprecedented spectacle, cascading lights flying headlong into and falling out of the sky.

But at the moment when Galka raised her eyes, her gaze fell on the poster opposite her, on the poster brightly illuminated by the triumphant light.

"Mama," asked Galya, transfixed. "Who is that?"

"That's Fritz," answered her mother.

And Galya did not take her eyes off the poster. She looked at this vile horned gorilla and quietly repeated:

"So, that's what Fritz is like . . . So, that's what he's like . . ."

Her mother was afraid of this whisper. She began to distract the girl:

"Galya, Galenka! You're not looking at the lights! Don't look at that trash!"

But Galya didn't look at the fireworks. She looked intently at her enemy, who had taken bread from her, who surely wanted to kill her; she looked and whispered:

"So that's what Fritz is like . . ."

Spring arrived. Vadik and Galya could now play all day long in the garden near their house, in the square near the Alexandrovsky Theater—because there was no longer shelling or bombing! And so once Galya returned at noon from a walk, unusually subdued, thinking somehow too deeply and consequentially for a child. Sighing, walking from window to window, she finally went to her mother and said:

"Mama, you know I saw a live Fritz today . . ."

Here it needs to be said that very few of us Leningraders saw a living German during the blockade. We had to deal with invisible enemies, and that was probably more painful than dealing with an enemy whose face you see.

"Where did you see him?" asked her mother.

"We were playing in the square, and suddenly boys ran in and shouted: 'Kids, kids, let's go taunt some live Fritzes. They're repairing the Alexandrovsky.' Well, we took off. And the boys surrounded them, jumping and taunting; and so I saw live Fritzes right there."

"Well, and what were they like?"

Galya hesitated, looked down, and quietly said:

"You know, mama, they were thin, green, just like our dystrophics."[18]

"Well, and how did you taunt them?"

Galya lowered her fair, round face even more; a confused, almost guilty smile lit up her face. But she whispered distinctly and firmly:

"I didn't taunt them. I went up to one of them and said, 'Guten morgen, Fritz.' And you know what?! He stroked my head! . . ."

And she looked at her mother and again smiled abashedly: she was ashamed of something, surprised and gladdened by something, something she was still unable to understand.

❁

I recalled Galina's "Guten morgen, Fritz" when after the meeting at the Astoria we walked around springtime Leningrad—illuminated by the morning sun—with our German comrades, as if cleansed by those songs, by the precious ideas and images called up by those songs that unite us for life.

We walked, overjoyed by the fact that despite the fathomless river of blood spilled because of the "Third Wheel" between our peoples—two of the world's most tragic peoples—we can still communicate with one an-other humanely, communicate sincerely and candidly, just as Galya said to the captured German: "Guten morgen, Fritz," which for her without a doubt meant: "Good morning, person!"

And how glad I was to address this greeting of Galina's to my new-found friends! But then I didn't tell them what this meant for me—it seemed out of place, and the evening was already oversaturated, and our hearts could only just bear its bitter, astringent happiness.

Twice after this I saw Anna Seghers, a person and writer whom I love more and more. Michael Tschesno-Hell came to Leningrad for a screening and discussion of his film about Thälmann, and we met two days in a row, and talked much and from the heart about the past, the present, and the future. And every time I would meet with German comrades or read their books or think about them—I invariably said to myself, always brighter and more firmly, "Guten morgen, Fritz." And I would think: yes, this is the most important, the simplest, the clearest thing that people must say to one another so that the horrors of the last war will never be repeated and the still greater pitch-black, hopeless horrors of an atomic war won't come.

"Good morning,   ," that is the most important thing we must say to one another.

No, I am not calling for universal forgiveness. We will never forgive the fascists—not present-day ones or their apologists—for Galina's tears or her hurt. But in 1945, Soviet soldiers going into Germany, punishing the Nazis, destroying fascism, before all else fed starving German children: these soldiers knew too well, from their own lives, the starving, hurt, crying child. After all, "the babe should weep no more"! No wonder that in Berlin, above the graves of the fallen victors, stands a soldier, lofty and unwavering, cleaving a swastika with a sword and pressing a child to his chest . . . And it always seems to me that this child is a girl—who looks like our little blokadnitsa, Galya . . .

I remembered Galya recently when Powers's plane was shot down near Sverdlovsk.[19] Of course I, like everyone else, didn't hear his flight, but thinking about it, I kept remembering how Galya would be frightened of the ferocious roar of the airplane above her—as if I once again hear it my-self. Yes, it is above Galya, above all the children, above the nation that experienced the most severe torments of war and managed to say: "Good morning people!"; above the nation that offered to do the only thing, the necessary thing so that the "Third Wheel" would disappear forever, so that war would disappear—during the Fatherland War, the shadow of the—fascist—airplane swept above it.

And this is bigger than espionage, bigger than the violation of our airspace: this is a provocative attempt to undermine the people's confidence in peace negotiations, an attempt to destroy their hope for peace, for the possibility and happiness of saying every day to one another: "Good morning, person!"

Powers's plane, and all those who equipped it, and all those who justified and are justifying this invasion of our sky—all of them once again offended Galya in the most severe way, insulted all those who yearn for peace.

They casually betrayed the meeting at noon on 25 April 1945 of American and Russian soldiers on the Elbe, when, crossing no man's land, on a shore drenched in blood, they embraced as brothers and vowed to one another to do everything in their power to create a better world. But our trust in people is lasting, our confidence in the possibility of peace is firm, it will not be broken—just as our hatred of fascists, of fascism—behind whatever national flag it may hide—will not be destroyed.

※

. . . My Uglich, my city of childhood—since returning there seven years ago, I no longer dream of it. Nor do I dream of it as it was when I saw it in 1953. Perhaps that's because between that journey and my present days lay the kind of joy that doesn't appear in dreams and sorrows that make it impossible to sleep.

But regrettably, I often dream of a future war. I dream that airships, resembling antiaircraft barrage balloons, appear in the sky. They move noiselessly toward me, toward my city. Here the chief terror is that everything happens noiselessly. This is the start of universal destruction, and first of all sound died in the world. No one and nothing produces a single sound . . . And that which should sing, doesn't sing; and that which should ring, doesn't ring; and even that which should whisper, doesn't whisper . . . Everything is mute, everything is happening in already dead silence.

The enormous silver cigar-dirigibles fly silently; bombs fall silently, not whistling, not rumbling as before.

And here I see—high in the sky, completely silent, a huge pink house rises above me. I'm lying on my back; I look at the deep blue sky and see how the house silently breaks in half, and its pink walls begin to fall on me. Destruction happens in complete silence. And even if I were to shout or try to groan—no one would hear me: sound was no longer being born into the world. The planet was deaf and mute. And here when it already seems that destruction is inevitable—sound is born, and I hear some kind of voice powerfully and distinctly say to me:

"Get up! It's a dream."

And I wake up and for a few minutes lie in deep exhaustion, powerless, somehow powerlessly rejoicing that it was a dream, and I recall it with disgust. I know that my motherland is powerful enough that this dream will never become a reality for it. But I don't even want to see such dreams; I don't want anybody anywhere to see them. I want to wake up with the feeling that outside my window is a vast, friendly, hardworking world. A world where there is no no man's land between allies or between opponents. There is no no man's land, but there is a land of flowers and grasses, a land of trees and animals, a land of labor and love—a humane Earth. The world, a million sounds reverberating. No, that's not quite it—it can say everything that it wants to say; it is not deaf—it hears every word of goodness and truth. And that which should speak—speaks, and that which should sing—sings, and that which should sound—sounds, and even that which should only whisper—whispers . . . I want to wake up and go to the window opening on such a world, and say, so that nations and each separate person would hear:

"Good morning, people!"

5

Blockade Bathhouse
Leningrad, April 1962 (published 1990)[1]

This was in the spring of 1942, in Leningrad. I went into the bathhouse.[2]
It was quiet. And the women's eyes were quiet, expressing neither
grief nor despair, but some frozen thought, weighty and hopeless, expressing
a long, sustained, silent reproach, but even the reproach was not screaming,
not passionate, but frozen, fixed. Leningrad women's famous eyes—empty,
heavy, and concentrated; a person cast a glance at something awful, and so
it remained within him.

They moved quietly around the bathhouse—weariness made itself felt
in all their movements. And they exerted no effort to make their movements
more vigorous—what for? So far had weariness already gone. They filled
the washbasins less than halfway—no one could lift more. Slowly, with
movements like the movements in a slow-motion, silent film, they scrubbed
one another's backs. Some kind of special politeness reigned in the bathhouse; no one squabbled; they ceded their places to one another, shared
the soap—and in this politeness there was something sickly and once again
weary. They were polite to each other in the way of people at a funeral.
Yes, it was dystrophic politeness.[3] And this was because we had become so
unaccustomed to a phenomenon like the bathhouse; a previously ordinary
and everyday place now seemed somehow fantastic—we arrived somewhere not knowing how to behave there. And the water flowed in a gaunt
trickle and was barely lukewarm—dystrophic water, too; even the water
in this city was dystrophic. Oh, sorrow, sorrow! At first I felt this terrible
sobbing for humanity, but then, like everyone, only weariness. I love
water, but the water did not gladden me but somehow irritated, like the

feeling of a child's powerless tears—so whimpers a convalescing, very weak child, who lacks the strength to hold a favorite old toy in his hands, or wind it up, or something . . . In any case, to do something that he did before with this same thing. And this gives him a sense of his hateful weakness and inflicts the profound pain of losing everything that had been "before." Closing my eyes, I splashed in the washbasin, in the barely lukewarm water. But it didn't bring me joy. I only remembered the facts, sensing that the sea "was," and I felt nothing in connection with this purely cerebral insight . . .

Then I looked at the women . . . The dark, stretched, rough skin of the women's bodies—no, not even women—they had ceased to resemble women—their breasts had disappeared; their stomachs were shrunken; the purple and deep blue stains of scurvy crawled across their skin. A few had horribly distended stomachs—on top of skinny legs—legs without calves, where the fattest part was the ankle. These black or bluish-white phantoms did not resemble women. On repulsively thin legs, they had been stripped of all womanly charm, all the womanly essence that humanity idolizes and admires—its highest delight, Madonna, its holy mother, its lover. Womanly beauty—what has become of it?! Into what horror and despair and shame had humanity sunk if its women became like this, if it allowed such a distortion of woman! I repeat, torn-off arms and legs are nothing compared to these bony bodies: You know, missing arms do not deform Venus. Here everything was in place and there was nothing. One should sob, looking at the multitude of these women; one should be amazed that they decided to bare in the light of day so profaned, emaciated, blemished, and spotted a body.

Oh, son of man, son of man! What have you done with your mother, sister, daughter, lover? How dare you allow her to stand here trampled, unashamed of the desecration of the purest of her riches—her body.

And suddenly a young woman came in. She was smooth, white, shimmering with little golden hairs. Her skin glowed, smooth and shiny. Her breasts were firm, round, almost buoyant, with brazenly pink nipples. A rounded belly, supple oval lines, shoulders without a single bone, downy hair, and the main thing—this pearly-milky Rubenesque skin color,[4] unbearable against the background of brown, blue, and spotted bodies. A skeleton coming into the bathhouse wouldn't have frightened us more, but a sigh rolled through the bathhouse when she entered. Oh, how terrible she was—terrible with her normal, radiant health, eternal female flesh. How could this have been preserved? She wasn't only more terrible than all of us. She was nauseating, repugnant, and disgusting—with her round breasts, created to be kneaded and squeezed by a man, panting with desire,

Berggolts describes the skin color of the healthy woman in the bathhouse as "Kustodiev-esque." She may have had in mind the painting *Russian Venus* (*Russkaia Venera*, c. 1925–26) by Boris Kustodiev. (Boris Kustodiev [Public domain], via Wikimedia Commons)

her thighs—all this intended for bed, for copulation, for conception—for everything that now could not and should not be, that was natural but had become shameful because it had become impossible, forbidden. And how did she dare—to come here like that, to this terrible room, where the most monstrous humiliations and horrors of war were exhibited—how dare she, the bitch, insult all this with her beautiful, healthy body?

The women, crazed by this blasphemy, whispered behind her back: "Healthy!"

"Rosy!"

"Fat!"

A quiet hiss of disgust, contempt, resentment swept toward her; almost every woman looking at her whispered:

"B . . . b . . . b . . ."

She shouldn't have been here.

"She's been sleeping with some canteen manager, and he's been stealing," the women said.

"She's probably been stealing and pilfering herself."

"She's been robbing us and our children."

A frightfully bony woman came up to her, lightly smacked her bottom and said jokingly:

"Eh, my pretty, don't come here—we'll eat you up."

A brief low laugh could be heard.

"Exactly. We don't have long . . ."

And to think that she might have come to aid Leningrad . . .

The sick and emaciated powerless people shunned her, shrank from her blooming health—they shrank from her as from a contagious patient, as from a leper, not wanting to touch her silky, glowing skin.

So disgusting she was—a vision of ordinary, healthy human life, an apparition of divine human flesh—the crown of creation—including how it should be, an apparition of miraculous female beauty, created for love, maternity, and work.

She cried out, started to sob, threw aside her washbasin, and ran out of the room.

Then there was another incident. I took my head out of the washbasin, and it was spinning. I sat down, breathing heavily, limp, even more tired, indifferent. A sobbing, humid whisper in which could be heard some remnant of passion caught my attention. It was a woman next to me whispering. Her eyes were fixed on something in front of her, and I looked there, too. I saw a little old woman dabbling in a shallow washbasin. Even amid all our ugliness, this old woman was an exceptional presence—she was scarcely human. She was as if intentionally invented. Not dark, not brown, her seemingly charred face was made up of prominent knuckles; she was completely bald; her very round bulging belly was supported by spidery legs, and what is more, a hernia was hanging under her belly—on the whole, she looked like a spider, not in the least like a person or even an ape, but exactly like a spider. She was alive, clearly alive! In her eyes, deeply, deeply set into her skull, something shined—she was splashing water, no not splashing but moistening her bald skull with her small nonhuman palms. And if it wasn't clear where the despicable, shameless, rosy one came from, then this, this one crawled out from somewhere! An animal! Is there really a place in our terrible, starving city where such old women can be found?

And my neighbor looked at her as if spellbound and whispered:

"Mine, handsome, young, is dead, and this one lives . . . died, and that lives . . . Suppose only those remain of us on earth? For what did he die? For these, for these, these . . ."

The old woman sat on the edge of the bench, alone. A generous, wide, softly shining ray of sunlight fell on her. A trickle of water spurted from the pipe that ran near the old woman's bald head, spraying out a tiny fan, and in this little fan of water a clear seven-colored rainbow danced— directly above the old woman's bald, black head, which she wet with her spidery claws—all brown, a bent wheel, skeletal, with a vile hernia beneath her belly. All our desecration was concentrated in her. She sat in a kind ray of sunlight, with a seven-colored halo above her head—she sat like Death herself, War herself . . .

I thought:

"Yes, that's what war herself looks like; she's not in the shape of a soldier, clad in iron, nor in the shape of a gorilla in a helmet, nor in the shape of a tank, but in the shape of this powerless, bald, barely alive, but living, deformed old woman with an accidental rainbow above her head . . ."

Notes

Foreword

1. Nikolai Ostrovskii, *How the Steel Was Tempered* (Moscow: Progress Publishers, 1976). For more on the Socialist Realist novel, see Katerina Clark, *The Soviet Novel: History as Ritual* (Chicago: University of Chicago Press, 1981).

2. Clark, *The Soviet Novel*, 3–24.

3. Ol'ga Berggol'ts, "Razgovor o lirike" [A conversation about lyric poetry], in *Sobranie sochinenii*, 3 vols. (Leningrad: Sovetskii pisatel', 1988–90), 2:367–78.

4. Nina Koroleva, "V gostiakh u Anny Akhmatovoi" [A visit to Anna Akhmatova], *Literaturnoe obozrenie*, 16 June 1989, 8.

5. Ol'ga Berggol'ts, "Na asfal't rasplavlennyi pokhozha" [Like molten asphalt], in *Sobranie sochinenii*, 1:171.

6. Ol'ga Berggol'ts, *Ol'ga: Zapretnyi dnevnik* [Ol'ga: The forbidden diary], compiled by Nataliia Sokolovskaia (St. Petersburg: Azbuka-klassika, 2010), 30.

7. Berggol'ts, *Ol'ga*, 31, 35.

8. Ol'ga Berggol'ts, *Blokadnyi dnevnik (1941–1945)* [Siege diary], compiled by Natal'ia Strizhkova (St. Petersburg: Vita nova, 2015), 239.

9. Diary entry for 1 April 1942, in Berggol'ts, *Blokadnyi dnevnik*, 277.

10. Ol'ga Berggol'ts, "Stikhi o sebe" [Verses about myself], in *Sobranie sochinenii*, 2:88–89.

11. Berggol'ts, *Blokadnyi dnevnik*, 106.

12. Berggol'ts, *Blokadnyi dnevnik*, 220.

13. Berggol'ts, *Blokadnyi dnevnik*, 156. In her diary entry for 8 February, Berggolts writes that she went to see her father "a few days ago" and records a few details of their conversation that appear in the third chapter of *Daytime Stars*. The diary account is dominated by her anxieties over her father's imminent deportation from the city, which does not feature in *Daytime Stars*.

14. Berggol'ts, *Blokadnyi dnevnik*, 108.

15. Records of some of the meetings at which Berggolts's case was discussed, and at which she attempted to defend herself, can be found in Mikhail Zolotonosov, *Okhota na*

Berggol'ts: Leningrad 1937 [The persecution of Berggolts: Leningrad 1937] (St. Petersburg: Mir'', 2015).

16. This document, which raises the possibility that Berggolts may have been beaten during questioning in 1937, is cited by Nataliia Sokolovskaia in Berggol'ts, *Ol'ga*, 351.

17. The poem is Mikhail Lermontov, "Poet," in *Polnoe sobranie sochinenii*, 5 vols. (Moscow: Academia, 1935–57), 2:42.

18. The scenario for the film *Dnevnye zvezdy*, directed by Igor Talankin, Mosfilm, 1968, is in Ol'ga Berggol'ts, *P'esy i stsenarii* [Plays and film scenarios] (Leningrad: Iskusstvo, 1988), 328–56.

19. Ol'ga Berggol'ts, *Vstrecha: Dnevnye zvezdy, pis'ma, dnevniki, zametki, plany* [Meeting: Daytime stars, letters, diaries, notes, plans] (Moscow: Russkaia kniga, 2000), 214.

20. Berggol'ts, *Vstrecha*, 272.

21. Berggol'ts, *Vstrecha*, 316–17.

22. Berggol'ts, *Vstrecha*, 220.

23. Berggol'ts, *Vstrecha*, 311.

Introduction

1. Page numbers refer to my translation in this volume.

2. The classic account of the blockade in English is Harrison Salisbury, *The 900 Days: The Siege of Leningrad* (New York: Harper and Row, 1969). More recent accounts include Richard Bidlack and Nikita Lomagin, *The Leningrad Blockade, 1941–1944: A New Documentary History from the Soviet Archives* (New Haven, CT: Yale University Press, 2012); Anna Reid, *Leningrad: The Epic Siege of World War II, 1941–1944* (New York: Walker and Co., 2011); Michael Jones, *Leningrad: State of Siege* (New York: Basic Books, 2008); Sergey Yarov, *Leningrad, 1941–42: Morality in a City under Siege*, trans. Arch Tait (Malden, MA: Polity, 2017).

3. Katharine Hodgson, *Voicing the Soviet Experience: The Poetry of Ol'ga Berggol'ts* (Oxford: Oxford University Press for the British Academy, 2003), 23–25. For memories of Berggolts's verses, see Ales' Adamovich and Daniil Granin, *A Book of the Blockade*, trans. Hilda Perham (Moscow: Raduga, 1983), 88.

4. Joan Scott, "The Evidence of Experience," *Critical Inquiry* 17 (Summer 1991): 777.

5. Alexis Peri, *The War Within: Diaries from the Siege of Leningrad* (Cambridge, MA: Harvard University Press, 2017), 12, 160. Ginzburg's account has been translated as *Blockade Diary*, trans. Alan Myers (London: Harvill Press, 1995). See also Polina Barskova, "The Corpse, the Corpulent, and the Other: A Study in the Tropology of Siege Body Representation," *Ab Imperio*, no. 1 (2009): 361–86.

6. Barbara Walker, "On Reading Soviet Memoirs: A History of the 'Contemporaries' Genre as an Institution of Russian Intelligentsia Culture from the 1790s to the 1970s," *Russian Review* 59, no. 3 (July 2000): 328; David Carlson, "Autobiography," in *Reading Primary Sources: The Interpretation of Texts from Nineteenth- and Twentieth-Century History*, ed. Miriam Dobson and Benjamin Ziemann (London: Routledge, 2009), 175–77.

7. Bidlack and Lomagin, *Leningrad Blockade*, 6, 314–23.

8. Hodgson, *Voicing the Soviet Experience*, 24.

9. Carlson, "Autobiography," 177.

10. Walker, "On Reading Soviet Memoirs," 329.

11. Jochen Hellbeck, *Revolution on My Mind: Writing a Diary under Stalin* (Cambridge, MA: Harvard University Press, 2006), 11, 13.

12. Paul John Eakin, *How Our Lives Become Stories: Making Selves* (Ithaca, NY: Cornell University Press, 1999), 117.

13. Choi Chatterjee and Karen Petrone, "Models of Selfhood and Subjectivity: The Soviet Case in Historical Perspective," *Slavic Review* 67, no. 4 (Winter 2008): 985.

14. Mary Jo Maynes, Jennifer L. Pierce, and Barbara Laslett, *Telling Stories: The Use of Personal Narratives in the Social Sciences and History* (Ithaca, NY: Cornell University Press, 2008), 43–51; Sidonie Smith and Julia Watson, *Reading Autobiography: A Guide for Interpreting Life Narratives*, 2nd ed. (Minneapolis: University of Minnesota Press, 2010), 24–25.

15. Polly Jones, *Myth, Memory, Trauma: Rethinking the Stalinist Past in the Soviet Union, 1953–70* (New Haven, CT: Yale University Press, 2013), 3.

16. On the cult of the war, see Nina Tumarkin, *The Living and the Dead: The Rise and Fall of the Cult of World War II in Russia* (New York: Basic Books, 1994), 125–57.

17. Robert Chandler, translator's introduction to *Life and Fate* by Vasilii Grossman (London: Collins Harvill, 1985), 9. The novel was published in the Soviet Union in 1988.

18. Tumarkin, *The Living and the Dead*, 134–35.

19. On the construction of the memorial at Piskarevskoe Cemetery and other early post-Stalin monuments to the blockade, see Lisa A. Kirschenbaum, *The Legacy of the Siege of Leningrad, 1941–1995: Myth, Memories, and Monuments* (New York: Cambridge University Press, 2006), 190–208.

20. George Gibian, *Interval of Freedom: Soviet Literature during the Thaw, 1954–1957* (Minneapolis: University of Minnesota Press, 1960), 3, 70, 73, 105.

21. Anatoly Pinsky, "The Diaristic Form and Subjectivity under Khrushchev," *Slavic Review* 73, no. 4 (Winter 2014): 805, 818.

22. Pinsky, "Diaristic Form," 821–22. The journal *Novyi mir* (New world) was founded in 1925 and is still published today. It was a literary periodical—a so-called thick journal—that continued the nineteenth-century tradition of periodicals that "functioned as major sites for public conversation and deliberately pursued a combination of literary, political, journalistic, and enlightenment aims." Under editors Konstantin Simonov and Alexander Tvardovsky, *Novyi mir* in the 1950s and 1960s was "by far the most prestigious literary periodical in the country." Especially under Tvardovsky it maintained an "independent, often semi-oppositional political stance." Denis Kozlov, *The Readers of* Novyi Mir: *Coming to Terms with the Stalinist Past* (Cambridge, MA: Harvard University Press, 2013), 4, 10.

23. Andrei Sinyavsky, "The Poetry and Prose of Olga Berggolts," in *For Freedom of Imagination*, trans. Lazlo Tikos and Murray Peppard (New York: Holt, Rinehart and Winston, 1971), 41.

24. Hodgson, *Voicing the Soviet Experience*, 173.

Chapter 1. Journey to the Town of My Childhood

1. These were among the most common foods that sustained Russians in times of famine, including the 1921 famine and the famine during the World War II blockade of

Leningrad. *Duranda* was a hard "cake" made from linseed or other oil plant seed hulls, the byproduct of oil extraction. *Vobla* is a small dried fish, the Caspian roach. *Kissel* is a starchy liquid jelly made from fermented oat flour, barley, wheat, or rye; it can also be made with berries. For a description of these and other famine foods, see Anya von Bremzen, *Mastering the Art of Soviet Cooking: A Memoir of Food and Longing* (New York: Crown, 2013), 40, 107–8.

2. These collections were intended to offset wartime shortages of fuel and pharmaceuticals. In 1919 the Chief Fuel Committee called for a "massive effort" to collect pinecones to replace firewood and other fuels. In a year-long experiment, pinecones were pressed into briquettes that tests showed had "one and one-half times the heat capacity of the best firewood." The project relied on invalids and children under ten to collect the pinecones. Lily of the valley had long been used in Russian medicine as a diuretic and "tonic of the heart" or vasopressor. The civil war interfered with the commercial cultivation of medicinal botanicals, and the collection described by Berggolts seems to be part of an effort to find local materials. Thomas F. Remington, *Building Socialism in Bolshevik Russia: Ideology and Industrial Organization, 1917–1921* (Pittsburgh, PA: University of Pittsburgh Press, 1984), 126. "The Convallaria Maialas—Its Actions and Uses," *The Medical Record* (16 June 1883): 653; Mary Schaeffer Conroy, *The Soviet Pharmaceutical Business during Its First Two Decades, 1917–1937* (New York: Peter Lang, 2006), 59.

3. From 1918 to 1920, Alexander Kolchak, a former tsarist admiral, led an anti-Bolshevik government based in Omsk, Siberia. He was captured and executed by the Bolsheviks in 1920. Jonathan D. Smele, *Civil War in Siberia: The Anti-Bolshevik Government of Admiral Kolchak, 1918–1920* (New York: Cambridge University Press, 1996).

4. Most Russian names have at least one diminutive form. Muska and Muskina are uncommon diminutives of Maria. On diminutives and their uses, see Genevra Gerhart, *The Russian's World: Life and Language* (San Diego, CA: Harcourt Brace Jovanovich, 1974), 21–27.

5. "Peter" was an affectionate nickname for the city of St. Petersburg, which had been renamed Petrograd during the war.

6. In Russia, children often use "uncle" and "aunt" to address unrelated adults.

7. The palace was named after Ivan IV's youngest son, Dmitry, who in 1584, after the tsar's death, was exiled to Uglich. For his story, see chapter 3.

8. The Komsomol (Young Communists League) was a Communist Party organization for young people, usually ages fourteen to twenty-eight.

9. A range of illnesses were classified as "typhus," which was rampant during World War I and the civil war. Here Berggolts refers to *sypniak*, a colloquial term for *sypnoi tif* or spotted fever. Also widespread were typhoid fever (*brishnii tif*) and relapsing fever (*vozvratnii tif*). Joshua A. Sanborn, *Imperial Apocalypse: The Great War and the Destruction of the Russian Empire* (Oxford: Oxford University Press, 2014), 162–64, 166–67.

10. Here Berggolts reproduces the man's nonstandard pronunciation of Russia (*Rossiia*).

11. Construction began on the Volkhov Hydroelectric Station in 1918 and was completed in 1926. It still supplies power to the Leningrad region. Paul R. Josephson, *Would Trotsky Wear a Bluetooth? Technological Utopianism under Socialism, 1917–1989* (Baltimore, MD: Johns Hopkins University Press, 2010), 51–53.

12. A verst is 1.067 kilometers or 0.6629 miles.

13. The region of St. Petersburg beyond the Nevsky Gate, called simply the Nevsky or Nevsky Gate, was a "large and at times politically explosive industrial and working-class neighborhood" in the far southeastern reaches of the city that extended beyond the city limit. Reginald E. Zelnik, trans. and ed., *A Radical Worker in Tsarist Russia: The Autobiography of Semën Ivanovich Kanatchikov* (Stanford, CA: Stanford University Press, 1986), 412n2.

14. H. G. Wells, *Russia in the Shadows* (New York: George H. Doran, 1921). The book was published in Russian as *Rossiia vo mgle* in 1922 and again in 1958.

15. The descriptions of the sailor's appearance and actions are Berggolts's inventions. The final quotation is from Wells, *Russia in the Shadows*, 117. Although Berggolts puts Wells on the "fast" train, he complained about the "slow train." Wells describes not the silver teapot but the drawing room it may have originally been found in as "charming" (62); he does not mention a monogram.

16. Berggolts presents this entire passage as a direct quotation from Wells. I have distinguished her additions from the original text by placing only Wells's words in quotation marks. The published Russian translation is closer to Wells's original, Gerbert Uells [Herbert Wells], *Rossiia vo mgle*, trans. I Vikker and V. Pastoev (Moscow: Gosudarstvennoe izdatel'stva politicheskoi literatury, 1958). Foreign intervention in the civil war included an economic blockade of Soviet Russia. Initially implemented during the world war, the blockade was lifted in 1920. David S. Foglesong, *America's Secret War against Bolshevism: U.S. Intervention in the Russian Civil War, 1917–1920* (Chapel Hill: University of North Carolina Press, 1995), 249–52.

17. The song emphasized the anti-Bolshevik forces' connections to foreign powers. The lyrics in Russian are available at http://a-pesni.org/grvojna/makhno/pprokoltchaka .php (accessed 2 December 2017).

18. See Wells, *Russia in the Shadows*, 158–59.

19. Krzhizhanovsky, an electrical engineer, headed the State Commission for the Electrification of Russia (GOELRO). Established in 1920, GOELRO devised a general plan for electrifying the entire country by constructing a network of power stations. At the Congress, Lenin famously announced, "Communism is Soviet power plus the electrification of the whole country." Richard Stites, *Revolutionary Dreams: Utopian Vision and Experimental Life in the Russian Revolution* (New York: Oxford University Press, 1989), 48–50.

20. Stalin implemented the First Five-Year Plan (1928–32) as a means of building industry, especially heavy industry, as quickly as possible. One of the plan's high-profile projects was the Dneprostroy dam and hydroelectric station on the Dnieper River. Anne D. Rassweiler, *The Generation of Power: The History of Dneprostroi* (New York: Oxford University Press, 1988). The Elektrosila plant in Leningrad produced generators and equipment for hydroelectric plants. It is still in operation.

21. Ulyanov was Lenin's last name. The Union of Struggle for the Emancipation of the Working Class was an early Social Democratic organization established by Lenin (before he took that name) in 1895 that worked to bring intellectuals and workers into contact with one another. Lars T. Lih, *Lenin* (London: Reaktion Books, 2011), 53–55.

22. "Varshavianka" (Warsawian) was a nineteenth-century Polish song popular in Russia. In 1897 Krzhizhanovsky wrote the Russian lyrics. Lyrics in English and Russian and

a recording are available at https://www.marxists.org/history/ussr/sounds/lyrics/varsha vianka.htm (accessed 2 December 2017).

23. Nadezhda Konstaninovna Krupskaya (1869–1939) was Lenin's wife. They married in 1898 so that she could join him in Siberian exile. Robert H. McNeal, *Bride of the Revolution: Krupskaya and Lenin* (Ann Arbor: University of Michigan Press, 1972), 48–66.

24. The Putilov metalworks had a legendary reputation as a center of worker radicalism before and during 1917. Renamed in 1934 after slain party leader Sergei Kirov, it remains in operation.

25. The Great Fatherland (or Patriotic) War refers to the war that began with the Nazi invasion of the Soviet Union in June 1941 and ended with the fall of Berlin in May 1945. The term is still used in Russia.

26. In early September 1941, German and Finnish troops cut Leningrad off from the rest of the Soviet Union. Relatively few Leningraders evacuated the city before the blockade closed, when it became nearly impossible to resupply the city or evacuate civilians. In the winter of 1941–42, hundreds of thousands of Leningraders died of starvation. In January 1943 the blockade was pierced; it was fully lifted in January 1944. For accounts of the blockade in English, see introduction, n. 2.

27. Vladimir Mayakovsky (1893–1930) was an avant-garde poet with prerevolutionary ties to the Bolshevik party. After October 1917, he put his poetry at the service of the revolution, writing propagandistic verse, which was nonetheless often criticized as too formally complex for newly literate proletarians to understand. In 1930 he committed suicide by shooting himself; Stalin later deemed him the poet laureate of the revolution. Mayakovsky's "Pro Eto" (About this, 1923) and the unfinished "Vo ves' golos" (At the top of my voice, 1930) are two of his most important long poems. Vladimir Mayakovsky, *Pro Eto: That's What*, trans. George Hyde and Larissa Gureyeva (Todmorden: Arc Classics, 2009). An English translation of "At the Top of My Voice" is available at https://www.marxists.org /subject/art/literature/mayakovsky/1930/at-top-my-voice.htm (accessed 2 December 2017). Nikolai Ostrovsky (1904–36) is best known for his novel *How the Steel Was Tempered* (1932). It became part of the Socialist Realist "canon" in which the "author's own life was deindividualized as he patterned it to recapitulate the great legends of the revolutionary hero." Katerina Clark, *The Soviet Novel: History as Ritual* (Chicago: University of Chicago Press, 1981), 44. It is available in English translation: Nikolai Ostrovskii, *How the Steel Was Tempered: A Novel in Two Parts*, trans. R. Prokofieva (Moscow: Progress, 1973). For thumbnail sketches of Mayakovsky, Ostrovsky, and other writers, see Victor Terras, ed., *Handbook of Russian Literature* (New Haven, CT: Yale University Press, 1985). For a discussion of the intertexts referenced in this section, see Katharine Hodgson, *Voicing the Soviet Experience: The Poetry of Ol'ga Berggol'ts* (Oxford: Oxford University Press for the British Academy, 2003), 155–60.

28. The New Economic Policy (NEP), implemented in 1921, allowed the return of small-scale trade and manufacture. It was designed to reduce peasant opposition to the Bolshevik regime by allowing some free trade in grain and to rebuild the economy after the civil war. Its opponents, who viewed it as compromising revolutionary ideals, feared that it would result in the "New Exploitation of the Proletariat." Simon Pirani, *The Russian Revolution in Retreat, 1920–1924: Soviet Workers and the New Communist Elite* (London: Routledge, 2008), 196.

29. Fedor Gladkov (1883–1958) is best known for the proto-Socialist Realist novel *Cement* (1925) that put idealized heroes into a realistic setting, telling the story of a veteran returning from the civil war who brought a cement plant back into production. Gladkov himself had served in the Red Army during the civil war. He published his autobiographical trilogy toward the end of his life. The first two volumes, *Childhood* (1949) and *Outlaws* (1950) both won Stalin Prizes (a state prize given in various categories). *Evil Days* was published in 1954. Unlike *Cement*, the trilogy has not been translated into English. Fedor Gladkov, *Cement*, trans. A. S. Arthur and C. Ashleigh (1980; reprint, Evanston, IL: Northwestern University Press, 1994).

30. Maxim Gorky (1868–1936) came from what he called the "lower depths" (title of a 1902 play). Orphaned at an early age, he worked from the time he was a child in a wide variety of jobs—from dishwasher on a Volga steamer to icon painter—that he describes in his autobiographical trilogy, *Childhood* (1913), *In the World* (often translated as *My Apprenticeship*, 1916), and *My Universities* (1922). Initially ambivalent about the October Revolution, he left Russia in 1921. He returned in 1931 as a firm supporter of the Soviet regime and was officially designated the "founder" of Socialist Realism—the template for which was his 1906 novel *Mother*—and originator of Soviet literature. Maksim Gorky, *My Childhood*, trans. Ronald Wilks (New York: Penguin, 1991); Gorky, *My Apprenticeship*, trans. Ronald Wilks (New York: Penguin, 1990); Gorky, *My Universities*, trans. Ronald Wilks (New York: Penguin, 1991).

31. Gorky's "Song of the Falcon" (1895) celebrates the romantic revolutionary hero. He wrote his most famous work, *Mother*, while visiting the United States in 1906; often judged of low artistic quality, the novel, which tells the story of a working-class woman who becomes a fearless revolutionary, had tremendous political and literary impact, providing an enduring model of revolutionary selflessness. Gorky, *Mother*, trans. Margaret Wettlin (Moscow: Foreign Languages Publishing House, 1950). An English translation of the "Song of the Falcon" by Janna Kaplan is available at http://people.brandeis.edu /~jannakap/writings_falcon.html (accessed 2 December 2017).

32. Alexander Herzen (1812–70) was among the most influential social and political thinkers of nineteenth-century Russia. When he began *Byloe i dymi* (Past and thoughts) in 1852, he was living in political exile in London, having left the notoriously repressive Russia of Tsar Nicholas I (1825–55) in 1847; he worked on his memoirs until 1868. As Berggolts suggests, the work presented a unique amalgamation of personal reminiscence, philosophy, social observation, and history. Berggolts was far from the only Soviet author who looked to Herzen as a model. The literary historian Irina Paperno traces the memoir's appeal to the fact that Herzen told "a paradigmatic Russian story: the story of a man forged by history." Paperno, *Stories of the Soviet Experience: Memoirs, Diaries, Dreams* (Ithaca, NY: Cornell University Press, 2009), 11; Herzen, *My Past and Thoughts: The Memoirs of Alexander Herzen*, rev. ed., trans. Constance Garnett (New York: Chatto and Windus, 1968).

33. Nikolai Gogol (1809–52) was nineteenth-century Russia's greatest comic writer. His often strange and mysterious works appealed to early twentieth-century modernists including Mayakovsky. In 1952 his centenary was marked in the Soviet Union with statues, productions of his plays, and huge print runs of his works. Mikhail Saltykov-Shchedrin (1826–89), who wrote under the pseudonym Nikolai Shchedrin, was nineteenth-century Russia's most important satirist; his work was praised by radicals, including Karl Marx,

both before and after the October Revolution. Robert L. Strong Jr., "The Soviet Interpretation of Gogol," *American Slavic and East European Review* 14, no. 4 (December 1955): 528–39.

34. Hiders (*Skrytniki*) were a branch of Old Believers, Russian Orthodox Christians who broke with the church over liturgical reforms in 1667 that they believed deviated from true Christianity. They lived in distinctive separate communities. Old Belief and non-Orthodox religious sects proliferated in prerevolutionary Russia and persisted after the revolution. Among the most extreme of the sects was the Eunuchs (*Skoptsy*), who engaged in ritual castration; they believed that making carnal relations impossible assured their salvation. Both pre- and post-revolutionary authorities persecuted the sect. Robert O. Crummey, *Old Believers in a Changing World* (DeKalb: Northern Illinois University Press, 2011); Oleg L. Shakhnazarov, "People of the Schism (1667–2007)," in *Religion and Politics in Russia: A Reader*, ed. Marjorie Mandelstam Balzer (New York: Routledge, 2015), 31–53; Laura Engelstein, *Castration and the Heavenly Kingdom: A Russian Folktale* (Ithaca, NY: Cornell University Press, 1999).

35. On the phenomenon of diary writing during the blockade, see Alexis Peri, *The War Within: Diaries from the Siege of Leningrad* (Cambridge, MA: Harvard University Press, 2017).

36. Genesis 2:7.

37. On the literary importance of diaries during the Thaw, see Anatoly Pinsky, "The Diaristic Form and Subjectivity under Khrushchev," *Slavic Review* 73, no. 4 (Winter 2014): 805–27.

38. Georgy Sedov was an arctic explorer who died in 1914 while attempting to reach the North Pole. The Moscow Canal, known before 1947 as the Moscow-Volga Canal, connects the Moscow and Volga Rivers, traveling 126 kilometers through 11 locks. It was constructed between 1932 and 1937 largely by convict labor. Karl Schlögel, "A City by the Sea: The Opening of the Moscow-Volga Canal," in *Moscow, 1937*, trans. Rodney Livingston (Malden, MA: Polity, 2012), 274–93.

39. Berggolts quotes Alexander Blok's poem "Oseniaia volia" (Autumn freedom, 1905). An English translation by Lyudmila Purgina is available at http://www.poemhunter.com/poem/a-blok-the-autumn-will-translation-rus/ (accessed 2 December 2017).

40. Completed in 1800, the Kalyazin Bell Tower was partially submerged in 1939 under the reservoir created by the Uglich dam. Berggolts saw the tower on her 1953 trip to Uglich.

41. Berggolts returns many times in her work to the city of Kitezh. According to legend, the city's inhabitants prayed for divine intervention against a Tatar attack, and the city was concealed beneath the waters of the lake on which it stood. Hodgson, *Voicing the Soviet Experience*, 164–75.

42. Arkhip Kuindzhi (1842?–1910) was a Russian painter of Greek descent. *Night on the Dnieper*, painted in 1880, depicts a full moon over the Dnieper River. It is in the collection of the Russian Museum, St. Petersburg, available at http://en.rusmuseum.ru/collections/painting-of-the-second-half-of-the-xix-century-beginning-of-xxi-century/artworks/lun naya-noch-na-dnepre/?sphrase_id=14500 (accessed 2 December 2017).

43. The 1854–55 siege of Sevastopol, during which Russian forces held out for a year against French, British, and Ottoman forces, was one of the most mythologized battles of

the Crimean War. Konstantin Stanyukovich (1843–1903) came from Sevastopol, where his father was an admiral, and witnessed the Crimean War as a child. His unfinished *Boy from Sevastopol* (1902) tells the story of the war from a child's point of view. Klavdiya Lukashevich (1859–1931 or 1937) was a popular children's author who wrote almost two hundred books. Berggolts and her sister may have read Lukashevich's *The Defense of Sevastopol and Its Glorious Defenders*, published in 1904 on the fiftieth anniversary of the Crimean War, or one of the smaller booklets that she wrote about the war. Her books told the stories of high commanders such as Admiral Pavel Nakhimov, the commander of the port; rank-and-file soldiers and sailors such as the legendary Petr Koshka, who among other heroic feats rescued a comrade trapped in front of the Russian defensive line; as well as women and children. Ben Hellman, *Fairy Tales and True Stories: The History of Russian Literature for Children and Young People* (Leiden: Brill, 2013), 214, 198–99.

44. A *duga* is a wooden shaft-bow, often decorated and hung with bells, that forms part of a traditional Russian horse harness, arching over the horse's neck and joining the vehicle's two shafts. The Valdai region was famous for these harnesses and their bells. See chapter 3.

45. The Time of Troubles denotes the period of civil war and foreign invasion between the death of Fedor Ivanovich, the last tsar of the Rurikid dynasty, in 1598 and the establishment of the Romanov dynasty in 1613. The Romanovs ruled Russia until the February 1917 revolution. Chester S. L. Dunning, *Russia's First Civil War: The Time of Troubles and the Founding of the Romanov Dynasty* (University Park: Pennsylvania State University Press, 2001).

46. The Soviet state categorized richer peasants as "kulaks." In practice, any peasant who opposed the collectivization of agriculture could be deemed a kulak, and kulaks became the scapegoats for any sort of agricultural shortfall or failure. They could be stripped of their land and possessions, arrested, exiled, or executed. Lynne Viola, *Peasant Rebels under Stalin: Collectivization and the Culture of Peasant Resistance* (New York: Oxford University Press, 1996).

47. In the winter of 1942, the only way for civilians to leave blockaded Leningrad was across frozen Lake Ladoga. The "Road of Life" was the marked truck route across the ice. Often under heavy artillery fire, the route was dangerous and often deadly.

48. Leningraders referred to the area outside the ring of the blockade as the "Main Land."

49. Blokadniki are survivors of the blockade of Leningrad.

50. On the importance of a mythic "Great Time" of heroic action in Socialist Realist novels, see Clark, *The Soviet Novel*, 39–41.

51. In the 1920s and 1930s, thousands of usually young activists established "house communes" and other types of communal living arrangements in dormitories, apartment buildings, and even single apartments in order to put the "new way of life" into operation immediately. Andy Willimott, *Living the Revolution: Urban Communes and Soviet Socialism, 1917–1932* (Oxford: Oxford University Press, 2017).

52. A "troika" was a group of three people working together usually for some administrative purpose. In the late 1920s and early 1930s, the Swiss architect Le Corbusier became deeply interested in the Soviet Union, which briefly embraced his style of functionalist

modern architecture. The headquarters of Tsentrosoiuz, the Soviet trade union, built to his 1928 design was his largest realized project before 1945. Jean-Louis Cohen, *Le Corbusier and the Mystique of the USSR: Theories and Projects for Moscow, 1928–1936* (Princeton, NJ: Princeton University Press, 1992).

53. Mikhail Chumandrin (1905–40) came from a working-class family and began his career as a worker correspondent. He was a member of the Russian Association of Proletarian Writers (RAPP) in the early 1930s. Working as a frontline journalist, he was killed in the Winter War with Finland. Matthew Lenoe, *Closer to the Masses: Stalinist Culture, Social Revolution, and Soviet Newspapers* (Cambridge, MA: Harvard University Press, 2004), 244.

54. French socialist Charles Fourier (1772–1837) imagined that the commune (or phalanx) needed a purpose-built and scientifically designed building, the phalanstery, that ideally would look something like the Palace of Versailles. The idea of the phalanstery resonated with many Russian radicals of the 1840s, and remained influential especially among non-Marxian Populists in the 1860s. Jonathan Beecher, *Charles Fourier: The Visionary and His World* (Berkeley: University of California Press, 1986), 242–45, 295.

55. Boris Chirkov (1901–82) was a popular Soviet actor who made the transition from silent to sound movies. He played Maxim in a trilogy of films directed by Grigory Kozintsev and Leonid Trauberg that tell the story of a young worker coming to revolutionary consciousness in tsarist Russia. *The Youth of Maxim* came out in 1934, followed by *The Return of Maxim* (1937), and *The Vyborg Side* (1938). Jamie Miller, *Soviet Cinema: Politics and Persuasion under Stalin* (London: I. B. Tauris, 2010), 94. Boris Babochkin (1904–75) gained international fame when he played the title character of the 1934 film *Chapaev* about the civil war commander Vasily Chapaev.

56. Ekaterina Korchagina-Alexandrovskaya (1874–1951) was already a well-known theater performer when she began appearing in Soviet films in the 1920s.

57. Chumandrin gives these toasts in Ukrainian.

58. The actor and singer Ernst Busch (1900–1980) was a lifelong communist. He fled Nazi Germany in 1933, living in the Soviet Union until 1937 when he joined the International Brigades to fight in the Spanish Civil War. Brigitte Studer, *The Transnational World of the Cominternians* (Basingstoke: Palgrave Macmillan, 2015), 65–66. Wedding was a working-class district of Berlin. Berggolts seems to be conflating "Der Rote Wedding" (Red Wedding, 1929, lyrics Erich Weinert, music Hanns Eisler) and the later "Das Einheitsfrontlied" (United Front Song, 1934, lyrics Bertolt Brecht, music Hanns Eisler). Recordings of "Der Rote Wedding" and lyrics in German are available at http://www.sovmusic.ru /english/alphabet.php?letter=D (accessed 2 December 2017). For an English translation, see "Der Rote Wedding," trans. Alexandra Chciuk-Celt, in *German Songs: Popular, Political, Folk, and Religious*, ed. Inke Pinkert-Sältzer (New York: Continuum, 1997), 78–81. A recording of "United Front Song" with English subtitles is available at https://youtu.be /cTM9J1PX4CI (accessed 7 December 2017). Here the translation is directly from Berggolts's Russian version.

59. Immediately after Stalin's death in March 1953, a group of top leaders, including Lavrenti Beria (1899–1953), the head of the political police, agreed to rule collectively. His growing power worried his peers, who had him arrested as a traitor and spy. He was executed in December 1953. The shake-up set the stage for Nikita Khrushchev (1894–1971) to

become the most powerful man in the leadership. Amy Knight, *Beria: Stalin's First Lieutenant* (Princeton, NJ: Princeton University Press, 1993), 176–224.

60. This was the fiftieth anniversary of the founding of the Bolshevik faction of the Russian Social Democratic Workers' Party. It did not take the name "Communist" until 1918. Communist Party of the Soviet Union, *The Fiftieth Anniversary of the Communist Party of the Soviet Union (1903–1953)* (New York: New Century, 1953).

61. Kliment Voroshilov (1881–1969) became associated with Stalin in 1918 during the civil war defense of Tsaritsyn (later Stalingrad, now Volgograd). He was an early and staunch political ally of Stalin's. In 1937, as people's commissar of defense, he played a central role in the purge of Red Army commanders. He was a member of the Politburo until 1960. Sheila Fitzpatrick, *On Stalin's Team: The Years of Living Dangerously in Soviet Politics* (Princeton, NJ: Princeton University Press, 2015).

Chapter 2. That Forest Clearing

1. "Gaudeamus Igitur" (So let us rejoice), known as "Gaudeamus" for short, was often played at graduations; it was also a student drinking song.

2. In 1921, as the Russian civil war was winding down, the sailors at the Kronstadt naval base in the Gulf of Finland mutinied against the Bolshevik regime, which they had strongly supported in 1917. The Red Army undertook a bloody attack across the frozen gulf to end the uprising. The mutiny helped persuade the Bolshevik leadership to adopt a more moderate program known as the New Economic Policy (NEP). Israel Getzler, *Kronstadt, 1917–1921: The Fate of a Soviet Democracy* (Cambridge: Cambridge University Press, 1983).

3. On the Nevsky Gate region of St. Petersburg, see chapter 1, n. 13.

4. This is a version of Yakov Prigozhego's 1911 song "Marusia otravilas'" (Marusya poisoned herself). Wildly popular in 1911, it was frequently performed and recorded before and after the revolution. A recording of Ivan Bobrov is available at http://www.russian-records .com/details.php?image_id=6770 (accessed 2 December 2017).

5. Gavrila Romanovich Derzhavin (1743–1816) was both a powerful official during the reign of Catherine II and the greatest Russian poet of his day. An English translation of his ode "Bog" (God, 1784) is available at http://max.mmlc.northwestern.edu/mdenner/Demo /texts/god.htm (accessed 2 December 2017). The University of Dorpat, founded as a German-language institution in 1682, is now the University of Tartu (Estonia).

6. Soviet popular culture in the 1930s was full of references to tractors and tractor drivers, who were considered heroes of the collective farm and also, because of their driving and mechanical skills, potential tank drivers. The musical *Tractor Drivers* (*Traktoristy*, 1939) directed by Ivan Pyryev, was enormously popular and epitomized the boy-meets-girl-meets-tractor genre that many Soviet authors, including Berggolts, criticized after Stalin's death.

7. Berggolts's difficulties during the purges began in May 1937, when she was accused of maintaining contact with a writer who had been deemed an "enemy of the people." In June 1937 she was excluded from the Writers' Union and the Communist Party; after a lengthy appeals process, she was reinstated in the summer of 1938. In December 1938 she was arrested and held in prison until July 1939; while in prison, she suffered a miscarriage.

She was rehabilitated and rejoined the party before the war. For additional information, see Katharine Hodgson's foreword.

8. This is a quotation from Derzhavin's "God."

9. A line from "Vozdushnyi korabl'" (Airship, 1840), part of Mikhail Lermontov's cycle of Napoleonic poems.

10. In the fairy tale "The Tsarevich Ivan, the Firebird, and the Gray Wolf," the wolf carries Ivan and aids him on his quests.

11. Petrushka is a stock character in Russian folk puppetry, similar to Punch and Judy. Catriona Kelly, *Petrushka: The Russian Carnival Puppet Theatre* (Cambridge: Cambridge University Press, 2009).

12. Berggolts likens the man to a jerboa, a small, jumping rodent with long hind legs, long tail, short forelimbs, and big ears that is native to the deserts of North Africa and northern Asia. During World War II, the British Seventh Armored Division fighting in North Africa took the jerboa as its mascot and became famous as the Desert Rats.

Chapter 3. The Nevsky Gate Campaign

1. Antoine Thibault was one of the protagonists of Roger Martin du Gard's multi-volume novel *The Thibaults*, published in France between 1922 and 1940. Berggolts refers to the epilogue, published during World War II, which Rafic Jouejati characterizes as focused "on the disparity between the aspirations for a better world and the inadequacy of the existing institutions to achieve the 'Ideal City,'" in *The Quest for Total Peace: The Political Thought of Roger Martin du Gard* (London: Frank Cass, 1977), 103. The translation is from Berggolts's Russian, a loose translation of the French: "Ma vrai source de force, c'était une secrète, une inaltérable *confiance en l'avenir*. Plus qu'une confiance: une certitude." Roger Martin du Gard, *Les Thibault*, in *Oeuvres complètes* (Paris: Éditions Gallimard, 1955), 2:995. Martin du Gard was a "fellow traveler," that is a writer sympathetic to the Soviet cause, and some of his works were translated into Russian in the 1930s. Ludmilla Stern, *Western Intellectuals and the Soviet Union, 1920–1940: From Red Square to the Left Bank* (New York: Routledge, 2007), 83. The novel has been translated into English: Roger Martin du Gard, *Summer, 1914*, trans. Stuart Gilbert (New York: Viking Press, 1941).

2. On the journal *Novyi mir* (New world), see introduction, n. 22.

3. Berggolts here quotes Psalm 137:5–6. The translation is the King James version. Berggolts's rendition deviates slightly from the standard Synodal Russian translation, suggesting that she may have been writing from memory.

4. On the Nevsky Gate region of the city, see chapter 1, n. 13.

5. Dunya is an affectionate nickname for Avdotya. On diminutives, see chapter 1, n. 4.

6. In Russian, the substitution is "ts" for "ch" and vice versa.

7. There is a rich folklore related to forest spirits and demons in Russia, perhaps particularly in densely forested north Russia. Elizabeth A. Warner, "Russian Peasant Beliefs and Practices concerning Death and the Supernatural Collected in Novosokol'niki Region, Pskov Province, Russia, 1995. Part I: The Restless Dead, Wizards and Spirit Beings," *Folklore* 111, no. 1 (April 2000): 67–90.

8. Berggolts overheard the Trisagion (or "Thrice Holy"), a standard Orthodox hymn. Not knowing the prayer, she mishears *sviati* (holy) as *svety* (lights), and decides that Dunya, who, with her Pskov accent, pronounces "ts" like "ch," must be saying *tsvety* (flowers). The hymn is commonly rendered in English as "Holy God, Holy Mighty, Holy Immortal, have mercy on us."

9. Those who wanted to join the party had to prove themselves as a member of the Komsomol and then as probationary (candidate) members of the party.

10. Gagra on the Black Sea coast is in present-day Abkhazia. It is about sixty kilometers south of Sochi. Both were popular Soviet resorts.

11. On the song "Marusya Poisoned Herself," see chapter 2, n. 4.

12. The British-owned Thornton Woolen Mill was nationalized after the October Revolution. In the 1930s it was named in honor of Ernst Thälmann, the German communist leader arrested by the Nazis in 1933 and shot in 1944 at Buchenwald. Martin Varley, "The Thornton Woollen Mill: St. Petersburg," *History Today* 44, no. 12 (December 1994): 62–63. On Kronstadt, see chapter 2, n. 2.

13. Berggolts is referring to Kaiser Wilhelm II, who ruled Germany during World War I.

14. Berggolts refers to the song "Na pole srazheniia" (On the field of battle), which repurposed the tune of the love song "Chaika" (The seagull) by E. Zhurakovsky. The first line is from Vladimir Nabokov's novel *The Gift*, trans. Michael Scammell with the collaboration of Nabokov (New York: Putnam, 1963), 140. A 1914 recording of Maria Emskaya singing the song is available at http://www.russian-records.com/details.php?image_id =8045&l=russian (accessed 2 December 2017).

15. Avdotya refers to the Cyrillic letter "ш," more properly rendered in English as "shch."

16. The First Five-Year Plan (1928–32), which aimed to industrialize the Soviet Union as quickly as possible, promoted "shock" or storming work, periods in which workers furiously overfulfilled the production norms set by the "plan." Berggolts's youngest daughter, Maya, not yet a year old, died in 1933; her oldest daughter, Irina, died in 1936. On Berggolts's experiences of the purges, see the foreword and chapter 2, n. 7. The "Great Fatherland War" is the name still used in Russia to denote the war between Germany and the Soviet Union that began with the German invasion of 22 June 1941.

17. Founded by mine engineer P. F. Semyannikov in 1857, the factory was also known as the Nevsky Shipbuilding and Machine Plant; its successors are still in operation. "Nevsky Plant," in *Saint Petersburg Encyclopedia*, http://www.encspb.ru/object/2855712771?lc=en (accessed 2 December 2017).

18. The Murzinka is a tributary of the Neva River, just beyond the city limits.

19. In the Soviet symbolic universe, the rubber plant evoked philistine or pettybourgeois values and bad taste. As literary critic Svetlana Boym explains, the rubber plant "was regarded as the last sickly survivor of the imagined bourgeois greenhouses," it was "domestic trash," a "bourgeois flower of evil." Boym, *Common Places: Mythologies of Everyday Life in Russia* (Cambridge, MA: Harvard University Press, 1994), 8, 9.

20. Kvass is a traditional drink made of fermented rye bread; it has a low alcohol content.

21. Physiologist Ivan Pavlov (1849–1936) is best known for his work on classical conditioning. On his death, see Daniel P. Todes, *Ivan Pavlov: A Russian Life in Science* (Oxford: Oxford University Press, 2014), 722–24.

22. The TASS news agency sponsored the creation of stenciled window-size posters with often innovative images and texts. Peter Kort Zegers and Douglas Druick, eds., *Windows on the War: Soviet Tass Posters at Home and Abroad, 1941–1945* (New Haven, CT: Yale University Press, 2011).

23. *Niva* was a popular, inexpensive illustrated magazine that was published from 1870 to 1918.

24. Generals Petr Wrangel, Alexei Kaledin, and Petr Krasnov led forces opposed to the Bolshevik seizure of power. In May 1918 Krasnov, with the support of the German army, briefly captured the Don region. Wrangel and Kaledin led the White (or Volunteer) Army organized by officers and nobles to oppose the Bolshevik seizure of power. Kaledin was an early leader; he committed suicide in February 1918. Wrangel, the last commander, oversaw the evacuation of White forces from the Crimea in 1920. Jonathan D. Smele, *The "Russian" Civil Wars, 1916–1926: Ten Years That Shook the World* (New York: Oxford University Press, 2015).

25. "First imperialist war" was the Soviet term for World War I.

26. On NEP, see chapter 1, n. 28.

27. The "white card" signified that Berggolts's husband was exempt from military service. He was released from military service in August 1941 because of his epilepsy. Katharine Hodgson, *Voicing the Soviet Experience: The Poetry of Ol'ga Berggol'ts* (Oxford: Oxford University Press for the British Academy, 2003), 23.

28. Mikhail Lermontov (1814–41) was a poet and novelist who achieved instant fame in 1837 with his poem "The Death of a Poet," which appeared shortly after poet Alexander Pushkin's death. He is best known for his novel *The Hero of Our Time*, whose protagonist Pechorin was the quintessential "superfluous man" of the 1830s—a man who could find no outlet for his ambitions in autocratic Russia. On Mayakovsky, see chapter 1, n. 27. Both poets influenced Berggolts's own poetry. Hodgson, *Voicing the Soviet Experience*, 161, 14–15.

29. Sergei Esenin (1895–1925) wrote far simpler verse than Mayakovsky and was celebrated as a true "people's poet," the most popular of the so-called peasant writers. He is perhaps best known outside of Russia for his brief (1923–24) marriage to the American dancer Isadora Duncan; he spoke no English, and she no Russian. In 1925 he committed suicide by hanging himself. Gordon McVay, "The Centenary of Sergei Esenin: A Survey of Publications," *Slavonic and East European Review* 76, no. 3 (July 1998): 494–528; Julia L. Mickenberg, *American Girls in Red Russia: Chasing the Soviet Dream* (Chicago: University of Chicago Press, 2017), 219–20.

30. Alexander Pushkin (1799–1837) is widely celebrated as Russia's "national poet," the most important poet of the Russian "Golden Age." Immediately after the October Revolution, the Bolsheviks banished him from the Soviet canon, but they rehabilitated him on the hundredth anniversary of his death (in a duel) in 1937. Nikolai Nekrasov (1821–78) was a leading "realist" poet; his poems depicted the difficult lives of Russian peasants—and he was thus a prerevolutionary poet endorsed by Soviet cultural authorities. Alexander Blok

(1880–1921), sometimes considered Russia's last romantic poet, achieved literary fame before 1917. His initial enthusiasm for the Bolshevik revolution quickly gave way to disillusionment. Nonetheless, he ascended to "the pantheon of Russia's 'great writers'" shortly after his death in 1921. He was an important influence on the younger Mayakovsky. Anastasia Felcher, "Public Festivities and the Making of a National Poet: A Case Study of Alexander Pushkin's Biography in 1899 and 1937," *European Review of History* 19, no. 5 (October 2012): 767–88; Evgeny Dobrenko, "Utopian Naturalism: The Epic Poem of Kolkhoz Happiness," in *Petrified Utopia: Happiness Soviet Style*, ed. Marina Balina and Evgeny Dobrenko (London: Anthem Press, 2011), 23–24; Galina Rylkova, "Literature and Revolution: The Case of Aleksandr Blok," *Kritika* 3, no. 4 (Fall 2002): 611–30 (quotation 616); Edward James Brown, *Russian Literature since the Revolution*, rev. ed. (Cambridge, MA: Harvard University Press, 1982), 45–46.

31. This may be a reference to book III, chapter 7:15 of Flavius Josephus's *The Jewish War*. The inhabitants of besieged Jotapata "begged that he [Josephus] would not abandon them," telling him, "if you go away, then we shall be captured!" H. Leeming and K. Leeming, eds., *Josephus' "Jewish War" and Its Slavonic Version: A Synoptic Comparison* (Leiden: Brill, 2003), 350 (Slavonic tradition). It also echoes the warning in Zechariah 11:17, "Woe to the idle shepherd that leaveth the flock!"

32. Revelation 10:6.

33. Berggolts quotes a line from Fedor Tyutchev's poem "Problesk" (The gleam, 1825). Tyutchev (1803–73) worked as a diplomat in Germany, where he was deeply influenced by German romanticism. The poem is available in Russian at http://www.ruthenia .ru/tiutcheviana/stihi/bp/26.html (accessed 2 December 2017).

34. The tsar was overthrown in February 1917; the Bolshevik revolution was in October 1917.

35. "Sovnarkom" is an abbreviation of the Council of People's Commissars (Sovet Narodnykh Komissarov), the new government formed by the Bolsheviks after the October seizure of power.

36. Berggolts quotes (and slightly rearranges) Mayakovsky's poem "My ne verim!" (We don't believe it), written in the winter of 1923 when Lenin suffered a stroke. A final stroke killed Lenin in January 1924. For information on when the verse was written, see Bengt Jangfeldt, *Mayakovsky: A Biography*, trans. Harry O. Watson (Chicago: University of Chicago Press, 2014), 285.

37. On Bloody Sunday, 9 January 1905, soldiers fired on unarmed men, women, and children carrying a petition to the tsar; the event touched off a year of revolution. "Hostile whirlwinds" are the first words of the song "Varshavianka" (Warsawian), a nineteenth-century Polish song popular in Russian Poland during the 1905 and 1917 revolutions. See chapter 1, n. 22. The revolutionary song "Tormented by a Lack of Freedom," written in 1876 by Grigory Machtet, remained popular into the 1920s. Lyrics in Russian are available at http://a-pesni.org/starrev/zamutchen.htm (accessed 2 December 2017).

38. The small makeshift stoves that were used during the civil war and reappeared during the World War II blockade of Leningrad were called burzhuiki, perhaps because they resembled contemporary caricatures of the potbellied bourgeois class enemy (*burzhui*) who consumed much and produced little or perhaps because the former bourgeoisie were

reduced to using them. Ales' Adamovich and Daniil Granin, *A Book of the Blockade*, trans. Hilda Perham (Moscow: Raduga, 1983), 325.

39. In May 1923 Lord Curzon, the British foreign secretary, threatened to terminate trade relations with the Soviet state unless it met certain conditions, including ceasing to disseminate anti-British propaganda in India, Persia, and Afghanistan. The ultimatum, coming at the time of Lenin's illness, produced a war scare in the Soviet Union. Authorities organized a large number of mass rallies against Curzon; they also met the British demands. Olga Velikanova, *Popular Perceptions of Soviet Politics in the 1920s: Disenchantment of the Dreamers* (Basingstoke: Palgrave Macmillan, 2013), 29–30.

40. The song "The Red Army Is the Strongest," popularly known as "White Army, Black Baron," was written by Pavel Gorenstein (words) and Samuil Pokrass (music) in 1920, during the civil war. The "black baron" is Petr Wrangel, the last leader of the White Army. The "British seas" took on new meaning during the anti-Curzon demonstrations. Russian lyrics and a recording are available at https://www.marxists.org/history/ussr/sounds/lyrics/belaia-armiia.htm (accessed 2 December 2017).

41. "Tears fill the boundless world" is the first line of the song "Krasnoe znamia" (Red flag). Russian lyrics and a recording are available at https://www.marxists.org/history/ussr/sounds/lyrics/krasnoe-znamia.htm (accessed 2 December 2017). English lyrics and a recording of "Smelo, tovarishchi, v nogu" (Boldly, comrades, in step) are available at https://www.marxists.org/history/ussr/sounds/lyrics/smelo-tovarishchi.htm (accessed 2 December 2017).

42. The translation is from the standard English version. "The Internationale" was written in 1871 after the defeat of the Paris Commune. It was the anthem of the Second International and, until 1944, the state anthem of the Soviet Union. Lyrics and recordings in English, Russian, and French are available at https://www.marxists.org/history/ussr/sounds/lyrics/international.htm (accessed 2 December 2017).

43. Lenin's first venture into activism among the working class was in 1895 during a strike of five hundred textile workers at the Thornton Mill; he wrote a leaflet and visited with strike leaders. Robert Service, *Lenin: A Biography* (Cambridge, MA: Harvard University Press, 2000), 106.

44. In the 1920s, the Soviet press encouraged workers to become "worker correspondents" (*rabkory*) and write about their daily experiences in their own terms. Jeremy Hicks, "Worker Correspondents: Between Journalism and Literature," *Russian Review* 66, no. 4 (October 2007): 568–85.

45. Berggolts quotes a fragment from Pushkin's *Eugene Onegin*. The translation is Aleksandr Pushkin, *Eugene Onegin: A Novel in Verse*, trans. Vladimir Nabokov (Princeton, NJ: Princeton University Press, 1975), 1:264.

46. Berggolts quotes Lermontov's poem "Listok" (The leaf, 1841). An English translation is available at http://max.mmlc.northwestern.edu/mdenner/Demo/texts/theleaf.html (accessed 2 December 2017). She also references "Na severe dikom stoit odinoko" (In the savage North there stands alone, 1841), "Utes" (The cliff, 1841), and "Parus" (The sail, 1832). The first two of these are available in English translation in David Powelstock, *Becoming Mikhail Lermontov: The Ironies of Romantic Individualism in Nicholas I's Russia* (Evanston, IL: Northwestern University Press, 2005), 248–49. For an English translation of "The Sail," see Laurence Kelly, *Lermontov: Tragedy in the Caucasus* (London: Tauris Parke, 2003), 197.

47. Berggolts quotes Lermontov's poem "Son" (The dream, 1841). The translation is from Powelstock, *Becoming Mikhail Lermontov*, 409.

48. Lermontov's poem "Rusalka" (The mermaid, 1832) includes a song sung by a mermaid about her love for a drowned knight, who lies at the bottom of a river.

49. This is a modified version of the English translation by Priscilla Meyer available at https://pmeyer.faculty.wesleyan.edu/nabokov/short-subtexts/the-mermaid/ (accessed 2 December 2017).

50. Lermontov wrote several versions of "Demon" (The demon) between 1829 and 1839. An English translation is available in Aleksandr Pushkin and Mikhail Lermontov, *Narrative Poems by Alexander Pushkin and Mikhail Lermontov*, trans. Charles Johnston (New York: Random House, 1983), 107–44.

51. Berggolts quotes Mikhail Lermontov's poem "Poet" (The poet), which can be found in his *Polnoe sobranie sochinenii* (Moscow: Academia, 1935–57), 2:42. An English translation by Denise M. Henderson is available at http://schillerinstitute.org/fid_02-06/034_lermontov.pdf (accessed 2 December 2017).

52. Blok's 1918 epic poem *Dvenadtsat'* (The twelve), his most famous work, was an ambiguous response to the revolutionary upheaval; it is set in postrevolutionary Petrograd during a blizzard. An English translation by Maria Carlson is available at http://russiasgreatwar.org/media/culture/twelve.shtml (accessed 2 December 2017).

53. Mikhail Svetlov (1903–64) was a poet and playwright who fought with the Red Army during the civil war. His 1926 poem "Grenada" (Granada) made him famous, but he fell out of favor in the late 1920s. His reputation was rehabilitated only after his death. The poem "depicts a Russian soldier of the civil war, dreaming romantically of the peasants in Spain, for whose freedom he is fighting." Katharine Hodgson, *Written with the Bayonet: Soviet Russian Poetry of World War Two* (Liverpool: Liverpool University Press, 1995), 26.

54. Berggolts refers to the beginning of her relationship with Nikolai Molchanov, in about 1930. The city of Leningrad is made up of a series of islands. The Tuchkov Bridge connects Vasilevsky Island and Petrogradsky Island. These may be "our" islands; she may also have in mind the islands north of Vasilevsky: Krestovsky, Elagin, and Kamennyi. She mentions "islands" in connection with her relationship with Molchanov in her sketches for part II of *Daytime Stars* and in her blockade diary. Ol'ga Berggol'ts, *Vstrecha: Dnevnye zvezdy, pis'ma, dnevniki, zametki, plany* (Meeting: Daytime stars, letters, diaries, notes, plans) (Moscow: Russkaia kniga, 2000), 262; entry for 1 October 1942 in Ol'ga Berggol'ts, *Blokadnyi dnevnik* (St. Petersburg: Vita Nova, 2015), 42. Thanks to Katharine Hodgson for these references.

55. Berggolts quotes Mayakovsky's long poem "Pro Eto" (About this, 1923). In this section, Mayakovsky gets stuck in the cupola of Ivan the Great's church tower in the Kremlin and is challenged to a duel. His appeal that he is "only poetry" is met with a reference to Lermontov, the "Hussar," who was killed in duel in 1841. For more on the poem, see Jangfeldt, *Mayakovsky*, 231–62, on this section, 250–51. See also chapter 1, n. 27.

56. A *duga* is a wooden shaft-bow that forms part of a traditional Russian horse harness. See chapter 1, n. 44.

57. Tsarevich (son of the tsar) Dmitry (1582–91) was Ivan IV's (the Terrible's) youngest son by his fifth (or seventh) wife Maria Nagaya. After Ivan's death, his older son Fedor became tsar, but the real ruler was the boyar (nobleman) Boris Godunov. To get rid of a

potential rival to the throne, Godunov in 1584 sent Dmitry and his mother to Uglich. In 1591 Dmitry died of a stab wound under mysterious circumstances, perhaps assassinated on Godunov's orders, perhaps accidently having killed himself during an epileptic seizure. A. M. Kleimola, "The Canonization of Tsarevich Dmitrii: A Kinship of Interests," *Russian History* 25, nos. 1–2 (1998): 107–17.

58. Budenny helmets were high-peaked felt hats worn by the Red Army in the civil war, named after cavalry commander Semen Budenny. Lev Trotsky wears one in the poster "Bud' na strazhe!" (Be on guard!) by Dmitry Moor. See https://en.wikipedia.org/wiki /File:Russian_Civil_War_poster.jpg (accessed 2 December 2017).

59. On these collections, see chapter 1, n. 2.

60. Mikhail Kutuzov (1745–1813) was a Russian general most famous for his leadership during the French invasion of Russia. In early 1813, he fell ill and died in Prussia.

61. On the cultural significance of the coachman, see John Randolph, "The Singing Coachman or, The Road and Russia's Ethnographic Invention in Early Modern Times," *Journal of Early Modern History* 11, nos. 1–3 (2007): 33–61.

62. This is a loose quotation from the song "Step' da step' krugom" (Only steppes around), based on I. V. Surikov's poem "V stepi" (In the steppe, 1865). Vadim Prokhorov, *Russian Folk Songs: Musical Genres and History* (Lanham, MD: Scarecrow Press, 2002), 133–35.

63. Berggolts quotes a version of a poem by F. N. Glinka (a distant cousin of the famous composer M. I. Glinka), "Son russkogo na chuzhbine" (A Russian's dream abroad, c. 1825), widely known as "The Troika." It was first set to music by A. Verstovsky around 1830 and exists in numerous variants. Thomas P. Hodge, *A Double Garland: Poetry and Art-Song in Early Nineteenth-Century Russia* (Evanston, IL: Northwestern University Press, 2000), 80–81, 144.

64. Cutting off an ear was a common form of punishment in this period; a person with a severed ear was marked as a felon. Nancy Kollmann, *Crime and Punishment in Early Modern Russia* (New York: Cambridge University Press, 2012), 242, 255–56.

65. The Nagoys were the family of Dmitry's mother, Maria Nagaya.

66. The quotation is from Dmitry Karamazov's dream, in which he recognizes his desire to mitigate suffering. Fedor Dostoevsky, *The Brothers Karamazov*, trans. Constance Garnett (New York: Macmillan, 1922), 547.

67. On the Time of Troubles, see chapter 1, n. 45.

68. Between 20 November and 25 December, the daily bread ration for office workers, dependents, and children in besieged Leningrad fell to a low of 125 grams. Although still meagre, the 250 gram ration represented a significant improvement.

69. On Le Corbusier, see chapter 1, n. 52.

70. Berggolts's father quotes a poem in prose by Ivan Turgenev, "Shchi" (Cabbage soup), in which the lady of the manor visits a peasant widow whose son has just died. The lady is appalled to find the peasant woman eating; the peasant explains to the lady that the cabbage soup mustn't go to waste because "after all, it is salted." The lady, who does not worry about the cost of salt, fails to understand. Ivan Turgenev, "Cabbage Soup," in *The Essential Turgenev*, ed. Elizabeth Cheresh Allen (Evanston, IL: Northwestern University Press, 1994), 879–80.

71. Stomatitis is a general term for oral inflammation including canker sores and cold sores.

72. Ephesians 5:32.

73. "Dystrophic" was the medical term Leningrad doctors applied to persons suffering from the blockade "disease" of "alimentary dystrophy" or starvation. By the end of 1941, doctors and ordinary Leningraders used the term. On the shifting meanings of this "unusual term," see Alexis Peri, *The War Within: Diaries from the Siege of Leningrad* (Cambridge, MA: Harvard University Press, 2017), 180–91.

74. Berggolts quotes from Pushkin's *The Tale of Tsar Saltan, of His Son, the Glorious and Mighty Knight Prince Guidon Saltonovich, and of the Fair Swan-Princess.* The poem tells the story of a prince cast out of the palace through the machinations of his mother's rivals. He saves a swan from death; ultimately, the swan turns out to be a beautiful princess, and the pair marries. This is Louis Zellikoff's translation, http://www.marxists.org/subject/art /literature/children/texts/pushkin/tsar.html (accessed 2 December 2017).

75. See n. 24.

76. Mercusal is mercurial diuretic; Luminal is phenobarbital.

77. Both Kornei Chukovsky (1882–1969) and Samuil Marshak (1887–1964) were beloved children's authors and both had literary careers that went well beyond children's literature. Chukovsky's children's verses, like "Crocodile" (1916), upended the canons of children's literature, and in 1928 were attacked in *Pravda* as "bourgeois muddle." Marshak's verses more often drew on themes from Russian and English folklore. Catriona Kelly, *Children's World: Growing Up in Russia, 1890–1991* (New Haven, CT: Yale University Press, 2007), 48–49, 88–92, 97–101.

78. This was likely the Forty-Second Army's Fifty-First Separate Tank Battalion, which defended the southern approaches to the city. David M. Glantz, *The Siege of Leningrad, 1941–1944: 900 Days of Terror* (Osceola, WI: MBI Publishing, 2001), 126, 202.

79. Berggolts refers here to Ivan Bunin's reworking of Buddhist ideas in stories such as "Brat'ia" (Brothers, 1914) and "Gospodin iz San-Frantsisko" (The gentleman from San Francisco, 1915). Bunin (1870–1953), who had supported the White forces during the Russian civil war, left Russia for Paris after the Red victory and was closely associated with the anti-Bolshevik emigration. Because of his hostility to the Soviet Union, his works were not published there after 1928. In 1933 he became the first Russian writer to win the Nobel Prize. He was rehabilitated after his (and Stalin's) death in 1953; a Soviet edition of his selected works was published in 1956. In evoking Bunin, Berggolts took advantage of and implicitly endorsed the relative loosening of controls on literature that characterized the post-Stalin Thaw. She is also careful to mark the distance between the émigré Bunin and herself as a Soviet author. Thomas Gaiton Marullo describes Bunin's idea of the "path of egression" and the "path of return" in *If You See the Buddha: Studies in the Fiction of Ivan Bunin* (Evanston, IL: Northwestern University Press, 1998), 10, 22–31.

Chapter 4. Good Morning, People!

1. Individual radio receivers had been confiscated in the first days of the war in an effort to prevent Soviet citizens from listening to foreign broadcasts. News within the Soviet

Union was closely controlled by the Soviet Information Bureau (Sovinformburo), set up just days after the German invasion. It provided few details in the catastrophic early months of the war (October 1941) that Berggolts describes here. While they may not have trusted news from Nazi Germany, the radio workers were in the privileged position of being able to listen to it, and may have hoped that comparing news from Germany with scanty Soviet reporting would yield some clues to the actual situation. Karel C. Berkhoff, *Motherland in Danger: Soviet Propaganda during World War II* (Cambridge, MA: Harvard University Press, 2012), 1–67.

2. During the blockade, a metronome sounded continuously on Radio Leningrad when there was no other programming. To warn of air raids, it increased its beat from a calm 50 to 55 strikes per minute to a frenetic 150 to 160 beats per minute. When air raids ceased during the winter of 1941–42, the metronome continued to sound as the "heartbeat of the city."

3. This long list of illustrious German communist or "antifascist" intellectuals reflects Berggolts's participation in and support for the renewal of internationalism that clearly set the post-Stalin Thaw apart from the xenophobia that marked Stalin's last years. Eleonory Gilburd, "The Revival of Soviet Internationalism in the Mid to Late 1950s," in *The Thaw: Soviet Society and Culture during the 1950s and 1960s*, ed. Denis Kozlov and Eleonory Gilburd (Toronto: University of Toronto Press, 2013), 362–401.

4. Anna Seghers (1900–1983) was best known for her literary depictions of World War II. Her 1939 novel *The Seventh Cross* depicts an escape from a Nazi concentration camp; in 1944 it was made into a film starring Spencer Tracy. Of Jewish ancestry, Seghers spent the war in emigration, first in France, then in Mexico. She returned to Berlin in 1947, and moved to communist East Germany in 1950, where she became president of the German Writers' Union. Helen Fehervary, *Anna Seghers: The Mythic Dimension* (Ann Arbor: University of Michigan Press, 2001); Catherine Epstein, *The Last Revolutionaries: German Communists and Their Century* (Cambridge, MA: Harvard University Press, 2003), 4, 90–91, 166–67.

5. Bernhard Kellermann (1879–1951) gained fame as an author before World War I. Unable to publish during the Nazi era, he returned to cultural life in postwar East Germany. Stephen Brockmann, *The Writers' State: Constructing East German Literature, 1945–1959* (Rochester, NY: Camden House, 2015), 43, 48.

6. Stephan Hermlin (1915–97) joined the German communist youth organization in 1931. He spent the war in emigration, returning to East Berlin in 1947. In the 1970s, he became an outspoken critic of the German Communist Party. Epstein, *Last Revolutionaries*, 225–26, 249–50.

7. Wolfgang Langhoff (1901–66) joined the German Communist Party in the late 1920s or early 1930s. The Spartacus League was one of the organizations that gave rise to the German Communist Party in 1918. Berggolts may call him a Spartacist because he was a communist of long standing. In 1933, while interned in a Nazi concentration camp in Emsland, he, along with another prisoner, Johann Esser, wrote the lyric for what would become the famous protest song "Die Moorsoldaten" (Peat bog soldiers); a fellow inmate, Rudi Goguel, supplied the melody. The song became an antifascist anthem during the Spanish Civil War. A 1937 recording made in Barcelona of Ernst Busch is available at "The

Soldiers of the Moor," https://www.ushmm.org/exhibition/music/detail.php?content=moor (accessed 2 December 2017). Langhoff fled to Switzerland after being released from Nazi custody in 1934 and returned to East Germany after the war. His postwar book on the concentration camp has not been translated into English: *Die moorsoldaten: 13 monate konzentrationslager* (Munich: Zinnen-Verlag, 1946). Max Reinhardt (1873–1943) was a prewar theater director who left Austria for Hollywood after the 1938 Anschluss. The Deutsches Theater in Berlin, where Reinhardt worked before the war and Langhoff after, was named in the former's honor.

8. Jürgen Kuczynski (1904–97) spent World War II in England, where in 1943 he helped to found the Free German Movement. After the war he returned to East Germany, where he became a prominent intellectual. In the mid-1950s he became a critic of the East German government but remained loyal to it. Epstein, *Last Revolutionaries*, 89, 164, 226.

9. Eduard Claudius (1911–76) began his writing career as a worker correspondent for the German Communist Party newspaper. After being wounded in Spain, he ended up in a camp for undesirable political refugees in Switzerland, where he wrote the novel *Green Olives and Bare Mountains* about the fall of the Spanish Republic. In the last days of World War II he fought with the Garibaldi partisan brigade in northern Italy before returning to East Germany. Hunter Bivens, "Ghostly Solidarities: Eduard Claudius, Green Olives, and Bare Mountains," in *Epic and Exile: Novels of the Popular German Front, 1933–1945* (Evanston, IL: Northwestern University Press, 2015), 154–87.

10. Günther Weisenborn (1902–69) immigrated to the United States in 1936 but returned to Germany in 1937, where he began working with the Resistance group Red Orchestra, while maintaining his career as a playwright. He was arrested in 1942 and convicted of treason, but his death sentence was commuted. In April 1945 Soviet troops liberated him from prison. After the war he returned to West Germany. Anne Nelson, *Red Orchestra: The Story of the Berlin Underground and the Circle of Friends Who Resisted Hitler* (New York: Random House, 2009).

11. Michael Tschesno-Hell (1902–80) together with Willi Bredel wrote the screenplay for the 1954 film *Ernst Thälmann—Sohn seiner klasse* (Son of his class) and its 1955 sequel, *Ernst Thälmann—Führer seiner klasse* (Leader of his class). Ernst Thälmann (1886–1944), a former Hamburg dockworker, became the leader of the German Communist Party in 1925; he was, according to historian Catherine Epstein, "a man who both slavishly followed Stalin's orders and who, by all accounts, was enormously popular among the communist faithful." Arrested by the Nazis in 1933, he was shot in 1944 at Buchenwald. Russell Lemmons, *Hitler's Rival: Ernst Thälmann in Myth and Memory* (Lexington: University Press of Kentucky, 2013), 160–74; Epstein, *Last Revolutionaries*, 34.

12. In April 1943 Yakov Babushkin (1913–44) was removed from his position as a radio producer, thereby losing his draft exemption. In February 1944 he was killed at the front. Anna Reid, *Leningrad: The Epic Siege of World War II, 1941–1944* (New York: Walker and Co., 2011), 380.

13. Yevgeny Lvovich Shvarts (1896–1958) was a playwright and writer of children's fiction that often incorporated fairy-tale elements. His plays *Golyi korol'* (The naked king, 1934), *Ten'* (The shadow, 1940), and *Drakon* (The dragon, 1943–44) offered a satirical look at Soviet reality through the prism of the fairy tale. He had difficulty getting them produced,

and they were revived only in the early 1960s. All three have been translated into English: Evgenii Shvarts, *Three Plays*, ed. Avril Pyman (Oxford: Pergamon Press, 1972).

14. On Ernst Busch and "The Reds from Wedding," see chapter 1, n. 58.

15. The Rote Jungsturm (Red Youth-Storm) was the name of the German Communist Party's youth organization in the early 1920s. The Roter Frontkämpferbund (Red Front Fighters League) was organized in 1924; Ernst Thälmann was its first leader. It popularized the greeting "Rot Front!" (Red front) accompanied by a raised, clenched fist. Between 1918 and 1922, German communists participated in a number of abortive uprisings; in this period Soviet and international communists considered Germany to be the most likely site of the next Soviet-style revolution. Aleksandr Vatlin, "The Testing-Ground of World Revolution: Germany in the 1920s," in *International Communism and the Communist International, 1919–1943*, ed. Tim Rees and Andrew Thorpe (Manchester: Manchester University Press, 1998), 117–26; Ben Fowkes, *Communism in Germany under the Weimar Republic* (London: Macmillan, 1984).

16. "Bandiera Rossa" (Red flag) is an Italian revolutionary song written in 1908 by Carlo Tuzzi. A recording and lyrics in Italian and English are available at https://www.marxists.org/subject/art/music/lyrics/it/bandiera-rossa.htm (accessed 2 December 2017). On "Warsawian" and the "Internationale," see chapter 1, n. 22, and chapter 3, n. 42.

17. The literary critic Lev Levin had been among those accused together with Berggolts in 1937 of maintaining a friendship with "enemy of the people" Leopold Averbakh. Katharine Hodgson, *Voicing the Soviet Experience: The Poetry of Ol'ga Berggol'ts* (Oxford: Oxford University Press for the British Academy, 2003), 19.

18. On the term "dystrophic," see chapter 3, n. 73.

19. In May 1960 Francis Gary Powers (1929–77) piloted a U-2 spy plane flying a reconnaissance mission for the Central Intelligence Agency that was shot down over Soviet airspace. Powers survived the crash and was taken into Soviet custody. He was tried, convicted of espionage, and spent about twenty-one months in a Soviet prison before being released in a prisoner exchange. US president Dwight D. Eisenhower's admission that he had authorized the overflights derailed a Paris peace summit already planned for mid-May and led to the cancellation of Eisenhower's trip to the Soviet Union. William Taubman, *Khrushchev: The Man and His Era* (New York: Norton, 2003), 442–72.

Chapter 5. Blockade Bathhouse

1. Berggolts completed this chapter in 1962, but it was not published until the years of glasnost. "*Dnevnye zvezdy*: Vtoraia chast'," *Ogonek*, no. 19 (1990): 15–16.

2. The public bathhouse (*bania*) has long been an important feature of Russian culture. It persisted into the Soviet period when many families lived in communal apartments, where a number of families shared a single bath, or in apartments that lacked running water. In the worst months of the blockade, few bathhouses operated in Leningrad. For a description of the traditional and contemporary bathhouse, see Genevra Gerhart, *The Russian's World: Life and Language* (San Diego, CA: Harcourt Brace Jovanovich, 1974), 8–10. On bathhouses during the blockade, see Alexis Peri, *The War Within: Diaries from the Siege of Leningrad* (Cambridge, MA: Harvard University Press, 2017), 155–60. For a different view

of the wartime bathhouse, see Ethan Pollock, "'Real Men Go to the Bania': Postwar Soviet Masculinities and the Bathhouse," *Kritika* 11, no. 1 (Winter 2010): 47–57.

3. On the medical term "dystrophic," see chapter 3, n. 73.

4. Berggolts refers not to the painter Peter Paul Rubens but to Boris Kustodiev (1878–1927). She may have had in mind his painting *Russkaia Venera* (*Russian Venus*, 1925–26), included in this chapter.

Contributors

Katharine Hodgson is a professor of Russian at the University of Exeter, UK. She is the author of *Voicing the Soviet Experience: The Poetry of Ol'ga Berggol'ts*, as well as numerous articles on Berggolts. From 2010 to 2014 she led a collaborative project investigating the post-Soviet reconfiguration of the twentieth-century poetry canon, examining questions of the canon and national identity, analyzing the role of anthologies, and exploring Boris Slutsky's position in the post-Soviet canon. She is also interested in Russian translations of foreign poetry, and has published work on translations of poems by Rudyard Kipling, Heinrich Heine, and Bertolt Brecht.

Lisa A. Kirschenbaum is a professor of history at West Chester University, Pennsylvania. She is the author of *Small Comrades: Revolutionizing Childhood in Soviet Russia, 1917–1932*; *The Legacy of the Siege of Leningrad, 1941–1995: Myths, Memories, and Monuments*; and *International Communism and the Spanish Civil War: Solidarity and Suspicion*. She is a coauthor (with Choi Chatterjee and Deborah A. Field) of *Russia's Long Twentieth Century: Voices, Memories, Contested Perspectives*.

Index

Page numbers in italics indicate illustrations.